Writing and Fantasy

Crosscurrents

General Editors:
Professor J. B. Bullen, University of Reading
Dr Neil Sammells, Bath Spa University College
Dr Paul Hyland, Bath Spa University College

Titles in the series:
William Zunder and Suzanne Trill, *Writing and the English Renaissance*
John Lucas, *Writing and Radicalism*
Gavin Cologne-Brookes, Neil Sammells and David Timms, *Writing and America*
Mpalive-Hangson Msiska and Paul Hyland, *Writing and Africa*
J. B. Bullen, *Writing and Victorianism*
Tim Youngs, *Writing and Race*
Ceri Sullivan and Barbara White, *Writing and Fantasy*

Writing and Fantasy

Edited by Ceri Sullivan and Barbara White

Longman
London and New York

Addison Wesley Longman Limited,
Edinburgh Gate,
Harlow,
Essex CM20 2JE,
United Kingdom
and Associated Companies throughout the world.

*Published in the United States of America
by Addison Wesley Longman Inc., New York*

First published 1999

ISBN 0-582-30911-5 CSD
ISBN 0-582-30912-3 PPR

Visit Addison Wesley Longman on the world wide web at
http://www.awl-he.com

British Library Cataloguing-in-Publication Data
A catalogue record for this book is available
from the British Library

Library of Congress Cataloging-in-Publication Data
Writing and fantasy/edited by Ceri Sullivan and Barbara White.
     p. cm. — (Crosscurrents)
    Includes bibliographical references and index.
    ISBN 0-582-30911-5 (CSD). — ISBN 0-582-30912-3 (pbk.)
    1. Fantastic literature, English—History and criticism.
  2. Fantasy in literature. I. Sullivan, Ceri, 1963– . II. White,
Barbara, 1952– . III. Series: Crosscurrents (London, England)
PR149.F35W75   1998
820.9′15—dc21
                                          98–26120
                                              CIP

Set 35 in 10/12 pt Sabon
Produced by Addison Wesley Longman Singapore (Pte) Ltd.
Printed in Singapore

Contents

Acknowledgements

We would like to thank the editorial team at Addison Wesley Longman for their interest and guidance, and the general editors of the *Crosscurrents* series for their advice and suggestions, particularly in the early stages of this project.

We are grateful to our contributors who have responded with patience, hard work and good humour to our queries and, in particular, to Karín Lesnik-Oberstein and Peter Stoneley for their valuable suggestions on an early draft of the introduction. Peter Field and Margaret Lockerbie-Cameron kindly read portions of the manuscript; Linda Jones helped with the administration of the project. Colleagues at *Advanced Studies in England* and the University of Wales, Bangor also offered generous support. Errors remaining are most certainly ours.

We are grateful to Robert Adam for making available the illustrations on pp. 237 and 251.

The publishers are grateful to the following for permission to use copyright material:

The Executor of the John Betjeman Estate for an extract from the poem 'Metro-land' by John Betjeman in *THE BEST OF BETJEMAN* ed. John Guest, Penguin Books 1978; Edouard Privat/ Dunod Editeur for an extract translated by Mark Philpott from *LE REGISTRE D'INQUISITION DE JACQUES FOURNIER, EVEQUE DE PAMIERS (1318–1325)* (3 vols) ed. Jean Duvornoy, Vol. 1, pp. 128–9; the author, Jeanette Winterson for extracts from *SEXING THE CHERRY*, Bloomsbury Publishing 1989, Copyright J. Winterson 1989.

General editors' preface

Crosscurrents is an interdisciplinary series which explores simultaneously the new terrain revealed by recently developed methodologies while offering fresh insights into more familiar and established subject areas. In order to foster the cross-fertilization of the ideas and methods the topic broached by each volume is rich and substantial and ranges from issues developed in culture and gender studies to the re-examination of aspects of English studies, history and politics. Within each of the volumes, however, the sharpness of focus is provided by a series of essays which is directed to examine that topic from a variety of perspectives. There is no intention that these essays, either individually or collectively, should offer the last word on the subject – on the contrary. They are intended to be stimulating rather than definitive, open-ended rather than conclusive, and it is hoped that each of them will be pithy and thought-provoking.

Each volume has a general introduction setting out the scope of the topic, the various modes in which it has been developed and which places the volume as a whole in the context of other work in the field. Everywhere, from the introduction to the bibliographies, pointers will be given on how and where the ideas suggested in the volumes might be developed in different ways and different directions, and how the insights and methods of various disciplines might be brought to bear to yield new approaches to questions in hand. The stress throughout the books will be on crossing traditional boundaries, linking ideas and bringing together concepts in ways which offer a challenge to previously compartmentalized modes of thinking.

Some of the essays will deal with literary or visual texts which are well known and in general circulation. Most touch on primary material which is not easily accessible outside major library collections, and where appropriate, that material has been placed in a portfolio of documents collected at the end of each volume. Here again, it is hoped that this will provide a stimulus to discussion; it will give readers who are curious to explore further the implications of the arguments an opportunity to develop their own initiatives and to broaden the spectrum of their reading.

The authors of these essays range from international writers who are established in their respective fields to younger scholars who are bringing fresh ideas to the subjects. This means that the styles of the chapters are as various as their approaches, but in each case the essays have been selected by the general editors for their high level of critical acumen.

Professor J. B. Bullen
Dr Paul Hyland
Dr Neil Sammells

This book is for
Neil and
Claire, Lucy and Mavis

Introduction

Ceri Sullivan and Barbara White

The fantastic is a paradoxical mode: it depends for its existence on an inverse relationship with what is perceived to be real. This has encouraged its appropriation by commentary – usually literary – on a post-romantic, fractured sense of self. *Writing and Fantasy* is a contribution to studies which have restored a sense of the fantastic as a political interpellation, a cultural artefact whose origin lies in a conscious response to daily events as much as it does in psychology or ideology.[1]

Much previous commentary has discussed the origins of phantasy in the context of nineteenth-century individualism. However, if the fantastic is read as political – involved in the creation and dissolution of social tensions – this narrow focus could be challenged. Changing circumstances produce the fantastic as a coping strategy, and privilege certain features of the mode over others. In this introduction we sketch distinctions currently made between phantasy and fantasy, the fantastic and the fictional. We then turn to recent debate over two prominent features of the fantastic: its interrogation of 'rules' by which reality is conceived, and its political engagement with the reader.[2] The volume brings together such historically specific fantasies as maternal and Edenic originary spaces, arielism, prophecy, credit, and the Western.

Most discussions of phantasy begin with its definition, as a constituent of the unconscious, in Sigmund Freud's *On Sexuality*. He argued that primary instincts in the infant, the need for food or protection, are manifested in desires ('libidinal drives') which, when they enter the conscious mind, become attached to symbols which are private to each individual.[3] Jacques Lacan developed this hypothesis, asserting the social determination of these symbols; they are, in effect, a form of language. The movement into this conscious state, which he called the symbolic order, depends upon the infant leaving behind an imaginary realm. There, Lacan suggested, the infant was in a state of undifferentiated desire; it had no separate identity, no cognition. The awakening consciousness of the child that it has a self simultaneously creates an understanding that it is not an other. The gaining of identity and of language entails an experience of separation, absence and loss which is repressed into the unconscious.[4] Psychoanalysis describes phantasies as compensatory stories, produced by the unconscious, which allow the individual to work over versions of this moment of loss of unity between the self and the other – the self-same moment in which meaning and language are created for the child. This moment is full of anxiety, so the unconscious repeatedly attempts to recapture the bliss of lost undifferentiation, and contain the fear of alienation. The unconscious's methods deal in the excessive, the extra-ordinary, its stories engage with the fantastic, with the 'not-real'; they 'express the demand of an Other, before which the subject ... "fades"'.[5] The displacement of feelings from one situation onto another, the focusing of wide-ranging concerns into a single symbol, or the splitting of a subject into opposing forces are characteristic methods used by such phantasy to rework the moment of initial loss, and also any subsequent variations of the experience which the mind recognizes. Thus, both the origin of phantasy in desire springing from absence and the 'unreal' forms of the consciously produced fantastic are explained by psychoanalytic theory as necessary – universal – features of the creation of the self, and credited with homeostatic functions.

As psychoanalysis acknowledges, this universalized model of the self needs to be supplemented: the forms of the fantastic are contingent on the historical and political circumstances surrounding human agents.[6] The fantastic acts as a secondary text to reality, variously acting as a commentary on, or a mimesis of it. In Rosemary Jackson's words,

> fantasy re-combines and inverts the real, but it does not escape it: it exists in a parasitical or symbiotic relation to the real. The fantastic cannot exist independently of that 'real' world which it seems to find so frustratingly finite.[7]

Yet the fantastic and real have an even stronger mutual dependency than this suggests. Commentary on fantasy frequently confines it to a psychoanalytic exploration of literary works, but it can be viewed as a cultural product, coming into being as a response to varied political exigencies. Sceptical formulations of knowledge see it as constructed by rules of discourse which decide what is admitted as fact.[8] Reality itself is seen as rhetorical; there is no simple perception of something, somehow, already 'there'. Such a formulation appears to bring fantasy under the aegis of an Althusserian notion of ideology, through which a subject unconsciously lives his or her relation to the 'real' conditions of existence. However, the fantastic is a conscious production, a deliberate response to a gap between the real and the desired, under the control of the individual. It may produce the subject examined, but does not claim any prior reality for it. The real and the possible are defined by the unreal and the impossible, whose boundaries are in a constant state of flux; as a result, the fantastic must be recognized as operating within a historical framework. Can, for instance, 'a story written in the Middle Ages be considered according to the concept of nature upheld in those times or according to our current understanding of reality?'[9] The shifts in these boundaries have a political and epistemological function, exposing repressive aspects within a society by making visible the culturally invisible, by tracing 'the unsaid and the unseen of culture: that which has been silenced, made invisible, covered over and made "absent"'.[10] Fantasy manifests social anxieties, taking the same compensatory role at the level of society as psychoanalytic theory provides for it at the level of the individual. Moving beyond boundaries into the empirically unknown or hypothetically impossible where codes for what is acceptable or right no longer apply – allowing the primary world to be interrogated by the secondary – is a central characteristic of the fantastic. For W.R. Irwin these movements between fantasy and the real provoke a politicized engagement:

> in a fantasy [the reader] is persuaded to play the new system of 'facts', which he has wilfully and speculatively accepted, against the established facts, which he only pretends to reject.[11]

Both reader and writer must make the choice of a non-mimetic mode of interpretation. They perform frequent, deliberate movements between the fantasy and reality; each must decide, within the social text, at what point the consumer will distinguish the fantasy from reality.[12]

This raises the question of how far the fantastic is a genre, with formal rules which allow certain texts to be admitted to it, rather than an effect of a political situation. The issue is debated widely: Kathryn Hume's definition of fantasy literature, for example, disqualifies realist novels as 'unrealistic but not a departure from what could physically happen in this world' and historical novels 'which use invented characters in real or imagined situations'.[13] An understanding of fiction as a conscious fantasy is present in the latter's etymology, from the Latin *phantasia* or 'making visible'. The meanings of 'fantasy' proliferated, from the process of making an object of sense visible to the mind, to the delusive perception of such an object, to the object itself as an hallucination. With 'fancy', 'fantasy' became the term for the deliberate creation of an imaginary object, and finally, the whimsical creation of an extravagant image or object. The term's perjorative annexation to the margins of poor-quality fiction is voiced by Samuel Taylor Coleridge:

> fancy and imagination [are] two distinct and widely different faculties ... The primary IMAGINATION I hold to be the living Power and prime Agent of all human Perception, and as a repetition in the finite mind of the eternal act of creation in the infinite I AM. FANCY, on the contrary, has no other counters to play with, but fixities and definites. The Fancy is indeed no other than a mode of Memory emancipated from the order of time and space ... and modified by ... CHOICE.[14]

The degeneration of 'fantasy' from science to caprice demonstrates its imbrication in the arguments about what is real and what is perceived. The most influential commentator on the fantastic as a literary mode, Tzvetan Todorov, describes fantasy as the creation of a moment of hesitation in interpreting between the two:

> in a world which is indeed our world, the one we know, ... there occurs an event which cannot be explained by the laws of this same familiar world. The person who experiences the event must opt for one of two possible solutions: either he is the victim of an illusion of the senses, of a product of the imagination – and laws of the world then remain what they are; or else the event has indeed taken place, it is an integral part of reality – but then this reality is controlled by laws unknown to us ... The fantastic occupies the duration of this uncertainty.[15]

Todorov portrays a reader who is unable to choose between uncanny (psychological) and marvellous (supernatural) explanations.

In commentary which is focused on the overtly political uses of fantasy three positions have developed: fantasy as conformist, as subversive, and as the hegemonic co-option of a challenge to the *status quo*. The mode is described as being conservative for two contradictory reasons as a compensation for social deprivation, where the satisfaction it offers reduces the individual's impetus to change conditions, and as escapist, in marshalling or creating desires for the purposes of control, as with advertising and pornography.[16] This practical and symbolic orchestration of a public mentality is credited by Jacqueline Rose with the power to produce a citizen:

> there is a common assumption that fantasy has tended to be excluded from the political rhetoric of the left because it is not serious, not material, too flighty and hence not worth bothering about. My starting premise works the other way round. Like blood, fantasy is thicker than water, all too solid . . . The modern state enacts its authority as ghostly, fantasmatic authority.[17]

The concept of fantasy as subversive relies on the opportunities it offers for the rehearsal of alternative scenarios from a position of safety, allowing them to be developed before being effected. It provides space for debate without the need to take responsibility for such commentary. Jackson has argued forcefully that subversion is a political function of literary fantasy. The violation of dominant assumptions of what is generally accepted as normative

> is not in itself a socially subversive activity: it would be naive to equate fantasy with either anarchic or revolutionary politics. It does, however, disturb 'rules' of artistic representation and literature's reproduction of the 'real'.[18]

Assaults on dominant ideologies need not always be subversive. Some new historicist readings, for instance, have pointed to the way fantastic challenges can modify prevailing ideologies to preserve social and economic order. José B. Monleón, for example, postulates that the history of the fantastic is the history of a class struggle. The fantastic helped 'modify hegemonic discourse in order to justify the survival of bourgeois society' by reflecting capitalist-engendered fears and creating 'a space in which those threats could be transformed into "supernaturalism" and monstrosity'.[19] Thus, he argues, the creation of a bourgeois state in the eighteenth century was expressed in gothic terms a fracture between order and chaos caused by a bourgeois reformulation of otherness which excluded everything it regarded as outside reason and order – madness, crime, or an emerging working class.

The chapters which follow accept the political imperative in fantasy, and the need to consider 'the changing historical meaning of the fantastic in different periods'.[20] They are organized chronologically to allow the reader to sample some of the genres which proved popular within a period. Here, however, we deliberately mix the periods, commenting on how certain modes of expression appear, become submerged, and reappear over time because of the dialectical nature of fantasy. We are not producing a history of the form but a series of vignettes of sites where it has become engaged with social necessities.

The first group of essays demonstrate how dependent fantasy is on modes of perception: rigid generic expectations are challenged by the fantastic. Contributors discuss the relationship between the writer and reader created by the choice of interpretation, particularly where non-canonical genres (such as the pamphlet or the Western) and marginalized constituencies (such as criminals and grotesqueries) are represented. Danielle Clarke argues that the classification of an artefact as fantastic depends on the desires of the consumer. Though Thomas Nashe's sixteenth-century poem 'The Choice of Valentines' is usually read within the twentieth-century category of 'pornographic fantasy', it can also be read as engaging in the period's Petrarchan and Ovidian debates about authorship as a fantasy of potency; sexual fantasy here is seen as a source of invention for the poet, and the reader's agenda changes the status of the object. A similar dependence on generic expectations is explored in Barbara White's use of factual records and fictional accounts of the lives of two notorious seventeenth-century female criminals, Mary Carleton and Jenny Voss. She exposes the processes of self-invention used by the women and by their biographers as a means of appealing to distinct audiences. Moving rapidly between the real, the expected and the desired, single texts simultaneously offer two contradictory fantasies: the subversion of gender, in suggesting to female readers an alternative life-style beyond male jurisdiction, and, for male readers, safe sexual fantasies where they maintain control over attempted female usurpation of male rôles. Mark Philpott notes how the purposes of the reporter infect the presentation of the ghost in medieval ghost stories, mediating the ontology of such fantasies. In discussing ghost stories from the twentieth century, Julian Thompson notes that the genre declined when its essential ambiguity was overridden by the desire to give rational explanations which reflected the latest political, sociological or psychological influences, to that which had hitherto been seen as unknowable. This position is challenged by Lucie Armitt's essay, which rejects the idea that fantasy is necessarily and solely a dialogue with reality. Armitt suggests the fantastic can be seen as a dialogue with the codes of a genre. She describes the twentieth-century utopia as a genre of bound spaces, paradoxically returned to by those who wish to 'go beyond'. Armitt argues that Jeanette Winterson's utopian spaces exhibit the desire for the originary space, repeatedly engaging with beginnings, longings, desires and absences. Monique Wittig's polychromatic, conflictual and strange utopias embody crossing points, understood by Armitt to be points of return to the imaginary and the potential.

A concern with the return to the originary or ideal space also marks the next group of essays, which concentrate on the movement towards an ideal space. This has been a traditional function of the utopian, though the process of getting to this space is infrequently described.[21] Travel becomes the escape to home. Such fantasies desire control over the material they advance over. Margaret Kean discusses *Paradise Lost* (1667) as a triple analogy between a fantasy of absolute control over the poem by the epic author, the reality of absolute control by God over his real world, and the creation by Adam of his perfect woman in a dream. The poem's monist drive, which permits a union of matter with spirit, means the body of the poem and the bodies in creation attempt to break free of their controlling author. Adam, like Milton, has to be taught the limits of such a fantasy. Timothy Mowl vigorously points out the dangers of homogeneity in ideal spaces. Twentieth-century British domestic architecture is conservative when contrasted with European stylistic experiments with Art Nouveau. In Britain the favoured styles have reflected a historicist fantasy which looks back to the Gothic, Italianate, Tudor and Neo-Norman for inspiration. In domestic architecture the fantasy has been the cottage idyll, seen by Mowl as a middle-class fantasy 'on behalf of' the working classes. In recent years the fantastic has given way to functionalism, impoverishing the urban landscape. The concept of childhood is discussed by Karín Lesnik-Oberstein as a fantasy constructed by adult viewers, where the content of childhood consciousness is also seen as fantastic. She establishes 'rules for reality' which are self-consciously varied in the construction of childhood by adults. Winnie-the-Pooh parades adult whimsy, colonizing the child's own subject position. Yet the film *Kids*, which appears to be an exposition of the brutal reality of childhood in the late twentieth century, is just as much a fantasy of childhood.

The frontier, a permeable membrane between the known and the unfamiliar, allows fantasy writers to maintain violate boundaries. Starting with an incoherence in the Western, between the genre's celebration of the cowboy who is hyper-masculine but who is also portrayed as isolated victim, Peter Stoneley looks at the feminization of the genre, by later romance writers. As the Wild West was tamed the demand grew for fictions about the 'hard man' of nineteenth-century Westerns. In twentieth-century Western romances, however, the silent hero shows maternal care for the heroine and the reader. A new incoherence arises in the genre, between the sexual desire of the heroine, which must look outside the family, and the maternal role which both partners must take up within it. Two essays examine the frontier as a re-flection of home. Julie Sanders uses Richard Brome's *The Anti-podes* (1638) and Ben Jonson's *The Alchemist* (1610) to chart the potential in armchair travel fantasies to satisfy desires for power and possession. These fantasies expand an understanding not of foreign lands but of 'home' and 'self'. In *The Antipodes* travels are staged by a fictitious doctor as a play-within-a-play, experienced in a dream by a madman, in order to bring him home to a sane understanding of reality. An examination of *The Alchemist* reinforces the political aspects of colonial fantasy, of going out in order to come back. In both plays, the boundaries between fiction, phantasy, fantasy, dreams and madness are eroded. In Daniel Carey's essay, however, travel involves a movement into the unknown, and therefore necessarily involves the imaginative. Practices which are taboo in the mother country are catalogued as though the writers have not been aroused or participated in them in their travels, though evidence from other sources suggests to the contrary. When imaginary voyages such as Henry Neville's *The Isle of Pines* (1668) are examined, the features of sexual fantasy which can be read out of the factual texts are exposed miscegenation, boundless fertility, and multiple sexual relationships.

The last group of essays suggests how dependent society is upon successfully creating and manipulating private desires. Fantasies are commercially and politically profitable. Ceri Sullivan argues that changes to the early modern money market created credit as an unreal product of rhetorical ethos, which nonetheless possessed value and could be circulated. Merchants developed techniques to control this reified fantasy, to give it credit-worthiness, and to profit from its risky nature. Jonson's *The Alchemist* is read as a comment on the means by which the fantasy of credit can be created, using speed, precision, a godly ethos and the tight maintenance of financial boundaries. The political uses of excess in Ben Jonson's masque *The Vision of Delight* (1617) are examined by Lesley Mickel. Jonson's boldest experiment with the literary fantastic is usually said to culminate in a fantastic pastoral masque which points up the hyperbole of self-praise in the early Stuart court. Mickel, however, shows how the antimasque comments on the fantastic within the masque proper, by forcing the audience's attention onto the somatic – real – court, rather than its spiritualized mirror in the masque. Christopher Pelling describes how classical historians moved from offering their readers an interpretation of dreams as prophecies towards seeing them as manifestations of unease by their characters. When Herodotus details Xerxes's dream of warnings from the gods about the dangers of conquering the Persians he provides a royal advisor, Artebanus, who interprets the dream as mere fantasy until he too dreams it in Xerxes's place. Tacitus takes a social and psychological position when relating Nero's fantasy of buried treasure; the emperor's inordinate greed is shared by his subjects, as state business is suspended under the power of a collective fantasy of wealth. The classical historians provide successive layers of doubt and belief about the dreams, as fantasies or as prophecies within each tale. Richard Kaeuper challenges the schoolroom image of the chivalry in medieval romances, such as the *Lancelot du Lac*, as a beautiful image of the perfectible society. Chivalry, he argues, was a fantasy which controlled violence by using violence. Three passages from the chronicles, *Perlesvaus*, the post-Vulgate *Merlin Continuation*, and Orderic's *Ecclesiastical History*, provide evidence of how the fear which the code inspired was dealt with. Finally, Carolyne Larrington's discussion of fairy mistresses undermines the traditional view of medieval romance as reinforcing notions of social order and knightly power. The stories of demonized women such as Mélusine and Morgan le Fay, who held knights in thrall, rehearse conflicts over the relationship between male honour and female domesticity and concerns over lineage and economic prosperity.

Topics which resurface over the period – ghosts, money, sexual desire, gods, criminals, idealized places – are predicated on the absence in reality of the thing longed for. They are discussed by texts which foreground a debate over the reality of what they present, both in the genres they use (dreams and prophecies, fictional autobiographies and docu-films, metadramatic presentations or mock Tudor cladding) and in their inclusion of characters who are sceptical or hesitant about the fantasy offered. Fantasies are one of the individual's deliberate responses to circumstances which are not ideal. In the sites which our contributors explore, they seem to keep the possibility of change alive.

Notes

1. For other instances of such an approach see Derek Jarrett, *The Sleep of Reason: Fantasy and Reality from the Victorian Age to the First World War* (London, 1988); José B. Monleón, *A Specter is Haunting Europe: A Sociohistorical Approach to the Fantastic* (Princeton, 1990); Jacqueline Rose, *States of Fantasy* (Oxford, 1996), ch. 1; Tobin Siebers, *The Romantic Fantastic*, (Ithaca, 1984); Meredith Veldman, *Fantasy, the Bomb and the Greening of Britain: Romantic Protest 1945–1980* (Cambridge, 1994).

2. On the interpellation of the subject and the transformation of social relations, see Louis Althusser, *For Marx*, trans. Ben Brewster (London, 1996), esp. pp. 227–31. On the knowledge (*savoir*) formed as a result of discursive formations which regulate what may be said, see Michel Foucault, *Discipline and Punish. The Birth of the Prison*, trans. Alan Sheridan (Harmondsworth, 1979), esp. pp. 25–8, and *The History of Sexuality*, trans. Robert Hurley, 3 vols (Harmondsworth, 1981–86). Foucault explains his project in the introduction to vol. 2.

   Students may refer to Lucie Armitt, *Theorising the Fantastic* (London, 1996) and Rosemary Jackson, *Fantasy: The Literature of Subversion* (London, 1981) for detailed introductions to the theory of fantasy.

3. Sigmund Freud, *Three Essays On the Theory of Sexuality* (London, 1949), pp. 51–8, 99–103.

4. Jacques Lacan, *Ecrits*, trans. Alan Sheridan (London, 1977), ch. 1.

5. Herman Rapaport, *Between the Sign and the Gaze* (Ithaca, 1994), p. 2. Since symbols are social, forming a language which can be accessed by others, Lacan suggests that phantasies do not belong solely to the individual. See also Anthony Easthope, *Poetry and Phantasy* (Cambridge, 1989), pp. 7–20.

   Hanna Segal, *Dream, Phantasy, and Art* (London, 1991) runs through the forms of 'dream-work' and argues that the maturing mind tests these unconscious and pre-conscious phantasies against reality, pp. 10–16, 25–9. Phantasies are scenarios which have been deliberately split off from reality-testing (as in art or day-dreams), or those where the mind cannot deal with a painful memory or experience without some form of mediation, pp. 20, 76–8.

6. Monleón, *Specter*, p. ix.

7. Jackson, *Fantasy*, p. 20.

8. See Karín Lesnik-Oberstein's essay below, pp. 197–206.

9. Monleón, *Specter*, p. 5.

10. Jackson, *Fantasy*, p. 4.

11. W.R. Irwin, *The Game of the Impossible: A Rhetoric of Fantasy* (Urbana, 1976), p. 67.

12. Gary K. Wolfe, 'The encounter with fantasy', in Roger C. Schlobin, ed., *The Aesthetics of Fantasy Literature and Art* (Notre Dame, Ind., 1982), p. 14.

13. Kathryn Hume, *Fantasy and Mimesis: Responses to Reality in Western Literature* (New York, 1984), p. 22. See also Neil Cornwell's discussion of the genre debate in *The Literary Fantastic: From Gothic to Postmodernism* (Hemel Hempstead, 1990), pp. 34–41.

14. Samuel Taylor Coleridge, *Biographia Literaria*, ed. J. Shawcross, 2 vols (1817; Oxford, 1907), vol. 1, pp. 60, 202.

15. Tzvetan Todorov, *The Fantastic: A Structural Approach to a Literary Genre*, trans. R. Howard (Cornell, 1973), p. 25.

16. For instance, the current debate about whether videos of violence arouse or reduce aggression in their viewers.

17. Rose, *States of Fantasy*, pp. 5, 9. See also Lauren Berlant, *Anatomy of Fantasy* (Chicago, 1991), p. 10.

18. Jackson, *Fantasy*, p. 14.

19. Monleón, *Specter*, pp. 14, 139.

20. Monleón, *Specter*, p. 17.

21. See, for example, A.G.H. Bachrach's essay in Dominic Baker-Smith and C.C. Barfoot, eds, *Between Dream and Nature: Essays on Utopia and Dystopia* (Amsterdam, 1987), pp. 70–90; Peter Ruppert, *Reader in a Strange Land* (Athens, 1986), chs 2, 3.

Part One
Early

1 *Modern fantasy and ancient dreams*

Christopher Pelling

Ancient dreams are in fashion. Enterprising historians are increasingly exploiting our knowledge of those dreams, especially those collected and discussed in the second century AD by Artemidorus, to give a variety of new perspectives on the ancient world. In particular, dreamers' preoccupations have illuminated the social construction of sexuality, or changing attitudes towards personal identity;[1] the various codes for deciphering dreams also afford insight into the symbolic modes of thought through which people would filter and process their perceptions.[2] Instead of dismissing dream-content as 'mere' fantasy, we can therefore see ancient dreams as an insightful mode of conceptualization, related in shifting and unstraightforward ways to the representational strategies of waking reality. Dreams and fantasy have something in common: both re-sort the ideological patterns of everyday existence at the same time as challenging them by their difference.[3]

This chapter will suggest that this contemporary historiographic trend mirrors one already present in the development of ancient historiography. Dreams had always been important in that genre, just as they are important in epic, the genre from which historiography ultimately sprang; but Greek and Roman historians and biographers found new ways in which dreams could illuminate aspects of an individual or a whole culture, and their ways of coping with reality.

There is, however, one obvious difference between ancient and modern perceptions. Ancient audiences were primed to expect a connection between dreams and the divine. Dreams could be 'invasive', sent from external powers to afford insight into the future or the otherwise unknowable present. Of course it was a familiar phenomenon for people to dream, and to realize that they had dreamed, about their daytime preoccupations (what Freud called 'the day's residue'); or for particular types of physical disorder to be seen to promote particular types of dreams. But there was still a tendency to think of dreams as most *interesting* when they came from outside. That was not merely a literary convention: the practising dream-interpreter Artemidorus drew a distinction between *enhupnia*, dreams inspired by the day's experiences, and *oneiroi*, prophetic dreams sent from outside, and it was the latter class which excited his interest.[4]

It remains a question how the classical historians fit into this pattern; and here one may find a further parallel with modern literary fantasy. Here, like Jackson, we may find useful Todorov's distinction between the 'marvellous', i.e. the readers' acceptance of a supernatural explanation for irregular phenomena, and the 'uncanny' (*l'étrange*), where strangeness is an effect produced by the distorting mind of the individual.[5] Jackson charts the development whereby '[f]rom Gothic fiction onwards, there is a gradual transition from the marvellous to the uncanny – the history of the survival of Gothic horror is one of progressive internalization and recognition of fears as generated by the self'. This chapter will explore a similar development within the ancient historians, and uses four dream narratives reproduced in the documents section on pp. 253–60 below.[6] Originally, dreams are indeed sent 'from without', are in Todorov's terms 'marvellous': they still illuminate human psychology, but typically by pointing the distinctive way in which the dreamer responds to such an invasive experience. But later writers incorporate more problematic patterns, whereby there is at least a *possibility* that the dreams may be generated 'from within', as an 'uncanny' product of the dreamer's pre-existent psychology: in other words, historians found interest in precisely the patterns which Artemidorus neglected. Still, this is often precisely that, a possibility. Matters are rarely clear, and, again as in much nineteenth- and twentieth-century fantasy,[7] some of the more interesting cases will be those which leave the reader uncertain – as uncertain, indeed, as the dreamers themselves must, or at least should, have been. This raises the further narratological question of the relation between the questions put to their experience by the dreamers and those put by the informed historiographic reader.

As we examine this development through some particular cases, we shall see continuity as well as change. Even in our later cases, it is important that the possibility of invasive, supernatural dreams remains; it is important also to notice some recurrent features of narrative technique. Here too it will be useful to apply some of Todorov's categories, namely his three conditions for the 'fantastic':[8] first, that the reader should hesitate between a natural and supernatural explanation of the events described; second (in most cases but not universally), this hesitation may be focused through the same hesitation on the part of a character; third, the reader must adopt a certain attitude in accepting the text's descriptions of strange experiences, rejecting non-literal and figurative interpretations of the sort Todorov terms 'allegorical' or 'poetic'. Naturally, not all of these terms will prove straightforward to project backwards onto ancient experience.[9] They can still serve as a useful starting point for our examination of four particularly thought-provoking passages.

Herodotus's dreams of Xerxes and Artabanus

Herodotus, writing in the second half of the fifth century BC, includes many dreams,[10] and by this stage of his History the reader has grown to expect them to be invasive and god-sent. This passage is his most elaborate and longest dream-sequence. It comes at the crucial moment of the entire narrative, where the Persian king Xerxes is deciding to launch his fateful invasion of Greece. The setting is Spring 484.

It follows an extended narrative of a Council meeting. Xerxes, still relatively new upon the throne, had first set out his reasons for wanting to attack Greece: expansion is a Persian tradition, driven on by some divine force; attack will bring glory and revenge. Therefore 'I am going to yoke the Hellespont and drive my army through Europe into Greece': the language captures both the fixity of the resolve and the way in which Xerxes's plan cuts across the natural boundaries of the Persian empire. This, he says, will enable him to extend the empire over every land seen by the sun, and everyone, guilty or not, will become their slaves. His counsellors are finally told to prepare their troops; but 'so that I should not seem to be self-willed, I am putting the matter for

public discussion . . .' (7.8). This, by Greek standards, is already
seen as a charade of consultation, a travesty of a debate.

The loyal Mardonius responds with eager, sycophantic flattery:
it will all be easy, there is nothing to fear from Greece, Xerxes is
invincible (7.9). Most keep silent. Only Artabanus, Xerxes's uncle
(and it is the relationship which made him so bold, 7.10.1), dares
to put a different view, and even he has to speak indirectly. It is
always good to hear an opposite view, just so that you can be sure
of the better course. Take your time, call another council once you
have reconsidered; the biggest animals, the tallest trees, the greatest houses are most vulnerable to the lightning-bolt. The direct
attack is reserved for Mardonius, whom Artabanus reviles for his
poor advice (7.10). Xerxes is furious: only the family relationship
with Artabanus saves him; it is unthinkable that a Persian king
could leave the Greeks unpunished . . . (7.11).

So much for the advice Xerxes sought, such is the nature of
council at a court. It contrasts eloquently with several debates on
the Greek side, most starkly with that at Athens at the end of
Book 8, where the Athenians, civilized and free as they are, listen
to unpalatable views and reply with urgency and dignity.

Then follows the long description of the dream (given on
pp. 253–5 below) – and so the greatest expedition of them all
begins.

This intriguing scene has provoked intense scholarly contro-
versy. Let us begin with Artabanus, particularly his suggestion
that Xerxes's dreams are simply the consequence of his daytime
preoccupation. That reluctance to accept the supernatural explanation reminds us of Todorov's second category, the presence of a
character to focus the reader's own doubtfulness. But readers' response to Artabanus's hesitation is more complex than this. On one
level, we understand, even empathize with it, as we empathize with
much in Artabanus's predicament. In everyday life, we would offer
similar rational doubts. The ancient reader would doubtless have
felt the same way: the fourth-century writer of the 'Hippocratic'
On Regimen 4.88 counts such dreams, representing the day's concerns, as utterly normal. Yet we know Artabanus is wrong. That
is partly because, by now, Herodotus's reader has heard of too
many other genuinely supernatural dreams; partly also because
we know that this is a critical moment, not a time for the trivial,
and Artabanus's casualizing is unlikely to capture the attitude of

concerned gods. But there is more. There is an implicit contract between the reader and writer of history, and we know that an occurrence would only be recorded if it were significant. Had Artabanus been right, the story would not be being told at all. So the reader is in a curious position of superiority over the character. However rational Artabanus's doubts, we know better, and we know that we know. Not for the only time, Artabanus is being over-rational. His contributions chart the limits of human insight into a complex world.[11]

It would, however, be a strangely insensitive reader who felt no doubts at all, even if they are not Artabanus's doubts. In particular, what is the relation of this sequence to the Council which precedes? That had seemed to give an adequate explanation for Xerxes's decision to invade; indeed, it had directed our attention in a subtle way to the dynamics of an autocratic court, where megalomaniac drives are unlikely to be successfully opposed. How do the human and divine sequences relate? Might this even be some sort of externalization of internal conflict, a shorthand way of remaining on the human level and dramatizing the inner disquiet of both Xerxes and Artabanus?[12]

This 'externalization' approach is unlikely to be sufficient, at least in a crude form: too many of Herodotus's other dreams resist that approach, for instance by conveying information that the dreamer could not possibly have known; and anyway that approach works better for Xerxes, who might well 'internally' regret his impulsiveness, than for Artabanus. We can certainly detect *some* unease in Artabanus's roundabout rhetoric, beautifully written and contrived as it is, but it is natural to relate this to the dangerous suggestion that he adopt the king's clothing and usurp his role.[13] It is harder to think him internally uncertain about the wisdom of his advice. It is always a mistake with Herodotus to collapse divine explanations into human: that is, after all, only another version of Artabanus's rationalizing mentality which is here seen to fail. In other words, we can here accept Todorov's third formulation, that we should not read a strange experience as some sort of figurative description for something other than what it is.

Still, the divine explanations are not wholly divorced from human, either. Here, much of what Xerxes's phantom says resonates with themes intimated by the preceding Council scene. Take his first words:

> Are you changing your mind, Persian, and deciding not to invade Greece, after telling the Persians to gather an army? You are wrong to change your mind, and there is not one here who will forgive you; just as you chose during the day, keep to that path.

Notice how he is addressed, 'Persian', and how this is echoed in 'after telling the Persians ...'. At the Council, an important element in Xerxes's argument had been the need to continue the great Persian tradition of expansion, and the dangers of quietude; the peril of abandoning that tradition is not far to seek – especially after making public such a plan. The phrasing 'there is not one here who will forgive you' is itself sinisterly vague. Does the phantom refer to itself, as many translators and commentators assume? Or is it referring to a threat from those Persian grandees present at the Council? True, they welcomed the abandoning of the plan, and 'fell at Xerxes's knees in delight'; but the loss of face involved in abandoning such a plan – even an unpopular one – is still very clear.

Then:

> Son of Darius, so you make it clear among the Persians that you have abandoned the expedition, and are dismissing my words as if they come from a nobody? Be certain of this, if you do not attack immediately, this is what will result for you: just as you became great and formidable in a short time, so swiftly will you be humbled once more.

This time he is 'son of Darius', and that too tells on a theme which Xerxes had aired: Darius had expanded the empire, and now there is a burden on Xerxes to live up to that tradition; and Darius had been rebuffed by the Athenians, and so there is a need for revenge. Artabanus had drawn a different moral from Darius's experience, stressing how close Darius's invasion of Scythia came to failure. Once again, too, the dream draws attention to the public quality of Xerxes's statements, 'so you make it clear among the Persians ...', and once again there are hints of the possibilities of unrest. Readers of Herodotus have by this point become used to the potential for dynastic intrigue at the Persian court, and these possibilities were focused only a few chapters earlier, with the court manoeuvrings which installed Xerxes, contentiously, on the throne (7.2–3). 'Just as you became great and formidable in a short time, so swiftly will you be humbled once more.' It is not difficult to relate this to the intrigue which could easily start again.

So there are earthly counterparts to much of the dream's content, just as there is a naturalistic earthly counterpart to the divine inevitability which drives the Persians on to empire, that imperialistic, expansionist, transgressive, ultimately self-destructive urge which readers have come to associate with king after king, and to see as embedded in the way the court works. But a counterpart is not an identification, and the divine content cannot be reduced to its human equivalent. The divine sequence re-sorts and reassembles elements of the human, and projects them in a different register. A parallel to the fantastic is again clear.

The parallel is the closer because this new register is distinctly elusive. We are still left with questions, but no answers, about this 'divine' element. Is this punishment for the transgressive aspirations which Xerxes made clear in the Council? Or is it rather that all Persia is under a divine 'curse'?[14] Or might this at least be a divine summation of its past expansionism, refusing to allow Persia to escape the climactic catastrophe for which its earlier imperialism had laid a foundation?

What, too, do we make of the response of the two characters at the end, where they are 'cheered' by the dream, and Artabanus takes it as intimating Persian triumph and Greek disaster?[15] Had this been 'a false dream' on the model of the one sent by Zeus to Agamemnon in *Iliad* 2, that response might have been natural. Homer's dream is indeed an intertextual presence here, and ironically Artabanus's 'some divinely wrought destruction is overtaking the Greeks' reproduces, not the dreams of the present, but the content of that Homeric dream – there, 'sufferings are fixed for the Trojans' (*Iliad* 2.15, cf. 32, 69). But Xerxes's and Artabanus's dreams never promised success: they were threats, not promises; and Artabanus's response is inadequate to the texture of the dreams in *this* text.

We should also consider the positive and encouraging response of everyone, dream-interpreters included, to the final dream of the olive crown. Evidently, that is an under-interpretation: no attention is paid to the sudden disappearance of the crown from Xerxes's head. Evidently, too, a Greek audience would have known what to make of it. The olive was Athens' sacred tree.[16] The Persian success will last so far, to Athens and Salamis, and then swiftly vanish.

The audience must notice the under-interpretation; can they explain it? The response of the dream-interpreters themselves is not puzzling: yet again, that can reflect the dynamics of the court, where even experts sense the dangers of telling the king anything but what he wants to hear.[17] But Xerxes and Artabanus themselves are more problematic. Do the audience feel that the demonic is active in a wider sense, blinding the human characters to the indications which the divine affords? Or do they toy with a more human, psychological explanation, with Artabanus and Xerxes so numbed and disconcerted that they now shy from anything but the most positive readings of supernatural signs – that, in fact, they create their own, new fantasies? The audience cannot know, any more than a little later they can know why Xerxes is blind to the sinister implications of divine signs at the Hellespont (7.34) and Athos (7.37), the two sites of his greatest natural transgressions.[18] But the audience notice; and they wonder. The supernatural, in Todorov's terms the 'marvellous', is both clearly present and perplexingly enigmatic.

So we readers ask questions, and we may feel particular empathy with a questioner in the text, Artabanus; but his questions are not ours, and we explore the supernatural register whereas he was inclined to reject it out of hand. His experience guides rather than reproduces our own hesitations.

Tacitus's dream of Caesellius Bassus

With Tacitus we have moved forward 500 years, to the beginning of the second century AD. He too has prophetic, 'from outside' dreams, though they tend to be distanced from his central field of vision. The cult of Persian Hercules on Mount Sanbulos features night-time appearances of the god (*Ann.* 12.13.3); 'they say' that Ptolemy founded the temple of Serapis after a dream (*Hist.* 4.83); but in each case we are dealing with distant, remote peoples. When Tacitus reverts to his central interest in the elite and the court, the treatment is more circumspect, and there are several cases where the reader is left uncertain whether the dream is 'from outside' or 'from inside'. Particularly interesting cases, which there is no room to discuss here,[19] are the mirroring dreams of Caecina at *Annals* 1.65 and Germanicus at 2.14, where we

are presented with the dreams non-committally, and left as uncertain about their interpretation as the original dreamer must
have been.

This passage (given on pp. 256–7 below) is less perplexing, but
very illuminating. It opens Book 16 of the *Annals*. We are in the
year 65 AD. In this story, in one sense, there is no hesitation at all,
on the part either of the reader – we are clear from the outset that
Caesellius Bassus is disturbed, and that would not have been said
if the dream were to turn out true – or of the spectators: the only
doubts are hinted in passing, those of the 'sensible folk', and even
these may have been divided.[20] The emphasis falls on the all-but-
universal credulity. If there is any lack of clarity on the reader's
part, it is only in defining exactly what is dream and what is
conjecture in Bassus's initial report. The phrasing ('he explained
that') leaves it open for us to believe that the cave he so confid-
ently described was real, and that the dream concerned only the
treasure: it is only at the end of the story that we discover it was
all, cave included, a dream. Notice especially the interpretative
comment which Bassus added about Dido, 'so conjecture makes
clear'. He is speaking as if the earlier part was absolutely incontro-
vertible. When all is delusion, it is a delightful touch to give Bassus
such a careful differentiation of certainty.[21]

So here too the reader feels superior, but not in feeling a deeper,
different sense of puzzled dubiety as with Herodotus. It is rather
in knowing that the characters should have felt a good deal more
puzzled and dubious than they did. But here again, as with
Herodotus, the encounter is most revealing about the nature of an
autocratic culture. In Herodotus too we noticed the interest in the
human response, but there it was the response of the dreamer
himself and his closest adviser; here it is the response of everyone,
the speed with which all rush onto the credulous bandwagon. This
is a world ripe for escapism, a world of easy living, easy money,
and easy believing. Dreams may be a good way of filtering and
coming to terms with realistic truth: here they eloquently distort
hard reality. Yet, once again, dreams juggle the elements of real
life even as they pervert them: and that is a question not merely of
the dreams' avaricious content, but also of the way they are dealt
with. At the beginning, where Bassus has to 'buy' his audience
with Nero, and at the end, where there is a glance forward to the
'public impoverishment' and the man's goods are confiscated, we

glimpse the shortages and the imperial moneygrubbing which rendered this world so susceptible to financial fantasy.

There is another way, too, in which this episode fits tellingly into its context. The previous book had ended with the long account of the Pisonian conspiracy, a dispiriting episode where most of the participants had cut figures as inglorious as the emperor they were plotting against. That too had been a story of rumours and hastiness, with the governing class swift to play upon the emperor's credulity; that too had shown the elite eventually playing along with the emperor and the court they despised, just as here the orators and poets show a sycophantic servility to match their 'heights of eloquence', as Tacitus sarcastically dubs the material of which he gives such an unimpressive example. That was a different sort of 'madness'; this replays some of the themes in a lighter tone. But the lightness is itself macabre: despite all the air of unreality, some elements are very real – the death or imprisonment, the confiscation, the impoverishment. Escapism is natural. There is a lot in this world to escape from.

Plutarch's dreams of Marius and Sulla

Plutarch was a contemporary of Tacitus, though living and working in a very different milieu. His *Parallel Lives* were written within a few years of the *Annals*.

There are many dreams in the *Lives*, and some are clearly prophetic:[22] the Vestal who dreams of her own death (*Romulus* 2), Pyrrhus dreaming of Sparta being blasted by a thunderbolt (*Pyrrhus* 29), Cicero dreaming of a strange young man with a great future, and next day coming across someone with the same features, the young Octavian (*Cicero* 44). But there are also those which, equally clearly, come from within and illuminate the dreamer's preoccupations: Marcellus so obsessed with the thought of fighting Hannibal hand-to-hand that he dreams about it nightly (*Marcellus* 28); Theseus so jealous of Heracles's exploits that they fill his dreams (*Theseus* 6); Brutus not being able to get dreams of killing Caesar out of his head (*Brutus* 13). There are also, arguably, some cases where dreams *both* illuminate the pre-existing psychology *and* afford new information from outside: thus the preoccupied King Mithridates dreams about the nearby army of Pompey and also is

given an indication of a devastating surprise attack (*Pompey* 32),
and the dispirited Medius dreams all too accurately about the
diminishing success of his king Antigonus (*Demetrius* 19). 'The
dream illustrates the curious characteristics of anxiety, prediction,
and vision of the future which we find in so many dreams of the
Lives.'[23]

In the passage given on pp. 258–9 below, Plutarch describes the
last days of Gaius Marius, locked in civil war with Lucius Cornelius
Sulla. Marius has returned to Rome and slaughtered many of his
enemies; but Sulla and his army are expected to arrive shortly
from the East, where they had just won a glorious triumph over
King Mithridates of Pontus.

'Dread is the lion's lair, e'en with the lion away': the lion, of
course, is Sulla, soon to return. The natural reading is that Marius's
dream comes from within, along with the other 'intense fits of
despondency and night-terrors', internalizing his fears of Sulla and
visiting on the man himself a version of the bloody horrors he
is causing others. Marius's mind breaks because it can no longer
summon the genuine ambition which dominated his earlier career:
he can only fight his wars in hallucination. His preoccupations
emerge strongly in that final crazed vision. It is not only ambition
but *jealousy*, an image of himself fighting the Mithridatic war
which had just brought Sulla such glory: this is a distorted version
of the genuine ambition he had been nursing for the Mithridatic
command a few years earlier (*Marius* 31). Such jealous rivalries
have been a major theme of the *Life*,[24] but never before have they
taken so bizarre a form. This internal, psychological register is
strong, and as readers we have no 'hesitation' in preferring it.

We may also take with it the account of Sulla's own death in
78 BC (given on p. 260 below). Plutarch probably wrote the *Sulla*
a few years before the *Marius*, but that does not exclude us from
regarding the passages as complementary.[25]

It is less clear what we should make of this. Sulla is already
very ill, of a wasting disease which filled his body with maggots
(ch. 36). Is this dream an internalization of his awareness of his
coming death? Or is it a genuine divine manifestation? Or is it
both? Sulla himself, Plutarch implies, had no hesitation in taking
it as the second: that is clear from the way Sulla bracketed it with
the prophecy from the Chaldaeans, and this is anyway the last of
a sequence of reliable, invasive, 'from without' dreams in the *Life*.[26]

Sulla has emerged as one who takes such things very seriously: 'trust nothing so much', he had said, 'as the instructions which the supernatural gives you by night' (6.10). But Plutarch's own narrative is not committed to that view: there are too many other cases in the *Lives*, including that of Marius, where internal generation of dreams is a clear likelihood. This, then, may be a case where we are left 'hesitating', in the way Todorov identified, between the supernatural and natural explanations – even though there is no one in the narrative who shares that hesitation.

What might seem clearer is the contrast between the two old adversaries in their terminal dreams, with Marius meeting his death in terror and Sulla calmly accepting the move to another, more peaceful world. That contrast can be felt whether Sulla's calmness is traced in the generation of the dream or just in his acquiescent, insightful recording of it – or in both. Yet there is a further twist: 'He should come and join Metella in peace . . .'. Caecilia Metella's death a few years earlier had fallen during an elaborate series of banquets which Sulla was giving to the people (35.1–2). The priests had advised Sulla that he should not visit her during her illness nor allow his house to be polluted during the festival. Sulla, 'god-fearing' (or 'superstitious', *deisidaimon*) as ever, had therefore written her a note of divorce before she died, and ordered her removal to another house; but he had her buried lavishly, transgressing his own regulations for funerary expenses (35.3). That reflects the respect in which Sulla had always held her, a theme stressed in the earlier narrative.[27]

A little later, Sulla had allowed himself to be captivated by the rather obvious public flirting of one Valeria, a beautiful noblewoman, and had married her. The morally sensitive Plutarch strongly disapproves:

> Perhaps there is no criticism of Valeria here, but there is of Sulla: even if she were the most chaste and highly-born woman alive, this started with a most unchaste and ignoble beginning. Sulla was led astray by her looks and her flirting charms, just as if he were a young lad – and that tends to be the source of the most dishonourable and shameless passions. (35.10–11)

Yet even after his marriage Sulla lived a wild life full of drink, flutegirls, actresses and theatre-musicians (36.1–2, recalling with terminal ring-composition 2.4–6): this played a part in leaving him susceptible to the final illness, with his flesh eaten away by all those maggots (36.3–4).

Now it is to a quiet life with his earlier wife Metella that he is beckoned. If the dream comes from outside, it might hint at divine disapproval at the recent moral and marital shenanigans, just as the maggots give a physical defilement of the flesh to go with its moral counterpart. If on the other hand it is internally generated, this may capture his own existential disquiet at how he has lived – an ancient counterpart of Richard's dream before Bosworth in Shakespeare's *Richard III*. Either way, or both ways, that 'calm acquiescence' in his death is not all there is to it, any more than the whole truth is captured by that complacent Chaldaean prophecy that he would die 'at the height of his good fortune': Fortune, which has been such a key-word in Sulla's life and public image.[28] Perhaps this end is not, after all, more serene than Marius's.

The circumstances of the death were certainly not tranquil. The illness is sordid; and his death itself was triggered by the strangling of a magistrate, Granius, at his bedside. The excitement of shouting the order stimulated Sulla to burst a blood vessel, and this hastened his demise (37.5). Marius was not the only man to meet his death amid bloodshed, terrorizing, and the slaughter of prominent Romans.

Sulla, it has been argued, is a particularly disorienting *Life*.[29] Time and again easy moral judgements are problematized and redirected by new suggestions; this is a story in which we never know quite where we are, or how we should judge. It is unsurprising that his death too should be thought-provoking in complex ways; and the register of his dream, like that of Marius's final hallucination, offers a new oblique perspective, a further way of denying us a single, simple, straightforward understanding.

We have continued to see ways in which dreams juggle critical elements of waking life, and by so doing both highlight them and submit them to a challenging new perspective. The reader is often left with a hesitation about the precise interpretation of the dream, but it is rare for our puzzlement to map precisely onto the puzzlement felt by the characters themselves, for the reader's role to be 'entrusted' (as Todorov puts it)[30] to a character: instead the reader typically possesses an insight denied to the characters. Either we are puzzled when they are not (Sulla); or, even if we have no hesitations ourselves, we feel that the characters ought to have asked more puzzled questions than they do (Bassus and Nero); or we are puzzled at a deeper level than the characters (Artabanus). These are not cases of simple focalization through a single participant's eyes: our writers have subtler ways. Yet the characters' response can still be crucial to our own reading, and in each case both dream and reaction afford an enriching glance into the forces at play, supernatural or psychological or both.

Dreams are good to think with,[31] and good for the illumination of how others thought about their lives. And the ancient historians knew it.

Notes

1. On the light shed by dreams into sexual 'protocols' see esp. John J. Winkler, *The Constraints of Desire* (New York, 1990), pp. 17–44. G.W. Bowersock, *Fiction as History: Nero to Julian* (Berkeley, 1994), pp. 77–98, gives a more sceptical view, but trivializes the position he is attacking by representing it as a claim that Artemidorus's dream-world was 'perfectly consonant with daily life' (p. 86): the juggling of everyday categories is evidently much more complex. On dreams and personal identity, see Suzanne MacAlister, *Dreams and Suicides: The Greek Novel from Antiquity to the Byzantine Empire* (London, 1996), esp. pp. 9–13, 33–5.

2. Patricia Cox Miller, *Dreams in Late Antiquity: Studies in the Imagination of a Culture* (Princeton, 1994), e.g. pp. 62, 79. Cox Miller's book ranges more widely than its title suggests, bringing out the value of dreams as a discourse for a culture to make sense of its world and itself.

3. See esp. Rosemary Jackson, *Fantasy: The Literature of Subversion* (1981; London, 1988), esp. p. 8, on the parallel between fantasy and dreams. On the relation between dreaming, day-dreaming, fantasy and phantasy, see more fully H. Segal, *Dream, Phantasy, and Art* (London, 1991), esp. pp. 16–17, 30, 64–5. In this volume Julie Sanders, pp. 137–50, examines the links between dreams, fiction, fantasy and madness.

4. On Artemidorus's distinction and the use he makes of it see S.R.F. Price, 'The future of dreams: from Freud to Artemidoros', in D.M. Halperin, J.J. Winkler and F.I. Zeitlin, eds, *Before Sexuality: The Construction of Erotic Experience in the Ancient Greek World* (Princeton, 1990), pp. 365–88, esp. 371–2; Winkler, *Constraints of Desire*;

Bowersock, *Fiction as History*, rightly warning that Artemidorus may be atypical; Cox Miller, *Dreams*, pp. 77–91.

5. Tzvetan Todorov, *The Fantastic: A Structural Approach to a Literary Genre*, trans. R. Howard (London, 1973), esp. pp. 41–57; cf. Jackson, *Fantasy*, pp. 24–32 (the quotation in the text is from p. 24).

6. I have discussed that development more fully in 'Tragical dreamer: some dreams in the Greek and Roman historians', *Greece and Rome* 44 (1997), pp. 197–213. Here I am concerned not to examine the development in detail, but to take some particularly suggestive examples and explore the connections with the fantastic.

7. Todorov, *Fantastic*, esp. pp. 24–31, 76, regards such uncertainty as a defining feature of the fantastic: as soon as the reader achieves clarity, the fantastic topples over into a neighbouring genre.

8. Todorov, *Fantastic*, pp. 31–4: this too is exploited by Jackson, *Fantasy*, p. 28.

9. 'Allegorical' and 'poetic' prove particularly problematic: the generic continuities between historiographic prose and epic poetry are too strong, and 'allegory' is too complex and ambiguous a term, for easy transcultural application. But one can still understand and explore Todorov's demand that the reader accept descriptions of strange experiences literally, without taking them as a figure for something different.

10. In fact sixteen or seventeen. They are listed and analysed by P. Frisch, *Die Träume bei Herodot* (Meisenheim, 1968).

11. I discuss other aspects of Artabanus's role, especially the limitations of his insight, in 'Thucydides' Archidamus and Herodotus' Artabanus', in M.A. Flower and M. Toher, eds, *Georgica: Greek Studies in Honour of George Cawkwell* (*Bulletin of the Institute of Classical Studies*, Supp. 58, 1991), pp. 130–40.

12. As suggested by e.g. L. Huber, *Religiöse und politische Beweggründe des Handelns in der Geschichtsschreibung des Herodotus* (Tübingen, 1963), pp. 147–8, arguing that in his heart of hearts Xerxes's mind is unchanged.

13. Cf. Frisch, *Die Träume*, p. 16. It was a capital offence in Persia to sit on the king's throne, as commentators observe. There are also anthropological parallels for individuals taking a king's role for a short time and being executed at the end (J.G. Frazer, *The Golden Bough*, 3rd edn, vol. 4 (London, 1930), pp. 113–19), or for disaster to threaten anyone using a ruler's clothes (Frazer, 3rd edn, vol. 3 (London, 1927), pp. 131–2). A Greek audience might anyway have felt it dangerous to test a deity in this way, and assume that someone as wise as Artabanus, even a Persian, might feel similarly. Cf. H. Klees, *Die Eigenart des griechischen Glaubens an Orakel und Seher, Tübinger Beiträge zur Altertumswissenschaft* 43, (Stuttgart, 1965), pp. 56–8.

14. See below, n. 17.
15. Notice also 7.47, where Xerxes is still sanguine ('Artabanus, if the dream had not been so clear, would you still have held your old opinion . . .'); Artabanus seems more nervous ('May the dream turn out as you and I would wish . . .'), but still only to shy away from the topic and turn to other reasons for concern.
16. The next hint of a royal dream will come at 8.54–5, when Xerxes has taken and burnt the Athenian acropolis and sent a messenger back to report the news to Artabanus (the name is itself a pointer back to this sequence). He then sends some Athenian exiles to the acropolis to perform traditional rites. Perhaps, Herodotus says, it was a matter of uneasy conscience, perhaps he was instructed by a dream. The exiles find a new shoot from Athena's sacred olive tree. The olive will eventually be on the Greeks' side, not the Persians'; and the gods will intervene accordingly.
17. There is something similar at 1.120, after Astyages has discovered that his grandson Cyrus has survived his attempts to kill him in infancy. The dream-experts give King Astyages the advice he clearly wants, that he should not kill him despite the earlier warning dreams of 1.107–8; Astyages is delighted (1.121.1); but the experts' persisting unease is reflected in their advice to send him away (1.120.6). There are several echoes of that sequence here: Cyrus's initiation of the Achaemenid dynasty is mirrored as Xerxes subjects it to its greatest crisis. And the dynasty had its birth amid kin-slaying and destruction of a household. Notions of a 'curse', very much in the manner of tragedy, are not far to seek; but neither are they clear and explicit.
18. Cf. Frisch, *Die Träume*, pp. 18–19; Klees, *Die Eigenart*, p. 58.
19. I discuss these in 'Tragical dreamer'.
20. The Latin *prudentes diuersa fama tulere* is ambiguous: either 'they talked about it in diverse ways', or 'they talked about it in a way diverse [from the commons]'.
21. There is a problem about the text here, but whether we read *ut coniectura demonstrabat* (Halm), 'as he made clear by conjecture', or the manuscripts' *ut coniectura demonstrat*, 'as conjecture makes clear', we should regard Bassus as marking a transition to guesswork. Professor Tony Woodman (to whom I am most grateful for helpful discussion) has persuaded me that, if we read the latter, we should take it as included in the indirect speech, not as a gloss of Tacitus himself. This is part of what Bassus said. I have translated accordingly.
22. They are analysed by Frederick Brenk in *Latomus* 34 (1975), pp. 336–49, and in his *In Mist Apparelled* (*Mnemosyne* Supp. 48, 1977), pp. 214–36.
23. Brenk, *In Mist Apparelled*, p. 222, discussing both these dreams. A fascinating marginal case is Caesar's dream of sexual intercourse with

his mother before crossing the Rubicon. Does it come from outside, and if so does it intimate divine disapproval for the most transgressive sexuality possible or promise success, conquest and domination of the earth, the mother of everyone? Or from inside, mirroring an inner disquiet? Or both? I discuss this case in 'Tragical dreamer'.

24. Cf. esp. *Marius* 10–11.1, 28.6–7, 32.
25. The relative chronology of the *Lives* is a scholarly minefield. The standard view is set out by C.P. Jones, *Journal of Roman Studies* 56 (1966), pp. 61–74, reprinted in B. Scardigli, *Essays on Plutarch's Lives* (Oxford, 1995), pp. 95–123. *Marius* 10.2 cross-refers to Sulla, and some complex arguments based on further cross-references suggest that a number of *Lives* lie in between the two. But this whole style of argument is very precarious. It is more important to see that the *Lives* are envisaged as a series, whatever their sequence of publication, and one *Life* can assume knowledge not only of its Greek or Roman pair but also of other *Lives*. Thus cross-reference to other *Lives* frequently excuses an abbreviated treatment of an episode (C. Stoltz, *Zur relativen Chronologie der Parallelbiographien Plutarchs* (Lund, 1929), pp. 43–55), and the Hellenistic *Lives* may well assume knowledge not only of Alexander's career but of Plutarch's own *Life* of Alexander: cf. J.M. Mossman, 'Plutarch, Pyrrhus, and Alexander', in P.A. Stadter, ed., *Plutarch and the Historical Tradition* (London, 1992), pp. 92–3, 103–4.
26. *Sulla* 6.10, 9.7, and especially 28.7–8, a mirroring dream of the dead Marius and *his* son: other prophecies and omens, 5.11, 7.3–13, 9.6–8, 11, 12.7–8, 14.12, 17.14, 27.1–3, 27.6–17, 29.11–13.
27. *Sulla* 6.18–23, 13.1.
28. Cf. esp. 6, 19.9, 27.6, 29.12, 34.3–5, 35.8, 38.5.
29. This is argued by Tim Duff in an important forthcoming book, *Plutarch's Lives: Biographies as Moral Texts* (Oxford), and in his 'Moral ambiguity in Plutarch's *Lysander-Sulla*' in J.M. Mossman (ed.), *Plutarch and his Intellectual World* (London, 1997), pp. 169–87.
30. Todorov, *Fantastic*, p. 33.
31. S.R.F. Price, *Journal of Roman Studies* 86 (1996), p. 242, reviewing Cox Miller, *Dreams*.

My thanks to other contributors, to Judith Mossman, and to Irene de Jong for very helpful comments.

2 The fairy mistress in medieval literary fantasy

Carolyne Larrington

The 'marvellous', the other world of fairies, enchantment and illusion which colours the genre of medieval European romance, tends to be regarded by modern theorists as simple to account for, and thus as inherently less interesting than the 'uncanny'. Some critics – Jackson and Apter for example – consider the medieval marvellous as continuous with the twentieth-century fantasy of J.R.R. Tolkien, C.S. Lewis and Charles Williams, a fantasy which 'defuse[s] potentially disturbing anti-social drives and retreat[s] from any profound confrontation with existential dis-ease'.[1] The fantasy of these writers tends to be relegated to a secondary, unproblematic category; the nostalgic, Christian-humanist character of their writing is impelled by a transcendentalism in which the twentieth century can no longer believe. The happy ending, reflecting Tolkien's '[j]oy beyond the walls of the world', seems assured in this kind of fantasy; the universe is one in which 'goodness, stability, order will eventually prevail'.[2] However, the over-simple elision of Tolkien-type fantasy with the medieval 'marvellous' entails the interpretation of the fantastic elements in medieval romance as merely compensatory: wish-fulfilment dreams open to all the criticisms of fantasy as unserious escapism, offering simplistic and implausible solutions to the problems of human existence.

To read medieval romance through the distorting lens of twentieth-century conservative, Christian re-creators of the genre is to miss both romance's historical particularity and the archaic and archetypal significances of the other world in romance texts. For, like Tolkien and Lewis's own 1950s nostalgia for a pre-war innocence, medieval romance is very much the product of a particular historical moment: the birth of feudal ideology in the twelfth century. By this time French had become the language of the aristocracy in both France and England. The Plantagenets were established on the English throne and held much territory in France, while the French kingdom was itself divided into a large number of competing duchies and fiefdoms; political unity in France was not to be achieved until the early thirteenth century. Nevertheless the European aristocracy had begun to become aware of itself as a universal class with a shared language, common ideals and class identity. With the increasing erosion of feudalism, and, from the thirteenth century onwards, the threat of infiltration of the aristocracy by the emerging bourgeoisies, it was in the interests of the nobility to formulate an elaborate, highly codified ideology to determine who was 'gentil' and who not, 'for an audience whose power and wealth depended on quite unchivalric practices but had need of a new imaginary because of their new position'.[3]

Who is 'gentil' and who is not? The profoundly held belief that nobility is a matter of birth was often troubled by empirical demonstrations that the aristocracy could and did behave ignobly; moreover, the tenet that rank is irrelevant to the achieving of Christian salvation appeared also to contradict the notion that the nobility's wealth and power were contingent on their virtue and were thus divinely ordained.[4] Taking its name from the Vulgar Latin vernaculars in which it was first composed, romance as a genre was comprehensible to both the illiterate secular courtly elite and the Latin-trained clerical classes; its appeal was to both men and women, to those who were born into the aristocracy and to those who longed to join its ranks.[5] Romance was, *par excellence*, the genre in which the nobility saw itself mirrored, the genre which defined and explained the nature of nobility. Thus ideas of exclusion and inclusion in the knightly in-group are fundamental to romance; the identity of the knightly hero is constructed equally by what he is and what he is not, and by what he does and does not do.

In a romance narrative, as Frederic Jameson argues, the naive hero, undergoing the process of identity formation in a quest or adventure, observes the operations of Good and Evil and learns accordingly.[6] Jameson asserts that, in romance, the Otherness against which the knightly class defines itself is found not in the enemy knights with whom the romance hero engages, for, once defeated, the enemy knight becomes simply another knight like oneself, a fellow-member of the noble elite. Rather, Otherness is displaced to the plane of magic and is here identified as evil: 'The point, however, is not that in such figures the Other is feared because he is evil; rather, he is evil *because* he is Other, alien, different, strange, unclean and unfamiliar' (p. 140).

Jameson generalizes too broadly here about the nature of the marvellous; by conflating Otherness with evil, he assumes that Christian ethics are all-embracing in the world of romance. Though, following Northrop Frye, he notes that romance is a 'debased form of myth', he misses the crucial fact that in myth the other world is morally neutral: a different, powerful, often cruel place. Its denizens have an agenda of their own in which humans play often only an incidental part. Hence the intervention of the Other in medieval romance is not necessarily beneficent, the wave of the fairy godmother's wand ensuring Tolkien's happy ending, but neither are its activities always as inimical as Jameson suggests. True, by the later thirteenth century, fairies were increasingly regarded as diabolical in operation, especially in clerically influenced works, but in many romance, and romance-related, contexts the other world is still seen as distinct from heaven and hell.[7] In the late medieval Scottish ballad of 'Thomas the Rhymer', the winding road to 'Elfland' lies between the path of righteousness, overgrown with thorns and briars, and the 'braid, braid road ... of wickedness'.[8] Even this categorization of the other world as an intermediate place should be refused, since it still seeks to enclose the other world within the Christian system.

Reading the marvellous in medieval romance requires an interpretative strategy which takes account of romance's historical conditions: nostalgia for a more secure past, before the collapse of feudalism and its concomitant social disruption, in combination with anxiety about the present. The aristocracy had much to be anxious about: powerful challenges to the value of chivalry were offered by the religious revivals of the thirteenth century; the constant drain on noble resources which the Hundred Years War entailed endangered the integrity of the great feudal estates; while the ideal of the knight as soldier of Christ had been tainted by the failure of the later Crusades. Meanwhile, back at court, the cash-rich bourgeoisie were becoming ever more influential in the nascent state bureaucracies and their daughters were increasingly marrying into the nobility, bringing substantial dowries. The place of women in aristocratic life was becoming altogether problematic. As the Church came increasingly to emphasize the importance of consent in marriage, the wife was no longer simply regarded as dynastic breeding stock, but rather as a helpmeet, adviser and companion. The distant and unobtainable damsel who inspired knightly service from afar became the wife who usually wanted her husband at home with her, administering the estates, training the children and keeping her company. The dilemma which new thinking about marriage posed for the knightly class is an important theme in twelfth-century romance.[9]

Apart from these immediate historical considerations, transhistorical structures, archetypes of human experience, also underpin the medieval romance genre. 'Even in the fantasy world, man is a social-historical animal, and he is free to create on his own by the proper use of themes and images drawn from the wider experience of the race', Harvey Cox suggests.[10] Cox's 'wider experience of the race' invites us to pay attention to recurrent themes and figures in the romances, relating them to human psychology in our interpretation: monitoring the psyche's reaction to extreme situations, and their function in identity formation. Thus a 'new historical' approach to the fantastic in medieval romance foregrounds the specific social and class conditions which contribute to the formation of the text, and upon which, in turn, the text itself exerts influence, reinforcing the ideology of the patrons of romance. At the same time a psychological reading, aware of the structuring function of archetype in romance, of the relevance to the individual of the questions raised by the text, and of the dangers and difficulties, both external and internal, which the romance hero faces, adds another dimension, helping us to gauge how both contemporary and modern readers may react to the fantastic elements of romance.

The theme of the fairy mistress, the other world woman who takes a human lover, demonstrates how a Celtic mythological motif is re-employed in medieval romance. The fairy mistress participates in the making, and unmaking, of her lover both in terms of his social and economic position in the medieval hierarchy and in the process of forging a knightly identity, the balancing of competing drives and forces in the hero's psyche. The other world woman and her human lover, a story type found universally,[11] can be traced back from medieval romance through the preservation of Celtic motifs in Breton oral tradition, as far back as Irish myth, notably in the stories of Cú Chulaind and Fand, and of Oisín and Niamh.[12] In 'The Wasting Sickness of Cú Chulaind', some members of the Tuatha Dé Danaan, other world inhabitants who live in a certain mound, need the human hero Cú Chulaind to help them in a battle against another other world tribe. As a reward Cú Chulaind gains the love of the other world woman Fand. She comes to the human world to be with her lover, but is driven away by Cú Chulaind's wife.[13] In the tale of Oisín the protagonist rides away with Niamh of the Golden Hair, queen of the land of eternal youth.[14] Oisín's stay in the other world is filled with every delight, but after three weeks he is ready to journey home to visit his kin. Niamh gives him a horse, warning him not to set foot on the ground or he will be unable to return to her. Back in this world, Oisín finds that 300 years have passed, and that Finn his father, and all the *fiana*, Finn's band of heroes, are long dead. Horrified, Oisín rides on, eventually forgetting the taboo when he alights to help an old man who has dropped a sack of corn. Immediately his 300 years descend upon him and he dies.[15] These Celtic motifs were most probably preserved and transmitted into French, and thence English courtly literature, by Breton *conteurs* or minstrels, bilingual in their own Celtic language and in French, who travelled widely around Europe, enabling in particular the spread of Arthurian myth.[16] Following the Celtic story patterns outlined above, medieval fairy mistresses fall broadly into two types: the woman who comes to the human world to marry or be with her lover, epitomized by the fairy Mélusine, and the woman who takes a human away into another world, the type of Morgan le Fay. An intermediate type comes to visit her lover in the human world but vanishes when a stipulated condition is violated. Only when her lover is in danger of his life does she return to rescue him, taking him away to the other world for ever.[17]

The story of Mélusine is in essence a dynastic origin myth for the noble line of Lusignan in Poitou, western France. Raimondin, an impoverished cousin of the count of Poitiers, accidentally kills his lord during a hunting party.[18] Distraught, he wanders away into the forest until he chances upon the Fountain of Fair Thirst; here he encounters a beautiful and noble woman who addresses him by name, telling him that she knows his story, and will bring him good fortune and prosperity if he follows her counsel. She adds:

have no fear that I do not belong to God, and that I don't believe in his miracles. I swear to you that I believe in the Catholic faith and each of its articles . . . Trust me and you will do well, you will be elevated to such high honours that you will be the noblest of all your lineage. (p. 50)

Raimondin agrees to marry the lady, accepting her stipulation that he must never seek to find out where she goes or what she does on Saturdays. The lady advises him and helps him obtain a fief. The marriage is celebrated with public ceremony; the lady, Mélusine, honours the guests with splendid presents, then sets about clearing the forest with the aid of workers of unknown origin. She builds the castle of Lusignan, henceforth the family seat. Thereafter Mélusine gives birth to ten sons; in between she founds many settlements, including Niort and La Rochelle, and constructs a number of churches. Seven of the sons have some kind of unusual blemish; the eighth, who has three eyes, one in his forehead, is simply named Horrible, while the last two are normal.

The marriage lasts for many years and the older sons grow up to be prodigious heroes, winning thrones in different parts of Europe, including Cyprus and Armenia, kingdoms historically ruled by members of the Lusignan lineage. Eventually the taboo is breached; Raimondin's brother tells Raimondin that his wife's Saturday disappearances are the subject of gossip: 'everyone is saying (God protect me) that she is breaking all moral rules, and that on that day she deceives you by giving herself to another. Others, you may as well know, say that on that day she goes away to the fairies' (p. 88). Raimondin feels forced to act. He pokes a hole in the door of his wife's chamber with his sword. Peeping through he sees:

Mélusine bathing; down to the waist he saw that she was white as snow on the bough, attractive and gracious, fresh and slender in form. Certainly one would never see a more beautiful woman. But her body ended in a serpent's tail, huge and horrible, banded with silver and azure with which she stirred up the water violently. (p. 89)

Mélusine is well aware that the prohibition has been transgressed, but neither husband nor wife raise the matter and life continues as normal. Then the seventh son, Geoffrey la Grand Dent, burns down the monastery of Maillezais, with all the monks inside, when he hears that his brother Fromont has joined the order. In his rage and grief, Raimondin refuses to listen to Mélusine's words of comfort, accusing her as well as his son: 'Ha, serpent! your progeny will never amount to anything worthwhile!' (p. 101). Once Mélusine's secret has been made public, the marriage is over. Sobbing piteously she takes leave of Raimondin, and flies out of the window in the form of a great serpent, circling three times around the tower, uttering a terrible cry. Raimondin never sees Mélusine again, though the nurses of his younger children report that she reappears at night to suckle them. Mélusine's cry is still to be heard whenever there is a change of seigneur at Lusignan. Raimondin dies shortly afterwards of grief, and the mighty lineage gradually declines in its fortunes, the main line becoming extinct in 1308.

Mélusine appears in Raimondin's life at the moment where his social alienation is complete. Already insecure because of his father's poverty, dependent on Aymeri, lord of Poitou, for material prosperity and social standing, Raimondin has just killed his lord and is lost in the trackless forest. Mélusine is able to help Raimondin, not only in covering up the circumstances of his lord's death and thus escaping censure, but also in gaining land from the new lord of Poitou by a variation of the trick used by Dido to found Carthage: asking for as much land as could be enclosed in a stag's hide, then cutting up the hide into narrow strips, capable of delineating a large area. In Jean d'Arras, Mélusine also reveals the truth of his parentage to Raimondin, enabling him to reclaim his exiled father's ancestral lands in Brittany and to clear his father's name of the accusation of treachery. Prefiguring Raimondin's own slaying of Aymeri, Raimondin's father had accidentally killed the nephew of the Breton king. Once Raimondin's fiefdom is established, Mélusine works indefatigably to lay the foundations of the lineage's future prosperity, producing sons and fortified towns in equal measure. Mélusine looks beyond the material: she establishes churches in order to assure her salvation and that of her husband. Through his liaison with the fairy, Raimondin gains social prestige and wealth, and becomes the ancestor of a unique lineage whose members become kings across Europe.

In an influential article, Jacques Le Goff re-situates the ancient figure of 'an autochthonous celtic fertility goddess' or 'Indo-European culture-heroine' who underlies the figure of Mélusine as a fairy of fertility.[19] She is the bestower of bounty in three distinct areas: the rural economy (as clearer of forests); as the builder of towns, castles and churches, 'la fée de l'essor économique médiévale', the fairy of the essence of the medieval economy; and in demographic terms, as the provider of a wealth of descendants. Le Goff emphasizes also the class position of Raimondin and the heroes of similar Melusinian tales – they are *milites*, not the sons of kings, but rather aspirant members of the lesser aristocracy for whom Mélusine is 'l'incarnation symbolique et magique de leur ambition sociale', the symbolic and magical incarnation of their social ambition (p. 601). Le Goff is right to point to the social mobility and prestige which Mélusine confers upon her husband, yet his article raises further questions not always easy to answer. Why should the story, unlike most 'fairy-tales' (and in contradiction to the modern definitions of the medieval marvellous outlined above), end tragically both for Raimondin and for Mélusine herself? Is the encounter with the fairy mistress to be regarded simply as a medieval equivalent of winning the lottery? Or, since the knights in Mélusine-type stories are emphatically chosen by their mistresses, who greet them by name and proceed to the question of marriage very quickly, is there some quality in the knights themselves which calls forth the fairy's munificence? In the tale of Mélusine, and in similar stories, the protagonist meets the lady when his need is greatest. She is the conduit through which he acquires land and riches, but she is, just as importantly, a source of advice, both practical and spiritual. Mélusine helps Raimondin devise a strategy for reporting Aymeri's death and she informs him of much about his lineage which he had not known. Raimondin insists on consulting Mélusine before Fromont is permitted to enter the monastery, while her sensible words of comfort after Geoffrey's burning of the monastery – that Geoffrey must make atonement and return to the Good – provoke the fatal revelation. Even at her departure she warns that her most deformed son, the aptly named Horrible, must be killed, for otherwise he would destroy all that his mother had achieved in Poitou.

Mélusine's strategic advice recalls the role which Georges Duby suggests the feudal lady plays in the education of the young noble: both maternal and erotic, she civilizes the wild and reckless young man, instructing him in courtly custom and the sphere of women.[20] Likewise Mélusine gives Raimondin the confidence and *savoir-faire* to break the pattern of his father's misfortune and to become a great lord, in character as well as in possessions. Like the Lady of the Lake and similarly nurturing other world females, Mélusine represents an anima-type figure for Raimondin, manifesting herself at a moment of psychic crisis and sending the young man in a new direction; she is symbolic of a continuing process within Raimondin's growth into the social identity of seigneur, the wisdom, confidence, and above all, trust, which the mature adult needs. Raimondin and Mélusine are a successful team; the psychic split which Raimondin's suspicion and anger causes in the breaking of the taboo is disastrous for both, bringing misery and an early death for him, and 'pain, misery and torment until the Day of Judgment' (p. 102) for her.[21]

In the social terms of the late fourteenth century, when the two main Mélusine narratives were composed, Mélusine's unspeakable origins, her fairy lineage and extraordinary blemish, align her with the wealthy bourgeois heiress, exchanged for social status in an aristocratic marriage. The heiress's dowry provides a much-needed cash infusion for the noble family's estates and the marriage may even bring happiness to the two individuals involved, but the common suspicion on the part of other members of the noble lineage that the strange wife is not quite *comme il faut*, the urge to make her social difference public, and the consequent sowing of mistrust between husband and wife suggests that Mélusine's tragedy was replicated in many ancient lineages as the aristocracy sought to bolster their depleted cash reserves by financially, but not socially, advantageous marriages. Le Goff argues that it is Mélusine's pagan ancestry, interpreted as demonic by clerical narrators of Mélusine-type stories, which makes it impossible for the couple to save one another. In many of the story's analogues, suspicion is aroused when the mysterious bride refuses to remain in church during the elevation of the Host; the unmasking and rout of the supernatural creature is regarded as a lucky and narrow escape for her husband.[22] But Mélusine is a good Christian, whose project is the salvation of her own soul, salvation which can only be achieved through marriage with a mortal and a Christian death.[23] Raimondin's own soul is never in danger; the only disadvantage his marriage brings are a brood of strange and somewhat unruly sons, though fit to be kings, and the envy of his brother who urges him to discover the truth about his wife. For Raimondin, the loss of Mélusine is disastrous, but for the fairy herself, the dénouement is truly tragic.

Morgan le Fay first appears in medieval narrative in the *Vita Merlini* (Life of Merlin) composed by Geoffrey of Monmouth in 1148. Here she is a beneficent healing fairy, one of nine sisters who live on the Fortunate island, later identified with Avalon; by the time Chrétien de Troyes was composing his Arthurian romances, some forty years later, she had become Arthur's sister, the kindly healer of his wounds after the final battle.[24] Only gradually during the thirteenth century is Morgan transformed into a malevolent figure, opposed to Arthur and Guinevere and the values of the Round Table. This transformation is, in part, dictated by the growth to prominence of Lancelot in the French Vulgate cycle, and consequently of his mentor, the Lady of the Lake, the good fairy with whom Morgan is increasingly contrasted.[25] Morgan is somewhat rehabilitated in the fifteenth century; in the romance *Ogier le Danois* she is shown cooperating with the will of God by sending her lover back from the other world to assist France in an hour of great need.[26] Typically, in thirteenth- and fourteenth-century texts, Morgan abducts human knights to be her lovers. Lancelot is frequently her victim, in part to spite Guinevere whom Morgan has hated since the queen thwarted her liaison with one of Guinevere's kinsmen, in part out of desire for Lancelot himself.

Two episodes from the *Lancelot* illustrate how Morgan's desire for control over her lovers manifests itself as hostility to knightly chivalry. In the first episode, Morgan decides to avenge herself on a faithless lover by creating an enchanted valley, the Val sans Retour. Any knight who strays there is unable to leave if he has ever been unfaithful to his lady in thought or deed. The ladies in question can come and go as they please; indeed they are quite content, since the knights' imprisonment keeps them at their ladies' side instead of wandering away after adventure. The spell can only be broken by the perfectly faithful knight. Armed with a magic ring given him by the Lady of the Lake, Lancelot overcomes two fierce dragons and three dangerous adversaries, breaking the spell. As the joyful knights depart, their ladies weep and Morgan curses Lancelot for destroying women's happiness, including her own, for she too was holding a lover in thrall.[27]

Later in the cycle Morgan captures Lancelot, keeping him prisoner for a long time, 'for she loved him for his great comeliness so much as woman may love man, and it grieved her sore that he would not love her, for she kept him not in prison from hatred, but she thought to conquer him by his misease'.[28] During his captivity, Lancelot whiles away the time by painting the story of his life, including the affair with Guinevere, on the walls of his chamber. Eventually Lancelot breaks the bars of his window and escapes. The paintings on the chamber wall will later, in the *Mort Artu*, be the final evidence Arthur needs to persuade him of Lancelot and Guinevere's treachery, and will set in motion the events leading to the downfall of the kingdom.[29]

By the time Morgan had been fully incorporated into the Vulgate cycle, the idea, originating in certain Irish tales, that departure from the courtly world with a fairy mistress might bring benefits such as immortality, youth, riches and other pleasures, had become problematic.[30] Captivity, however pleasant the prison, equates with loss of masculinity. Although the metaphor of the lover's imprisonment by the lady was popular in courtly rhetoric, it is clear that the knights released from the Val sans Retour are overjoyed to escape, not only from Morgan, but also from their *amies* who have rejoiced in their lovers' bondage.[31] During their imprisonment the honour of the captive knights gradually diminishes as they are prevented from performing new heroic deeds which would maintain their reputations. Instead they sink into an effeminate domesticity. Morgan's womb-like valley tropes with peculiar clarity one of the fundamental dilemmas explored in the debate about the role of women in chivalry: how can a knight establish the balance between devotion to his lady, expressed by spending time in her presence, and the maintenance of knightly honour, possible only by absenting oneself from her in pursuit of adventure?[32] The version of the other world which the fairy offers – domestic comforts, feminine attention, sensual pleasures – is sternly resisted as antithetical to knightly identity, sapping the strength, separating the knight from kin and peer group and weakening his will and desire for autonomy.[33] New ideas about love and friendship as desirable concomitants to marriage, recognition of the alluring comforts of the home as opposed to the dangers of court and battlefield, together with a growing awareness of the control over a couple's destiny which a bourgeois heiress-wife could exert, lie, to some extent, behind the popularity of the Morgan-type story. Aristocratic ideology is challenged by the woman who chooses to use her material and sexual powers to discourage her man from aggression, competition and the pursuit of masculine honour; thus Morgan's plots – and those of other fairy mistresses – are frequently made to fail.

The damage suffered by the imprisoned knight on an individual and psychological level is made clear in Lancelot's final captivity. Lancelot feels his chivalric identity to be under threat through forced inactivity. He seeks to re-establish his sense of self through textualization: illustrating and, crucially, writing revelatory titles to the story of his growth into knighthood – an identity formed by his attachment to Guinevere. Morgan's exultation when she realizes that Lancelot has unwittingly provided the evidence which will convince Arthur of the lovers' guilt, underlines the fatal nature of his last meeting with Morgan. Even though Lancelot defies her and is successful in escaping from every prison she devises for him, ultimately, in the French tradition, it is the encounter with the fairy mistress which brings about his destruction. Just as the Celtic hero's visit to the other world woman separates him from all he holds dear and deprives him of a normal hero's life (a few brief days in the other world turn out to have absorbed more than an entire mortal lifespan), so the captives of Morgan le Fay and her sisters in medieval romance become the unhappy victims of women's wiles. The fairy mistress theme becomes a site for the exploration of the fear of domesticity, of loss of masculinity, and of the maintenance of knightly honour, underpinned by general ecclesiastical mistrust of women and the Church's elision of the female with the diabolical.

The theme of the fairy mistress in medieval romance contradicts the supposition that the project of medieval fantasy is to give assurance of transcendance, order and consolation for the trials of the knightly hero. Originating in the pagan, Celtic past, the motif circumvents questions of Good and Evil, focusing upon the effects of a powerful, female-gendered force on masculine identity and illuminating the preoccupations of the feudal nobility and those who aspired to imitate them: the noble and bourgeois classes. These preoccupations may be summarized as the larger questions of economic prosperity, heirs and inheritance, the maintenance of masculine honour in the face of the demands of female desire and domesticity, and of class privilege when noble blood, the channel through which 'gentil' values are transmitted, becomes diluted by marriage with bourgeois heiresses. Lesser concerns are also addressed: the disparity between public appearance and private character in the women one encounters, the dangers of opportunism and slanderous gossip in the courtly setting when the knight is absent, and the threat constituted by sexual temptation.

The commentary on the two story-types above has been predicated on the idea that the intended readership of the tales was a male one and that male anxieties are particularly addressed.[34] Yet one of the most distinctive features of romance is that, from its earliest emergence in vernacular, as opposed to Latin, the elite language, romance was accessible to both readers and listeners, men and women. Evidence shows that medieval women, like their modern sisters, were avid consumers of romance. Chaucer makes sarcastic reference to the esteem in which women held stories about Lancelot of the Lake, while noble and bourgeois women's wills show that women were more likely to own romances than any other kind of book, except for devotional works.[35] What did women think when they read, or heard read, these fairy mistress stories? We may speculate that they enjoyed the fantasy of female autonomy, the capacity to own property and bestow gifts freely, to choose a lover and to hold the power of life or death over him, and that the fantasy of keeping the beloved ever beside one, attentive and happy in the domestic sphere, would have been a compelling one. However, just as the male consumer of these stories would recognize the impossibility of keeping the simple promise asked by a Mélusine or by Launfal's mistress, Triamour, in the face of complex social pressures, and the inevitability of loss and disillusionment that the narratives provide, so the female consumer would have noted the demonization of the woman who keeps her lover captive, the discontent of the knight in a woman's power, and the doomed nature of the love between Mélusine and Raimondin, with the consequent jeopardizing of Mélusine's salvation.

The fairy mistress may, at first sight, appear to be a straightforwardly escapist fantasy in which immediately pressing problems are solved at a stroke by a transcendent power. But, as the narratives analysed above demonstrate, the fantasy both perpetuates and challenges the dominant ideology of the mid- to late medieval periods, engaging closely with fundamental social and economic questions, while, at the same time, by tapping into archetypal and universal processes of identity formation and gender differentiation, the fairy mistress fantasy retains its ability to speak to medieval and modern readers alike.

Notes

1. Rosemary Jackson, *Fantasy: The Literature of Subversion* (London, 1981), p. 9.
2. J.R.R. Tolkien, 'On fairy stories', in *Tree and Leaf*, ed. Christopher Tolkien (London, 1992), p. 62; Jackson, *Fantasy*, p. 174.
3. Stephen Knight, 'The social function of the Middle English romances', in David Aers, ed., *Medieval Literature: Criticism, Ideology and History* (Brighton, 1984), p. 116. See also Richard Kaeuper's essay in this volume for a consideration of the contemporary ambivalence about chivalry as a social force.
4. The debate about gentility is set out most clearly in Chaucer's 'Wife of Bath's Tale'; Geoffrey Chaucer, *The Riverside Chaucer*, ed. L.D. Benson (Oxford, 1988), p. 120.
5. For the development of European romance see W.J.R. Barron, *English Medieval Romance* (London and New York, 1987), pp. 11–15; significantly, Chaucer's Franklin tells a 'Breton lai' as his contribution to *The Canterbury Tales*, a type of romance already old-fashioned in Chaucer's time, but which perfectly suits the Franklin's *arriviste* pretensions.
6. Frederic Jameson, 'Magical narratives: romance as genre', *New Literary History* 7 (1975), p. 139.
7. This was particularly the case in texts strongly influenced by the Celtic; the Middle English romance of *Sir Orfeo*, in which Queen Heurodis is snatched by the fairies, is a case in point. See *Sir Orfeo*, in *Middle English Verse Romances*, ed. Donald B. Sands (Exeter, 1986), pp. 187–200.
8. Tolkien, 'On fairy stories', p. 10; 'Thomas Rymer', *The English and Scottish Popular Ballads*, ed. F.J. Child, 5 vols (New York, 1956), p. 324. This version of 'Thomas Rymer' was collected, like most of Child's ballads, in the eighteenth century, but traditions about Thomas are known in Scotland from the thirteenth century onwards.
9. See Carolyne Larrington, *Women and Writing in Medieval Europe: A Sourcebook* (London, 1995), pp. 7–19, for changing views of marriage in the period.
10. Harvey Cox, *The Feast of Fools: A Theological Essay on Festivity and Fantasy* (New York, 1969), p. 78. See also Knight, 'The social function'.
11. Stith Thompson, *Motif Index of Folk Literature*, 6 vols (Bloomington, Ind., 1932–36), vol. 3, types F300–305, pp. 55–66.

12. The dating of myth beyond its first recording in oral tradition is problematic. However the Cú Chulaind traditions probably originated in the eighth century, judging from the descriptions of Iron Age warfare which they contain.

13. 'The Wasting Sickness of Cú Chulaind' and 'The Only Jealousy of Emer', in *Early Irish Myths and Sagas*, ed. J. Gantz (Harmondsworth, 1981), pp. 153–78. Compare also the Welsh 'Pwyll, Lord of Dyved', in *The Mabinogion*, ed. J. Gantz (Harmondsworth, 1976), pp. 45–65.

14. The tale of Oisín is first recorded in the eighteenth century, but its features – the approach of the fairy woman, the description of the other world and the effects of the return to this world – correspond with medieval traditions in Irish and other Celtic-influenced texts.

15. Several different versions of the Oisín story exist; the version above is summarized from E. Hartland, *The Science of Fairy Tales* (London, 1891), pp. 196–8.

16. R.S. Loomis, 'The oral diffusion of the Arthurian legend', in R.S. Loomis, ed., *Arthurian Literature in the Middle Ages* (Oxford, 1959), pp. 52–63.

17. The best example of this type is Marie de France's *lai Sir Lanval*; other such *lais* include Marie's *Guigemar* and the anonymous *Graelent* and *Guingamor*. See *Lais de Marie de France*, ed. and trans. Laurence Harf-Lancner (Paris, 1990). In the Lanval-type story, the pleasures of success in this world, the terror of losing lover, wealth and social standing, and escape from this world with its fallible institutions (usually a treacherous queen or failure of the king to dispense justice adequately) are combined with arresting effect. A full study of the fairy mistress in medieval literature is the indispensable Laurence Harf-Lancner, *Les Fées au Moyen Age* (Geneva, 1984).

18. There are two principal versions of the story of Mélusine in French: Jean d' Arras's 1393 prose *Roman de Mélusine* and Coudrette's early-fifteenth-century verse *Le Roman de Mélusine*. Editions: Jean d'Arras, *Mélusine*, ed. Louis Stouff (repr. Geneva, 1974); Coudrette, *Le Roman de Mélusine ou Histoire de Lusignan*, ed. E. Roach (Paris, 1982). All quotations here translated from Coudrette, *Le Roman de Mélusine*, trans. Laurence Harf-Lancner (Paris, 1993).

19. Jacques Le Goff and Emmanuel Le Roy Ladurie, 'Mélusine maternelle et défricheuse', *Annales Economies Sociétés Civilisations* 26 (1971), p. 599.

20. Georges Duby, *Medieval Marriage: Two Models from Twelfth-Century France* (Baltimore, Md., 1978), p. 14; see also Larrington, *Women and Writing in Medieval Europe*, pp. 41–3.

21. Mélusine, herself the product of a fairy–human union, has been cursed by her mother which requires her to marry a human and remain

married until death if she wishes to be saved (Jean d' Arras's prologue, Coudrette, pp. 115–19; 136–7). She has now lost her chance of salvation (see n. 23 below).

22. See Harf-Lancner, *Les fées*, pp. 119–54, and compare in particular the story of Gerbert of Aurillac in Walter Map's *De Nugis Curialium: Courtiers Trifles* ed. and trans. M.R. James, rev. Christopher Brooke and R.A.B. Mynors (Oxford, 1983), pp. 350–65.

23. Paracelsus, *Werke*, vol. 2, ed. W.-E. Pueckert (Basel, Stuttgart, 1967), pp. 489 ff., reports a similar belief: that *mélusines* lack a rational soul and will disappear at the Day of Judgement, unless they marry a human.

24. See Harf-Lancner, *Les fées*, pp. 264–7 and bibliography there.

25. The Vulgate cycle is the great French prose account of the Arthur–Lancelot saga, incorporating *Lancelot do Lac*, the *Queste de Saint Graal* and the *Mort Artu*.

26. Harf-Lancner, *Les fées*, pp. 279–88.

27. *Lancelot: roman en prose du XIIIe siècle*, ed. A. Micha (Paris, Geneva, 1978–83), 9 vols. Here bks. XXII–XXV.

28. *Lancelot*, ed. Micha, LXXXVI, p. 21; *The Book of Lancelot of the Lake*, trans. Lucy Paton (London, 1929), p. 322.

29. *Le Mort Artu*, ed. J. Frappier (Lille, Geneva, 1954), chs. 51–4; *The Death of Arthur*, trans. James Cable (Harmondsworth, 1971), pp. 70–4.

30. For example, the tales of Loegaire and of Condle; see Harf-Lancner, *Les fées*, pp. 214–19; *Silva Gadelica: A Collection of Tales from the Irish*, ed. Standish O'Grady, 2 vols (London and Edinburgh, 1892), vol. 1, pp. 290–1.

31. For a good example of this trope, see *Book of the Knight of the Tour-Landry*, trans. W. Caxton, ed. M.Y. Offord (Oxford, 1971), pp. 27–8; Larrington, *Women and Writing*, pp. 30–1.

32. The question is the theme of two of Chrétien de Troyes's most psychologically complex romances, *Yvain* and *Erec et Enide*. See Chrétien de Troyes, *Arthurian Romances*, trans. C.W. Carroll and W.W. Kibler (Harmondsworth, 1991).

33. Knight, 'The social function', p. 117, notes the castration anxieties suffered by romance heroes, especially in the popular motif of the lover breaking window bars and cutting his hands severely.

34. See Knight, 'The social function', p. 101.

35. Chaucer, *The Riverside Chaucer*, p. 258; Carol Meale, 'Laywomen and their books in late medieval England', in Carol Meale, ed., *Women and Literature in Britain 1150–1500* (Cambridge, 1992), pp. 139–42.

3 Haunting the Middle Ages

Mark Philpott

In the Middle Ages the dead were universally present with the living. Bishop Jacques Fournier of Pamiers was told that Arnaud Gélis, a household servant from near Pamiers, had said that 'those who move their arms and hands from their sides when they rush about do great harm ... moving arms about like that flings many of the souls of the dead to the ground'.[1] Perhaps few would have gone quite as far as this reported remark; nonetheless, whenever medieval people went to church, for example, they found themselves surrounded by the dead. They were buried in the churchyard or the church itself, or, in the case of the sanctifying relics of the saints, enshrined with great honour or embedded in the altar. Prayer was offered through the intercession of dead saints and for the welfare of dead kinsfolk and benefactors. Indeed, by Scripture and ritual the medieval Church proclaimed the abolition of death by the death and resurrection of Jesus, in which all were encouraged and often virtually compelled to participate by baptism and by sharing in Christ's Body and Blood in the Mass. It is scarcely surprising then that the dead, both the sanctified and the more ordinary dead, should have been, as large numbers of different types of medieval writings testify, a real presence in everyday lives and preoccupations.

In the last twenty years or so, the history of the dead and of (attitudes to) death has begun to receive the scholarly attention it deserves. However, medieval accounts of ghostly visits to this world have been comparatively little studied.[2] This chapter will explore the ways in which they can be considered 'fantasy' and sketch some of the important insights into medieval cultures this provides. The first step will be an examination of the nature of the evidence for medieval ghosts. It will be argued that our evidence for medieval ghosts can be loosely categorized under three headings: 'literary', 'educational' and 'documentary'. Secondly, the difficulties posed by the evidence will be explored with the aid of an example from each of the three categories. Thirdly, on the basis laid by the first two sections, we will be able to suggest some frutiful lines of enquiry, in which medieval and modern ideas of fantasy can help to understand medieval ghosts and the society to which they belonged.

Before we can proceed any further it is essential first to get a good understanding of the evidence. Medieval ghosts are part of an extremely ancient and widespread tradition. It seems safe to assume that everybody in the Middle Ages who reported seeing a ghost would have known some older tradition in which ghosts played a part. Certainly, the claim of the psychologist Nicolas Abraham that 'belief that the spirits of the dead can return to haunt the living exists either as an accepted tenet or as a marginal conviction in all civilisations, ancient or modern' seems true of all the past cultures known to the Middle Ages.[3] Since Homer, the Greeks had told stories of the return of the ghosts of loved ones, and of bribing the dead with sacrifices to prophesy truth about past or future.[4] The Romans believed the dead walked among the living on a number of occasions in the year.[5] The ancient Israelites also allowed that the dead could communicate with the living, as Saul's terrifying encounter with the dead Samuel testifies.[6] The New Testament suggests that the early Christians did not differ in this respect either from their predecessors or contemporaries, Jewish or Graeco-Roman. Peter, James and John saw Moses and Elijah talking to Jesus, and in one of the parables it is assumed that someone could be sent from the dead to warn the thoughtless rich of the fate awaiting them.[7] Similarly, it is clear that the traditions of Celtic, Germanic and Scandinavian peoples also had a place for ghosts.[8] Thus in assessing the accounts of medieval ghosts we must take into account the traditions that lay behind them.

Extensive testimony survives of ghosts throughout the medieval period, from the fifth century when Augustine of Hippo discussed the nature of apparitions of the dead, to the fifteenth century and beyond.[9] Ghosts can be discovered in a variety of forms from one end of medieval Europe to the other, from North Africa to Iceland, and in a number of different types of text, composed and preserved for a variety of reasons.[10] These accounts can conveniently be grouped into three categories: the literary, the edificatory, and the official. Some ghost stories clearly belong in a literary context and seem to have been composed in order to entertain. Thus the twelfth-century Anglo-Cambrian writer, Walter Map, offers 'the insipid and bloodless follies' of his work, presumably including the ghost stories, 'for the sake of recreation and play'. A good example of Walter's ghosts (and the example on which we shall be concentrating in the rest of this chapter) is the story of the knight of 'Lesser Britain' who had lost his wife and went on mourning her for a long time. One night in a valley in the midst of an uninhabited area he found her dancing with a crowd of women. He was amazed and afraid to see revived the woman he had buried. He decided to snatch her, so either he would have the joy of embracing her, or if the phantasm eluded him, nobody could accuse him of cowardice. So he grabbed her, and they enjoyed a long and happy marriage, producing several children known as 'the sons of the dead woman'. 'This', Walter notes, 'would be an incredible and portentous injury to nature, did not trustworthy evidence of its truth exist.'[11]

Other accounts of ghosts were collected primarily for edificatory or educational purposes. The thirteenth-century German Cistercian, Caesarius of Heisterbach, for example, claimed he wrote his *Dialogue on Miracles*, including its ghost stories (one of which is translated on p. 263 below), as part of his duties as master of the novices and 'for the edification of posterity'.[12] Literary and edifying ghosts are not, however, mutually exclusive. Master Walter explains his stories as part of divine incomprehensibility, while Caesarius's stories have a certain literary polish.[13]

A third group of medieval ghosts, often mentioned only in passing, is to be found in official documents. A number of canon law texts, for example, deal with belief in ghosts.[14] Among the most interesting of these ghosts are those which haunt Bishop Fournier's inquisition *Register* (extracts from the formal deposition of Arnaud Gélis are translated on pp. 261–2). Initially this type of evidence seems more straightforward, but in fact it overlaps with the others. The ghosts reported in sober official records bear a striking family resemblance to those that populate the literary and educational texts. As Gurevich notes,

> medieval man was predisposed by the whole cultural order to see the other world . . . he saw what folklore tradition and religious ideology imposed on him, and in his intimate mystical experiences

he found the images and situations which the parish priest or wandering preacher told him about and which he saw represented in his church and cathedral.[15]

Thus, many of the views attributed to Gélis in Fournier's *Register* seem to owe something to a tradition ultimately derived from Gregory the Great, presumably by way of sermons that Arnaud had heard.[16] However, it is also true that the answers recorded in the *Register* seem to reflect the inquisitors' expectations of what the answer should have been. Thus, William Agasse, head of the lepers of Pamiers, confessed to involvement in a conspiracy to poison the wells, a fantasy spread throughout France, seemingly derived from the imagination of the prosecutors rather than the activities of the accused.[17]

An essential part of considering the nature of the sources is thus to reflect on their difficulties and limitations. Three more must be noted, the first self-imposed. Accounts of ghostly visitors to this world form only a small section of the vast and multifarious body of medieval writing relating to the dead, which, in turn, is dwarfed by the volume of works concerning the supernatural. We must not forget the consequences of limiting the scope of the inquiry. For example, we have excluded apparitions of the saints, the 'happy dead', from consideration, so we can hardly then be surprised to discover that in our sample no one returns to tell of the joys of heaven; certainly, we could not legitimately conclude, for example, as Abraham has, 'to be sure, all the departed may return, but some are destined to haunt: the dead who were shamed during their lifetime or those who took unspeakable secrets to the grave'.[18]

Secondly, not all the ghost stories that were told in the Middle Ages now exist, since not all of the stories were written down, and not all that were have survived. Indeed, a number of our best sources only survived through frighteningly unlikely series of events. Bishop Fournier's *Register*, for example, survives because he took the notes of his inquisitional sessions with him when he was translated to the diocese of Mirepoix. There he had them written up into a *Register*, which he took to Avignon when he became pope. After his death unknown bureaucrats decided to put this *Register* into the library, and some years later others had it transferred to the Vatican. Even so, only one of the original two volumes of the *Register* survives. Without it, our knowledge of medieval ghosts would have been completely different. Similar examples of the tenuousness of our knowledge of medieval ghosts might be multiplied almost endlessly.[19] With such a transmission, it is necessary to exercise great caution about making arguments based on the absence of evidence, drawing conclusions about the relative popularity or commonness of various sorts of ghost story, and still more about changes in their proportions.[20]

Thirdly, care must be taken about drawing sweeping conclusions from this comparatively thin evidence base. Not all that has been written about the history of death has taken sufficient note of the (seemingly obvious) point made by Dr Whaley:

> attitudes to death in all ages are characterised by the most diverse emotions – fear, sorrow, anger, despair, resentment, resignation, defiance, pity, avarice, triumph, helplessness. And if fear and sorrow predominate, it is by no means unusual to find complex mixtures in individuals.[21]

Professor Caciola demonstrates precisely the sort of cautious and nuanced approach which is necessary to avoid forcing the evidence. Some of her revenants are diabolically revived corpses, whereas others seem to return from the dead by their own volition; which explanation was preferred depended, she suggests, on 'local ideas', but also on the 'characteristic' views of individuals.[22] On the other hand, Dr Park's attempt to draw a sharp contrast between Italian interpretations of 'apparitions of the dead as visible manifestations of the *souls* in purgatory' (her italics) and 'northern (and eastern) European belief in "revenants" or vampires – recently buried corpses who refused to lie passively in their graves' goes considerably beyond what the evidence will bear.[23]

Now we have explored the nature of the sources and the limitations that they impose on the sort of interpretations that are possible, we can move on to an exploration of how ideas of fantasy can help to understand medieval ghosts and medieval society. Professor Schmitt's work provides a good starting point. His fundamental premise is, 'the dead have no other existence than that which the living imagine for them'; thus he sees the exploration of medieval believing in ghosts (he prefers *croire*, 'to believe', to *croyance*, 'belief') as 'a contribution to a social history of the imagination'. Noting that while 'everyone "believed in ghosts"', not all the dead returned, and when they did, they did not appear at random, he argues that the dead who returned to haunt were those for whom something had gone wrong with 'the good Christian death', the normal separation of living and dead through ritualized action. For Schmitt, liturgical commemoration (*memoria*, literally 'memory') of the dead was not a form of collective memory, rather 'a social technique of forgetting':

> it had as its function 'cooling down' memory under the cover of maintaining it, of soothing the painful remembrance of the deceased until it faded. A classifying technique, it put the dead in their place as dead, so that the living if they happened to recall their name could do so without fear or passion.

In short, in studying 'the living and the dead in medieval society', Schmitt believes himself to be exploring the social function of memory in 'forgetting and what prevents forgetting'.[24]

Medieval thought about memory and forgetting was deeply influenced by Augustine.[25] For him memory was vital to cognition, and fantasies were vital to the working of memory. Dr O'Daly explains Augustine's self-confessedly difficult ideas:

> sense-perception is perception of incorporeal images of the objects perceived. These images are stored in memory, and when we call something to mind it is an image that we recollect. Remembering is, for Augustine, a form of imagining. Imagination can merely be *reproductive* of the images in the memory, but Augustine can also talk of the *creative* exercise of the imagination.

Among the terms Augustine used for such images were 'phantasia' and 'phantasma'. Sometimes he distinguished between them. Fantasies were mental images of objects perceived, products of sensory motion and counter-motion, and themselves motions of the mind, vital to O'Daly's 'reproductive imagination'. Phantasms, 'like images of images', were the result of memory working on itself; they were the vital link between memory and the creative use of the imagination,

> for I know in one way my father whom I have often seen, and my grandfather whom I have never seen in another. The first is a fantasy, the other a phantasm. The former I find in memory, the latter in that movement of the mind which arises from those memory has.[26]

In Augustinian terms, then, ghosts described as 'fantasia', 'fantasma', or even 'fantastic apparitions' are placed exactly where
Schmitt would position them, in the history of imagination and
memory.[27] Caesarius of Heisterbach in the thirteenth century, for
example, put his ghosts into the Augustinian framework of 'bodily
vision', 'spiritual vision' and 'intellectual or mental vision', and
uses Augustine's synonym for 'phantasia', 'imago'.[28]

Nonetheless, Augustine's particular ideas of fantasy were not the
only ones available in the Middle Ages. The Vulgate translation of
Ecclesiasticus testifies to another strand:

> like a woman in labour your heart shall suffer fantasies (*phantasias*),
> unless the visitation has been sent out from the Most High, do not
> give your heart to them; for dreams have made many err and those
> who have trusted in them have been cut off.[29]

These fantasies, potential instruments of good or evil, similar to
dreams, seem rather like the ' "I am having a fantasy" experience'
identified by the psychologist Maria Torok, which 'calls attention
to itself because of its incongruous relation to one's immediate
concerns'.[30] Walter Map saw it similarly, '*fantasma* is derived from
fantasia, that is a passing apparition', although some fantasies
(*fantastica*), like the story about the knight snatching his dead
wife from the dance, lasted an inexplicably long time. Here he
adopts a diabolical explanation for all *fantasma*, whereas elsewhere he does not.[31] Arnaud Gélis's contact with the dead was
dismissed by Fournier's clerk, 'having been deluded by diabolical
phantasms, he had deluded a number of others'.[32] Thus it is clear
that one of the ways in which the living imagined (or constructed)
the existence (or reality) of the dead was as *fantasia* (or *phantasma*),
a concept that bears comparison to modern ideas of fantasy and
phantasy. For example, there are some intriguing parallels between
the centrality attributed to *phantasiae* by Augustine and the role
attributed to phantasy by some Freudians; Julia Segal, for example,
wrote, 'phantasies make up the background to everything we do,
think or feel: they determine our perceptions and in a sense *are*
our perceptions'.[33] It is therefore legitimate to turn to those ideas
as tools in the interpretation of the medieval belief in ghosts.

One of the biggest issues for historians wanting to use these
texts is in what sense they are 'true'. Caesarius of Heisterbach
calls God to witness that he has not made up (*fingo*, from which

'fiction' derives) any of his chapters.[34] Indeed his ghosts are portrayed with a wealth of corroborative detail; in the story of Henry Nodus (below p. 263) we have names, places, a date (Archbishop John reigned 1189–1212), what laid the ghost, and, delightfully, that when hit with a sword he made 'a sound like a soft bed being struck'. However, such unsubstantiated details cannot guarantee the literal truth of the story, especially since, as in modern 'urban myths', several of these details put the story just out of reach 'not long ago' in a neighbouring province. Walter Map is even more worrying: although, as we have seen, he sometimes claims his work is for entertainment, many of his stories bear quite close resemblance to ghosts from the other traditions.[35] Some of his other stories were clearly jokes and are still funny; it seems possible some of his ghosts were also originally intended to be jokes.[36] Is the amazed hesitation of the knight at the edge of the dance in which his dead wife has joined 'that hesitation experienced by a person who knows only the laws of nature, confronting an apparently supernatural event' which Todorov notes the reader of fantastic literature often shares with the chief character; is it just how the knight told it, with 'trustworthy evidence of its truth'; or is it intended to be comic, especially in the light of his (perhaps excessive) concern about being thought cowardly?[37] Even Gélis's confession raises difficulties. For the author of the *Register*, Gélis's belief in ghosts was a delusion; Guillemette, the wife of Pierre Battegay, claimed that she did not believe him; and his nickname 'botheler' (bottle-man or butler) may have alluded to his favourite hobby rather than his profession.[38]

Ideas of fantasy point to a way out of these dilemmas. What Gélis saw in his nightly wanderings, what he remembered having seen 'the morning after', what he told Fournier he had seen, or what Fournier wanted to believe that Gélis had been deluded into seeing – whichever it is that the *Register* recorded – speaks of the Segalian (and Augustinian) phantasies of the individuals and the society in which they lived. Thus Gélis (thought he) met the dead and accompanied them on their penitential wanderings between churches or to their posthumous parties; whereas some modern people see (or think they see) UFO's or creatures from outer space or believe themselves to have been abducted for obscene experiments. The different fantasies surely tell a great deal about the difference between the two societies, as well as about the individuals concerned. Edifying ghosts similarly testify to medieval fantasies. Caesarius's pupils might not have believed particular stories, but for the stories to have fulfilled any didactic function, the novices must have believed that they were the sort of thing that *could* have happened. Seeing them as fantasy even brings fictional ghosts into the historian's purview. Even if Walter Map and his colleagues wrote stories entirely derived from their imaginations and incredible to the audience (and the similarities with the other types of ghost suggest this was not the case), they are still part of the history of fantasy.

Modern ideas of fantasy can draw the historian's attention to aspects of medieval ghosts that might otherwise have escaped attention. For example, on the issue of the (latent) social function of the ghosts and their stories, Todorov's observation that the social function of fantastic literature is to allow discussion of otherwise unmentionable subjects raises some fascinating lines of thought. Certainly, Henry Nodus's story deals with extra-marital and possibly non-consensual sex, illegitimacy, and incest between father and daughter. Many others deal with familial neglect of duty, very often the failure to ensure proper funeral rites or to carry out bequests.[39] Indeed, some commentators have argued that, as a means of encouraging penance and benefaction, medieval churchmen deliberately fostered the trauma and horror associated with haunting.[40] Certainly, some of the evidence points to a horror being felt towards ghosts; Arnaud Gélis was frightened by his first ghostly visitor, as was Walter Map's knight when he found his dead wife dancing, while Henry Nodus's daughter was sufficiently distressed to get someone to hit her father repeatedly with a sword. However, this does not give a complete picture of medieval fantasy-construction of the dead. Both the living and the dead asked Arnaud to find their relations and to get news of them.[41] Several of Caesarius's ghosts returned by arrangement, indeed Abbess Ermentrude of Ditkirgen was reproved by her sister for not coming sooner.[42] In this fantasy-constructed world ties between people, of kindred especially, transcended death, and the dead tended to appear to those closest to them.[43] The return of a dead loved-one may initially have provoked fear, but the subsequent nature of the encounter seems to have depended on the previous relationship of dead and living.[44] Thus Nodus's daughter was scared and wanted to get rid of her abusive father, whereas the knight of Little Britain seized his wife back and lived happily with her for many years.

Thus, exploring medieval stories of ghosts as fantasy clearly provides a most important way of understanding how medieval people saw the world. The purpose of this chapter has been to suggest the possibilities of this approach rather than to present hard and fast conclusions. Nonetheless, it is clear that ideas of fantasy can be used without departing from the careful and minute exploration of the evidence, respecting the nature of each individual source, which is the hallmark of good historical scholarship. Perhaps the greatest of the merits of 'fantasy' as an interpretative tool is that it allows for complexity. As we have seen, medieval ghosts were the result of a complex process. Caciola rightly concludes that 'the border between popular and élite culture was subject to a process of dynamic exchange':[45] so were the imaginations of individuals. Here, as elsewhere in this volume, we see 'fantasy as re-sorting the ideological patterns of everyday existence at the same time as testing and challenging them by their difference'.[46]

Notes

1. *Le Registre d'Inquisition de Jacques Fournier, Évêque de Pamiers (1318–1325)*, ed. Jean Duvernoy, 3 vols (Toulouse, 1965; with a vol. of corrections, Toulouse, 1972), vol. 1, pp. 544–5, from the confession of Mengarde de Pomiès, my translation. There is a French version, *Le Registre d'Inquisition de Jacques Fournier (Évêque de Pamiers) 1318–1325*, ed. and trans. Jean Duvernoy, 3 vols (Paris, 1978), but it is a paraphrase rather than a translation.

2. For an introduction to the historiography of death, see Paul Binski, *Medieval Death: Ritual and Representation* (London, 1996) and Christopher Daniell, *Death and Burial in Medieval England 1066–1550* (London, 1997). On medieval ghosts, see Jean-Claude Schmitt, *Les Revenants: les Vivants et les Morts dans la Société Médiévale* (Paris, 1994); supplemented by Nancy Caciola, 'Wraiths, revenants and ritual in medieval culture', *Past and Present* 152 (1996), pp. 3–45. This chapter prefers 'ghost' to its Francophone synonym 'revenant'.

3. Nicolas Abraham, 'Notes on the phantom: a complement to Freud's metapsychology', in Nicolas Abraham and Maria Torok, *The Shell and the Kernel: Renewals of Psychoanalysis*, ed. and trans. N.T. Rand (Chicago, 1994), p. 171.

4. Homer, *Iliad*, bk 23: ll. 62–107, the dead Patroklos demands burial from his lover, Achilles; *Odyssey*, bk 11: ll. 23–333 and 404–61, Odysseus conjures up and questions the dead.
5. See Ovid, *Fasti*, bk 5: ll. 419–92, in *Works*, ed. and trans. James George Frazer, rev. G.P. Goold, 2nd edn (Cambridge, Mass., and London, 1989), pp. 290–7; also Lacy Collinson-Morley, *Greek and Roman Ghost Stories* (Oxford, 1912).
6. I Samuel 28.
7. The Transfiguration, Matthew 17:1–3; Dives and Lazarus, Luke 16:19–31.
8. Much attention has been devoted to these, see Caciola, 'Wraiths', pp. 15–17 and refs, esp. n. 43.
9. Augustine, *De Cura pro Mortuis Gerenda*, ed. J. Zycha in *Corpus Scriptorum Ecclesiasticorum Latinorum* 31 (Vienna, 1900), esp. cc. 10–13, pp. 619–60. For fifteenth-century ghosts, see M.R. James, 'Twelve medieval ghost stories', *English Historical Review* 37 (1922), pp. 413–22.
10. On the (conceptual) boundaries of medieval Europe, see Robert Bartlett, *The Making of Europe: Conquest, Colonization and Cultural Change 950–1350* (Harmondsworth, 1993). On the *draugr* of Icelandic saga, see, for example, Aron Gurevich, *Historical Anthropology of the Middle Ages*, ed. Jana Howlett (Cambridge, 1992), pp. 116–21.
11. Walter Map, *De Nugis Curialium: Courtiers' Trifles*, ed. M.R. James, rev. Christopher Brooke and R.A.B. Mynors (Oxford, 1983), dist. 3: prologue, pp. 210–11; dist. 4: c. 8, p. 344; and dist. 2: c. 13, p. 160. Medieval ghosts tend to be quite solid; might the knight's wife owe her potential insubstantiality to Walter's classical reading? See, for example, Propertius, *Elegies*, ed. and trans. G.P. Goold (Cambridge, Mass., and London, 1990), bk 4: no. 7, l. 96, pp. 418–9.
12. Caesarius of Heisterbach, *Dialogus Miraculorum*, ed. Joseph Strange (Cologne, 1851), preface, vol. 1, p. 1.
13. Map, *De Nugis*, dist. 2: c. 13, pp. 160–1.
14. See, for example, Burchard of Worms, *Decretum*, bk 19: c. 5, in *Patrologia Latina*, ed. J.P. Migne (1861), vol. 140, col. 973; and Gratian, *Decretum*, C. 13 q. 2 c. 29.
15. Gurevich, *Historical Anthropology*, p. 52.
16. *Le Registre*, trans. Duvernoy, vol. 1, p. 170, n. 5; compare *Le Registre*, ed. Duvernoy, vol. 1, p. 134.
17. *Le Registre*, ed. Duvernoy, vol. 2, pp. 135–47. See Malcolm Barber, 'Lepers, Jews and Moslems: the plot to overthrow Christendom in 1321', *History* 66 (1981), pp. 1–17.
18. Abraham, 'Notes on the phantom', p. 171. Schmitt also falls into this trap, *Revenants*, pp. 18–19.

19. On Fournier's *Register* (n. 1 above) see Emmanuel Le Roy Ladurie, *Montaillou: Cathars and Catholics in a French Village 1294–1324*, trans. Barbara Bray (Harmondsworth, 1980), esp. pp. xi–xvii; and the criticisms of Leonard E. Boyle, 'Montaillou revisited: *mentalité* and methodology', in J.A. Raftis, ed., *Pathways to Medieval Peasants* (Toronto, 1981), pp. 119–40. Other examples of slim transmission include Map, *De Nugis*, (see pp. xxxi and xlv), and James, 'Twelve medieval ghost stories', p. 414.

20. *Pace* Megan McLaughlin, 'On communion with the dead', *Journal of Medieval History* 17 (1991), pp. 23–34, especially p. 31, on the 'passive even pathetic' ghost and 'the angry ghost'.

21. Joachim Whaley, 'Introduction', in Joachim Whaley, ed., *Mirrors of Mortality: Studies in the Social History of Death* (London, 1981), p. 9.

22. Caciola, 'Wraiths', esp. pp. 14–22, quotations from pp. 11 and 32.

23. Katherine Park, 'The life of the corpse: division and dissection in late medieval Europe', *Journal of the History of Medicine and Allied Sciences* 50 (1995), p. 117. Contrast Gregory the Great, *Dialogues*, bk 4: cc. 53, 55 and 57 (ed. A. de Vogüé, *Grégoire le Grand, Dialogues, Tome III, Livre IV* (Paris, 1980), pp. 178–9, 180–3 and 184–7). Also note that not all corporeal revenants were 'vampires'.

24. Schmitt, *Revenants*, pp. 13, 19, 22, 14–18, 19 (my translations). Schmitt is not always above criticism. His reliance (p. 17) on the idea of the 'good death' is too absolute (see Whaley, quoted above p. 52). His claim (p. 15) that medieval Latin authors derived their idea of 'corporeal revenants' from the *hamr* of Germanic folklore does not take account of other possible influences such as the 'corporeality' of the Risen Christ in the Gospels. See also n. 18 above.

25. See Mary Carruthers, *The Book of Memory: A Study of Memory in Medieval Culture* (Cambridge, 1990), esp. pp. 51, 64 and 146.

26. Gerard O'Daly, *Augustine's Philosophy of Mind* (London, 1987), pp. 106–8 and 144, quotation from p. 106. For the development of Augustine's thought, see also James J. O'Donnell, *Augustine, Confessions II, Commentary on Books 1–7* (Oxford, 1992), p. 180. The quotation is from Augustine, *De Musica*, bk 6: c 11. 32, in *Patrologia Latina* vol. 32, cols 1180–1.

27. Map, *De Nugis*, uses all three for his ghost stories, for example dist. 2: c. 13, pp. 160–1. Walter starts *De Nugis* (dist. 1: c. 1, pp. 2–3) by quoting Augustine, but he may not consciously be referring to him here.

28. Caesarius, *Dialogus*, dist. 8: c. 1, vol. 2, pp. 80–1, and the Novice's comment at dist. 12: c. 22, vol. 2, p. 332.

29. Ecclesiasticus 34:6–7 (my translation; the Vulgate differs from modern translations).

30. Maria Torok, 'Fantasy: an attempt to define its structure and operation', in Abraham and Torok, *The Shell and the Kernel*, pp. 27–35 (also p. 24), quotation from p. 35.

31. Map, *De Nugis*, dist. 2: c. 13, pp. 160–1. On causation, contrast, for example, dist. 2: cc. 27–30, pp. 202–7. Caciola, 'Wraiths', p. 19, fails to take account of this inconsistency (which actually supports her case); and her description of *De Nugis* as a chronicle is rather unconventional.

32. Translated below pp. 261–2.

33. Julia Segal, *Phantasy in Everyday Life: A Psychoanalytical Approach to Understanding Ourselves* (Harmondsworth, 1985), p. 22. See Susan Isaacs as quoted by Torok, 'Fantasy', pp. 27–8, esp. p. 27(a). The relationship between phantasy and words (f) also concerned Augustine, see O'Daly, *Augustine's Philosophy*, p. 144.

34. Caesarius, *Dialogus*, preface, vol. 1, p. 2.

35. For example, Map, *De Nugis*, dist. 2: c. 29, pp. 205–7, where a clerk who interferes with bequests by one of Charlemagne's knights is lifted into the air near Pamplona and eventually found three days' journey away 'amongst rocks with all his limbs smashed'. The moral thrust of the story is obvious. It was reported to Fournier as 'commonly said in the Pays de Sault and d'Aillon' that the souls of the evil went about among rocks and precipices, being thrown down by demons and breaking their limbs (*Le Registre*, ed. Duvernoy, vol. 1, pp. 447–8, confession of Guillaume Forte).

36. See the joke made at St Bernard's expense, Map, *De Nugis*, dist. 1: c. 24, pp. 80–1.

37. Map, *De Nugis*, dist. 4: c. 8, pp. 344–5. See Tzvetan Todorov, *The Fantastic: A Structural Approach to a Literary Genre*, trans. Richard Howard, 2nd edn (Cornell, 1975), pp. 25, 33, 157.

38. For Arnaud's beliefs as delusion, see below pp. 261–2, Guillemette's scepticism, *Le Registre*, ed. Duvernoy, vol. 1, p. 537; the nickname, *Le Registre*, trans. Duvernoy, vol. 1, p. 169, n. 1. Several witnesses claimed Gélis told them about the 'souls' drinking; for example, Arnaud de Montesple (*Le Registre*, ed. Duvernoy, vol. 1, pp. 533–6).

39. Todorov, *The Fantastic*, p. 158. Abraham, 'Notes on the phantom', *passim*, discusses the relationship between trauma and haunting. Henry's story below p. 263; for insufficient rites, see Gélis's confession, below pp. 261–2; for interference with bequests, n. 35 above.

40. For example, Daniell, *Death and Burial*, pp. 2 and 11, and Schmitt, *Revenants*, p. 21.

41. *Le Registre*, ed. Duvernoy, vol. 1, pp. 540–5, Mengarde de Pomiès testifies that she went to see Arnaud to inquire after her daughter;

and vol. 1, pp. 128–37, Arnaud testifies that a number of dead people give him messages.

42. Caesarius, *Dialogus*, dist. 12: cc. 31, 41, 43 (Ermentrude) and 44, vol. 2, pp. 341–2, 349–50 and 351–2.

43. Gurevich, *Historical Anthropology*, pp. 57–60, found other-worldly visions similarly parochial. Daniell, *Death and Burial*, p. 11, asserts as a fundamental distinction between medieval and modern hauntings that 'they were revealed to individuals, rather than being located in one place'. However, the fear expressed by Gausia, according to her friend, Mengarde de Pomiès, that Gélis would not be able to meet the dead if he had not known them when alive, was unfounded (*Le Registre*, ed. Duvernoy, vol. 1, pp. 540–1). In James, 'Twelve medieval ghost stories', the ghosts are sometimes linked to places and appear to strangers.

44. Compare Luke 24:36ff.

45. Caciola, 'Wraiths', p. 45.

46. Christopher Pelling, 'Modern fantasy and ancient dreams', above p. 15.

It is a pleasure to thank those who have helped me with this chapter; in particular, my parents, Ms Paula Gooder, Dr Matthew Kempshall, Dr Timothy Leary, Dr Karín Lesnik-Oberstein, and the Revd Richard Smail. Naturally, none of them is responsible for abuses of their generosity, all errors are my exclusive property.

4 Chivalry: fantasy and fear

Richard W. Kaeuper

School books teach that chivalry internalized restraints in noble males: it was the noble code of noble men in shining armour who used minimal force to right wrongs, preserve religion, and protect those regarded as weak. Chivalry entered into the formula of forces producing what historians often label High Medieval civilization, that time from the later eleventh century, if not earlier, when remarkable socio-economic, political, religious and intellectual activity is so evident in Europe: Charles Homer Haskins's 'renaissance of the twelfth century', Marc Bloch's 'second feudal age', Roberto Lopez's 'age of commercial revolution', Sir Richard Southern's age of 'medieval humanism'.[1] Chivalry could easily be viewed as a purely positive force for order.

Yet it could be argued that chivalry was an ambivalent force, inextricably involved with the violence troubling a developing society.[2] The best evidence comes from medieval chivalric literature, especially *chansons de geste*, romance, chivalric biography and vernacular manuals. Here are gilded fantasies about ideal chivalry, brutal fantasies about the sheer power of warriors wielding edged weapons, and a complex interplay of fantasy, idealized and feared, over the effects of omnipresent violence. The fear sometimes informs and shapes the fantasy in these medieval texts; but much modern writing on chivalry resonates only to aspects of the medieval ideal that appeal to contemporary sensibilities. Such a view generates its own soft-hued modern fantasy about the Middle Ages, missing the crucial importance of violence altogether. Yet as Rosemary Jackson has argued, fantasy as a literature of desire simultaneously expresses and expels desire, revealing dark areas in the dominant order of society.[3] The violence inherent in chivalry – desired, feared and debated – makes a good case in point. This chapter will contrast an idealized view of knightly powers in the thirteenth-century *Lancelot do Lac* with three more ambivalent works: the *Perlesvaus*, the *Ecclesiastical History* of Orderic Vitalis, and the *Merlin Continuation*.

Medieval writers used the term chivalry in three distinct but related ways: great deeds done with edged weapons; the body of men who did those deeds (meaning all those in one particular location or even all knights considered as an 'order' in society); and, more broadly, the code animating such men, their ideals and ideal practices. The range of meanings steers us away from simplistic readings of a single chivalric practice set against a single chivalric ideal. There was probably – within flexible limits – a fairly common chivalric practice over centuries.[4] William Marshal, the model knight of the late twelfth century, whose life is told in a fascinating contemporary biography, would perfectly understand Geoffroi de Charny, the leading French knight of the mid-fourteenth century, who wrote *The Book of Chivalry*, an important handbook for knights, and Sir Thomas Malory, the active knight and author of the famous *Morte Darthur* in the late fifteenth century.[5] Yet moving beyond a core of beliefs – martial prowess winning honour, piety embodied in ideal knightly practice and expiatory suffering, the mutual inspiration of prowess and love – there is no single theory, no detailed code agreed upon by all. Royal administrators, monks, bishops, scholars, and the knights themselves all had plans for what chivalry should ideally be.

The focus in their debates over the three-fold usage of the term chivalry falls on prowess, on the expert, bloody, sweaty, muscular work done with sword and lance. Chivalry was one of the problems in medieval Europe, not just one of its creative solutions to problems. Modern commentators avoid concentrating on the actual prowess so essential to chivalry, wanting the Middle Ages to be less violent, chivalry to function as escapist fantasy. But prowess as the central strand of chivalry means hacking, slashing and eviscerating all opponents. The young Arthurian heroes in *The Story of Merlin* in the Lancelot–Grail Cycle have fought so well in a battle against the Saxons 'that their arms and legs and the heads and manes of their horses were dripping with blood and gore'. They are described as having done 'many a beautiful deed of knighthood and struck many a handsome blow for which everyone should hold them in high esteem'.[6] A maiden whose rights Bors defends in the *Lancelot* (Vulgate Cycle) gives him a white banner to attach to his lance. After combat with her enemies, Bors 'saw that the banner which had been white before, was scarlet with blood, and he was overjoyed'.[7] A knight who has seen Lancelot perform in a tournament, in the *Lancelot* (Vulgate Cycle), can scarcely find words sufficient to praise his prowess:

> it takes a lot more to be a worthy man than I thought it did this morning. I've learned so much today that I believe there's only one truly worthy man in the whole world. I saw the one I'm talking about prove himself so well against knights today that I don't believe any mortal man since chivalry was first established has done such marvelous deeds as he did today.

He explains explicitly what these marvels were:

> I could recount more than a thousand fine blows, for I followed that knight every step to witness the marvelous deeds he did; I saw him kill five knights and five men-at-arms with five blows so swift that he nearly cut horses and knights in two. As for my own experience, I can tell you he split my shield in two, cleaved my saddle and cut my horse in half at the shoulders, all with a single blow ... I saw him kill four knights with one thrust of his lance ... if it were up to me, he'd never leave me. I'd keep him with me always, because I couldn't hold a richer treasure.[8]

All of the ambiguity about violence pivots on knightly prowess. Is all knightly violence licit and admirable? Should it be praised? Should it be stopped? Can it be channelled? Does God approve? Does it prove a knight's masculinity?

We can examine the idealistic fantasy through a splendid conversation in the *Lancelot do Lac*, written early in the thirteenth century. Lancelot is instructed in chivalry by his foster mother, the Lady of the Lake. Her teaching and the responses evoked from the young Lancelot by her Socratic questions paint an ideal representation of chivalry.[9] In the misty past,

> envy and greed began to grow in the world, and force began to overcome justice ... And when the weak could no longer withstand or hold out against the strong, they established protectors and defenders over themselves, to protect the weak and the peaceful and to maintain their rights and to deter the strong from their wrongdoing and outrageous behaviour.

So 'the big and the strong and the handsome and the nimble and the loyal and the valorous and the courageous, those who were full of the qualities of the heart and of the body' were elected as knights. Each knight learned that he must

> be courteous without baseness, gracious without cruelty, compassionate towards the needy, generous and prepared to help those in need, and ready and prepared to confound robbers and killers . . . a fair judge without love or hate.
> [He must not] for fear of death do anything which can be seen as shameful; rather he should be more afraid of suffering shame than of suffering death.

There is a moral core in a knight, chivalry is a quality of the heart rather than the body. Asked to differentiate these qualities of heart and body, Lancelot answers:

> It seems to me that a man can have the qualities of the heart even if he cannot have those of the body, for a man can be courteous and wise and gracious and loyal and valorous and generous and courageous – all these are virtues of the heart – though he cannot be big and robust and agile and handsome and attractive . . . qualities of the body . . . that a man brings . . . with him out of his mother's womb when he is born.

We moderns might expect this analysis to conclude that a kind and pacific man is worth more than a mere warrior. But Lancelot takes this line of thought in a different direction, as Geoffroi de Charny would a century and a half later.[10] He tells his Lady: 'so I believe that it is only indolence which prevents a man from being valorous, for I have often heard you yourself say that it is the heart alone which makes a man of valor'. Since all men are descended from one man and one woman, he has already asked her, rhetorically, how one would become noble except through prowess? The Lady of the Lake concludes their conversation with an insistence that the knight was established to protect the Holy Church, and gives a long set of symbolic interpretations of each piece of knightly equipment: the shield symbolizes the knightly protection of the Holy Church from robbers and pagans, and so on.

The *Lancelot do Lac* was influential, leaving its traces across much later writing on chivalry, including the important book of Ramon Llull. His *Book of the Order of Chivalry*, published in

Catalan and translated quickly into French before Caxton's English translation, presents again a myth of origins in which chivalry
appears in the role of saviour after a Fall; his book likewise gives
idealized, symbolic interpretations of each piece of knightly gear.[11]
Writing near the end of the thirteenth century, Llull thinks chivalry so important it should be taught in schools. Chivalry and
learning must cooperate; if the science of the knights and that of
the clerks both flourished, all would go well in the world. His
comment brings readily to mind the famous words of the great
romance writer Chrétien de Troyes in the opening of his romance
Cligés:

> this our books have taught us, that Greece once stood preeminent
> in both chivalry and learning. Then chivalry proceeded to Rome in
> company with the highest learning. Now they have come into France.
> God grant that they be sustained here and their stay be so pleasing
> that the honor that has stopped here in France never depart.[12]

The ideal sounds familiar to us, through its presence in many
books, having sometimes slipped almost unnoticed, in its hazy,
pre-Raphaelite colouration, from the realm of fantasy into the
supposedly sharper interpretion of actual historical representation.

Does the ideal blot out fears about the proud violence of knights?
These fears show up with convincing regularity, and sometimes
with stunning effect. The early-thirteenth-century romance *Perlesvaus; the High Book of the Grail* more than once introduces huge,
terrifying knights in black armour.[13] We first see these dread figures
through the eyes of Perceval's sister when she comes to the Perilous
Cemetery.

> As the maiden peered around the graveyard from where she stood
> among the tombs, she saw that it was surrounded by knights, all
> black, with burning, flaming lances, and they came at each other
> with such a din and tumult that it seemed as though the whole
> forest were crumbling. Many wielded swords as red as flame, and
> were attacking one another and hewing off hands and feet and
> noses and heads and faces; the sound of their blows was great
> indeed . . .

Later in the story when Arthur, Lancelot and Gawain journey
on a Grail pilgrimage they find themselves in the midst of a dense
forest without the accommodation that usually appears in such

stories as if on cue. After sending a squire up a tree to try to discover some sign of hospitality in the engulfing darkness, they move toward an open fire he has sighted in the distance. The fire is burning inexplicably, they find, in the ruined courtyard of a fortified but deserted manor house. When they send the squire in search of food for the horses, he returns in utter terror, having in the dark stumbled into a chamber filled with fragments of butchered knights' bodies. Suddenly a maiden appears in the courtyard, bearing on her shoulders half a dead man. For her sins against knighthood this unfortunate maiden has had to 'carry to that chamber all the knights who were killed in this forest and guard them here at the manor, all alone without company'. She warns the Round Table companions against a fearsome band of knights who will come at night, 'black they are, and foul and terrible, and no-one knows where they come from. They fight one another furiously, and the combat is long.' On her advice Lancelot draws a magic circle all around the house with his sword – just in time, for the demon knights

> came galloping through the forest, at such a furious speed that it sounded as though the forest were being uprooted. Then they rode into the manor, clutching blazing firebrands which they hurled at one another; into the house they rode, fighting, and made as if to approach the knights, but they could not go near them, and had to aim the firebrands at the king and his company from a distance.

Though the maiden warns Lancelot not to step outside the protective magic of his circle, with characterestic valour he attacks the knights. Inspired by his example, Arthur and Gawain join in; swords swing, sparks and hot coals fly, the evil are defeated. As the swords of the heroes cut through them,

> they screamed like demons and the whole forest resounded, and as they fell to the ground and could endure no more, both they and their horses turned to filth and ashes, and black demons rose from their bodies in the form of crows.

With hardly a moment's rest Arthur, Lancelot and Gawain confront another band, 'even blacker men, bearing blazing lances wrapped in flames, and many were carrying the bodies of knights whom they had killed in the forest'. Flinging down the bodies they demand of the maiden that she deal with them as with all the others. She refuses, declaring her penance done. They attack the three companions, seeking revenge for their defeated fellows; the combat is terrible until a bell sounded by a hermit saying mass causes them to flee suddenly. Near the end of the romance shapes that are apparently these same demon knights put in a final, chilling appearance. Lancelot at the Perilous Chapel,

> came to the door of the chapel, and there in the graveyard he thought he saw huge and terrible knights mounted on horseback, ready for combat, and they seemed to be staring at him, watching him.

These astonishing and terrifying images have been read in the framework of elaborate religious symbolism so evident in this romance. This imagery works in other dimensions as well. Jackson's recognition that fantasy uncovers the 'dark areas' of the 'dominant order' could scarcely be better illustrated than in the portrayal of these demon knights lurking in the forest shadows or suddenly emerging to hack at each other and at the innocent with their flaming weaponry. Their appearance in the *Perlesvaus* takes on even more force when we consider that the author seems to be drawing the raw material of his images from a folkloristic tradition known as 'la Mesnie Hellequin' or Herlequin's Hunt, a wild nocturnal ride by a hunting party or armed host across the countryside. The use of such images in this romance calls to mind what Marjorie Chibnall called 'one of the most unforgettable passages in the *Ecclesiastical History*' of the twelfth-century chronicler Orderic Vitalis.[14]

Orderic tells us the story given to him in person by Walchelin, a priest who claimed to have witnessed the fearful procession on the first night of January 1091, while returning from a visit to a sick parishioner. Hearing them approach, Walchelin mistook the noise to mean a troublesome contemporary force, the household troops of Robert of Bellême, on their way to the siege of Courcy, and feared being 'shamefully robbed'. His initial fear is useful evidence in itself. What happened was yet more terrifying, however, for he saw pass before him in the clear moonlight not an army of mortals, but four troops of tormented spirits: first commoners on foot, then women riding side-saddle, then a great troop of clergy and monks, all groaning under torments. The last troop was

a great army of knights, in which no colour was visible save black-
ness and flickering fire. All rode upon huge horses, fully armed as if
they were galloping to battle and carrying jet-black standards.

To the watching priest these forms are thoroughly real, recalling
Todorov's distinction between the truly marvellous or supernatural in fantasy and the merely uncanny or psychological.[15] Wanting proof that he had actually seen 'Herlechin's rabble', the priest
foolishly tried to seize one of the coal-black horses, which easily
galloped off. His yet more foolish second attempt brought an attack
by four of the demon knights. Orderic assures us that he saw the
scar on the priest's throat caused by the knight's grasp, 'burning
him like fire'. One of the knights who proved to be the cleric's
dead brother, who spared Walchelin, told him of the torments the
ghostly knights suffer, and begged for his priestly prayers as his
hope for relief:

> I have endured severe punishment for the great sins with which I
> am heavily burdened. The arms which we bear are red-hot, and
> offend us with an appalling stench, weighing us down with intoler-
> able weight, and burning with everlasting fire. Up to now I have
> suffered unspeakable torture from those punishments. But when
> you were ordained in England and sang your first Mass for the
> faithful departed your father Ralph escaped from his punishments
> and my shield, which caused me great pain, fell from me. As you
> see I still carry this sword, but I look in faith for release from this
> burden within the year.

Walchelin noticed what seemed to him 'a mass of blood like a
human head' around his brother's heels where his knightly spurs
would attach. It is not blood, he learns, but fire, burning and weighing down the knight as if he were carrying the Mont Saint-Michel.
His brother explains:

> because I used bright, sharp spurs in my eager haste to shed blood
> I am justly condemned to carry this enormous load on my heels,
> which is such an intolerable burden that I cannot convey to anyone
> the extent of my sufferings.

The knight's message is clear: 'Living men should constantly have
these things in mind'. It seems likely that the author of the *Perlevaus*,
a century later, had them much in mind. Both he and Orderic

testify vividly to a fear of knightly violence at the deepest level of human psychology. Both writers show the fear that can accompany desire in fantasy.

An image of similar vividness and power, much better known, involves a 'dolorous stroke' with frightful consequences to whole kingdoms. The incident points us toward the significant theme of wasteland, of terrible and sweeping devastation. As portrayed in the story of Balain, contained within the Post-Vulgate *Merlin Continuation* (written probably soon after 1240), the dolorous stroke gives us particularly useful evidence of fears generated by knightly violence and the devastation it causes.[16] This story is all the more powerful for being a part of a major structural contrast built into this cycle: Balain, the source of misery and misfortune, is set opposite Galahad, the bringer of joy and release; the Unfortunate Knight stands on one side, the Good Knight on the other. Balain brings into being the oppressive 'adventures' of the Grail when he wounds King Pellehan; Galahad lifts this curse when he cures him. In a society accustomed to thinking about fall and redemption, it seems significant that Balain is compared to Eve, Perceval to Christ.

Doggedly pursued by an invisible knight who repeatedly kills his companions without warning, Balain finally finds the man in conveniently visible form at the castle where King Pellehan is holding court. Wasting no time, Balain kills his enemy with a sword stroke, splitting the man from his head down through his chest. King Pelleham is even more outraged at this act of vengeance in his court than Arthur was when Balain had similarly killed a lady in his presence. In his hot wrath King Pellehan personally attacks Balain with a great pole and breaks the knight's sword. A wild chase through the castle ensues, with Balain searching in desperation for any weapon to resist the pursuing king.

Disregarding an unearthly voice warning him not to enter so holy a place, Balain rushes into a marvellous and sweet-smelling room containing a silver table upon which stands a gold and silver vessel. A lance suspended miraculously in mid air, point down, is poised over this vessel. Ignoring another voice of warning, Balain seizes the lance just in time to thrust it into the genitals ('through both thighs') of King Pellehan who falls to the floor grievously wounded. Although it first seemed to Balain that this stroke was justified, his error becomes progressively clear. This time Balain cannot ignore the voice which trumpets the following sentence,

the entire castle trembling all the while as if the world were coming to an end:

> Now begin the adventures and marvels of the Kingdom of Adven-
> tures which will not cease until a high price is paid for soiled,
> befouled hands having touched the Holy Lance and wounded the
> most honored of princes and the High Master will avenge it on
> those who have not deserved it.

Balain has, of course, seized the sacred lance that pierced the side
of Christ on the cross, the Lance of Longinus, and has used it
against the king into whose care God had entrusted the keeping of
the Holy Grail.

The result – certainly miraculous rather than merely uncanny
– approximates an atomic bomb explosion, with rings of gradually decreasing devastation. A great part of the castle wall falls;
hundreds within the castle die from pure fear; in the surrounding
town many die and others are maimed and wounded as houses
tumble into rubble; no one dares to enter the castle for several
days, as a sense of divine wrath akin to radiation lingers. Merlin
finally leads people back into the site, accompanied by a priest
wearing 'the armor of Jesus Christ', which alone will guarantee
them safe entry. Finding Balain, Merlin leads him out, even providing him with the necessary mount. Everywhere he rides the
prospect is cheerless:

> as he rode through the land, he found the trees down and broken
> and grain destroyed and all things laid waste, as if lightning had
> struck in each place, and unquestionably it had struck in many
> places, though not everywhere. He found half the people in the
> villages dead, both bourgeois and knights, and he found laborers
> dead in the fields. What can I tell you? He found the kingdom of
> Listinois so totally destroyed that it was later called by everyone the
> Kingdom of Waste Land and the Kingdom of Strange Land, be-
> cause everywhere the land had become so strange and wasted.

So powerful and complex an incident as the dolorous stroke
can only be considered a polyvalent symbol. Yet we can see immediately its significance for our inquiry. A man who is recognized as
one of the best knights in the world takes perhaps understandable
vengeance for unprovoked attacks. Fleeing for his life, weaponless,
he commits the great sin. A knight, whatever his good qualities,

has laid profane hands on the weapon that pierced God in the course of divine redemption and has used it in his private quarrel to wound one of his fellow knights and one of God's chosen agents. Devastation, like lightning – or war – blots out or blights the lives of innocent people throughout an entire region. Pure knightly prowess, highly praised at the opening of this story, has produced these stunning results near its close.

Balain must not be viewed in isolation in this work, of course. At the other end of the scale of knighthood, in other works of the great Vulgate or Lancelot–Grail Cycle, stands his counter, Galahad, the Good Knight, being everything, achieving everything his clerical creators wanted in knights.[17] Perhaps it puts us in mind of the word-play regularly employed by clerical reformers interested in chivalry. Was chivalry to be considered *militia* (idealized, pure knighthood), or simply *malitia* (evil)?

In important works of literature, medieval society engaged with the basic issue of violence through the mode of fantasy. Knightly obsession with the hands-on violence of personal prowess was celebrated in accounts of superhuman strokes with sword and lance. The obvious dangers of knightly violence were more indirectly but no less powerfully portrayed in accounts of a dolorous stroke or demon knights. In works like the *Lancelot do Lac* authors proposed fantasies of ideal chivalry which upheld social order and never troubled it. The nineteenth century may have brought the flowering of fantasy, but six or seven centuries earlier fantasy was already rooted in social realities through a literature which not only presented fundamental truths about society, but also tested them by raising troubling questions.[18]

Notes

1. Charles Homer Haskins, *The Renaissance of the Twelfth Century* (Cambridge, Mass., 1927); Marc Bloch, *Feudal Society*, trans. L.A. Manyon (Chicago, 1961); Roberto Lopez, *The Commercial Revolution of the Middle Ages* (New York, 1971); Richard W. Southern, *Medieval Humanism and Other Studies* (Oxford, 1970).
2. A theme developed in my book, *Chivalry and the Problem of Violence*, forthcoming from Clarendon Press, Oxford.
3. Rosemary Jackson, *Fantasy: The Literature of Subversion* (London, 1981), pp. 2–4, 15, 26.

4. As Maurice Keen claims for the twelfth to fifteenth centuries, *Chivalry* (New Haven, 1984).

5. Marshal's life studied in Sidney Painter, *William Marshal, Knight-Errant, Baron and Regent of England* (Baltimore, 1933); Georges Duby, *William Marshal, the Flower of Chivalry*, trans. R. Howard (London, 1986); David Crouch, *William Marshal: Court, Career and Chivalry in the Angevin Empire, 1147–1219* (Harlow, 1990). The French original has at present not been translated into English. On Charny: Richard W. Kaeuper and Elspeth Kennedy, *The Book of Chivalry of Geoffroi de Charny: Text, Context and Translation* (Philadelphia, 1996). The bibliography on Malory is immense; see Page West Life, *Sir Thomas Malory and the Morte Darthur: A Survey of Scholarship and Annotated Bibliography* (Charlottesville, 1980). For his great book, see *The Works of Sir Thomas Malory*, ed. Eugene Vinaver, 3rd edn, 3 vols, revised by P.J.C. Field (Oxford, 1990).

6. *The Story of Merlin*, trans. Rupert T. Pickens, in *Lancelot–Grail, The Old French Arthurian Vulgate and Post-Vulgate in Translation*, Norris J. Lacy, gen. ed., 5 vols (New York, 1993–96), vol. 1, p. 268.

7. *Lancelot Part IV*, trans. Roberta Krueger, in *Lancelot–Grail*, vol. 3, pp. 42–3.

8. *Lancelot Part V*, trans. William W. Kibler, in *Lancelot–Grail*, vol. 3, pp. 161–2.

9. The quotations that follow are drawn from *Lancelot of the Lake* trans. Corin Corley (Oxford, 1989), pp. 50–8.

10. Charny's leitmotif is 'he who does more is of greater worth'. Kaeuper and Kennedy, *The Book of Chivalry*, pp. 86–99.

11. *The Book of the Ordre of Chyvalry*, ed. Alfred T.P. Byles (London, 1926), presents Caxton's English translation.

12. *The Complete Romances of Chrétien de Troyes*, trans. David Staines (Bloomington, Ind., 1990), p. 87.

13. The following quotations appear in *The High Book of the Grail: A Translation of the Thirteenth Century Romance of Perlesvaus*, trans. Nigel Bryant (Totowa, New Jersey, 1978), p. 144, and pp. 176–8.

14. *Orderic Vitalis. The Ecclesiastical History* ed. and trans. Marjorie Chibnall, 6 vols (Oxford, 1969–80), vol. 4, pp. xxxix–xl; the following quotations appear in this volume, pp. 236–51.

15. Tzvetan Todorov, *The Fantastic: A Structural Approach to a Literary Genre*, trans. Richard Howard (Cleveland, Ohio, 1973), pp. 41–57.

16. *The Merlin Continuation*, trans. Martha Asher, in *Lancelot–Grail*, vol. 4, chs 8, 10–13, 16–23.

17. For the story of Galahad, see *The Quest for the Holy Grail*, trans. E. Jane Burns, in *Lancelot–Grail*, vol. 4.

18. Jackson, *Fantasy*, pp. 2–3, 15.

Part Two
Early Modern

5 Dreaming of Eve: Edenic fantasies in John Milton's Paradise Lost

Margaret Kean

The composition of an epic poem was taken to be the defining act of the Renaissance poet, indisputable proof of individual ability and of a nation's cultural achievement. Even within this literary hierarchy, John Milton's 'adventurous song' (I.13) claims supremacy by means of its subject matter.[1] To direct and expound events within an epic of creation is to expand the boundaries of human knowledge and aesthetic control. The choice of subject allows an unprecedented opportunity for metaphysical inquiry into the nature of man but the narration of *Paradise Lost* simultaneously sustains misgivings over the surety for such audacious speculation. The poem may preside over the fundamental myths of Western man, both in terms of the Judaeo-Christian religious heritage and of the Graeco-Roman cultural inheritance, but it foregrounds the exercise of authority as a major preoccupation within such an undertaking.

This chapter intends to approach *Paradise Lost* as a text charged by the need to control its own creative potential. By focusing on specific 'author'izing processes within the epic, one can show how the desire for true liberty of thought within the poem activates its own policies of containment and regulation. Concentrating on the Edenic books of Milton's poem, it will be argued here that, in its presentation of the world in its creational perfection, the poem discovers a new space where, freed from the limitations of mortal existence, desires for unrestricted access and activity can be entertained and an ideal fiction can be developed. Despite the reader's overriding knowledge of the fallen state of man, the prelapsarian presentation within *Paradise Lost* admits the development of fantasies of authorial power, attempting to secure, firstly, the perfect system of Edenic life and, secondly, the composition of the ideal woman.

One opportunity presented by the choice of an epic not just of Genesis but more inclusively of genesis is the chance to detail a new world, to act as creator to one's own ideal society. A description of the original perfection of Edenic human existence will involve the construction of a truly promised land. The literary endeavour can be compared not just to hexameral commentary but also to early modern texts that aim to construct ideal sociopolitical systems for the readership's judicious evaluation. Such works as Thomas More's *Utopia* (1516), Francis Bacon's *New Atlantis* (1627), or more immediately James Harrington's *The Commonwealth of Oceana* (1656) set out to depict the organization of an ideal state, detailing political, scientific, social or theological order, and from the base of that controlled experiment to offer explicit or implicit comparison with the disarray of contemporary society. Writing of humanity's paradisal existence, the Miltonic epic can venture one step further than such texts in its moral authority, for the Edenic estate as it is presented within the epic is an inspired revelation, the authorized truth of divine creational perfection.

Foregrounded within the presentation of Eden within *Paradise Lost* is the metaphor of the garden. The innocence of the garden state is of course biblically endorsed and also classically pastoral in setting but grounding this epic exploration of man's core identity in such a locale also proves to be deeply indebted to the monist theory of substance advocated in Milton's later writings. The metaphysics of monism and, by extension, of animist materialism advances a singular concept of Eden that underpins a daring poetics and unorthodox philosophical, political and theological positions.[2] The doctrine of monism emphasizes an irreducible union of matter and spirit throughout the created universe. Such a logic of spiritualized substance is for Milton based upon a theory of matter as inherent in the divine creative process.

The doctrinal argument is to be found in Milton's theological treatise, *De Doctrina Christiana*.[3] In Book I, chapter vii, 'Of the Creation', Milton defends his view of the universe as created *ex deo*, that is directly from God, in contrast to the orthodox view as found in the writings of Augustine where God's creation of the universe is *ex nihilo*, that is from nothing. For Milton, it simply stands to reason,

> So the material cause [of creation] must be either God or nothing. But nothing is no cause at all; (though my opponents want to prove that forms and, what is more, human forms were created out from nothing) ... It is, I say, a demonstration of God's supreme power and goodness that he should not shut up this heterogeneous and substantial virtue within himself, but should disperse, propagate and extend it as far as, and in whatever way, he wills. For this original matter was not an evil thing, nor to be thought of as worthless: it was good, and it contained the seeds of all subsequent good. It was a substance, and could only have been derived from the source of all substance. It was in a confused and disordered state at first, but afterwards God made it ordered and beautiful.[4]

God as the first, absolute and sole cause of all things, necessarily comprehends within himself the material cause of Creation, for 'there had been some bodily force in his own substance, for no one can give something he has not got'.[5] Matter then is an essential attribute of the divine and the act of creation is the action of forming or ordering that unlimited divinity within finite structures. The ontological premise of monism concurs with that of animist materialism, the theory of agency or vitalism as extant within the material body. However, implicit in the extension of the theory of vitalism is a libertine creational autonomy that threatens to break free from the epic's Christian frame. The focus on constant, obedient acknowledgement of the original Creator is endangered by a pluralist view of autonomous life-forces. As the poem engages with the concept of a monist universe it also needs to regulate its own creational activities, in effect to restrain its volatile energies.

The sensual delights of Eden are explored at length in the initial description of Paradise as a garden planted by God. The interactive syntax and intersensual experience of the descriptions of Eden in Book IV have been commented on by many critics but what remains to be shown is that this Edenic dynamic has been activated by the philosophical tenets of animist materialism.[6] Charting Eden by mapping the course of its rivers (IV.223–63), the landscape is presented both as a specific physical locale and as a model for the creational process. As if expounding upon a biblical verse, the progress of the text explores creational organicism in the ongoing activity of 'water[ing] the garden' (IV.230). The common religious metaphor of water as a life-giving force functions literally in the Edenic setting, where 'Southward through Eden went a river large . . .' (IV.223). For over forty lines the narration traces and duplicates the flow of the river as it infuses all material substance with an energy amounting to a vitalizing pulse.[7] The water circulates, penetrates and regenerates the land as the narration describes how the river divides its streams and saturates the earth, only to be reconstituted in the sap of the plants, morphosed into plant matter and then into scent. Finally, to complete the cycle, the waters regroup and decant into a lake, a clear mirror reflecting back the creation sustained by the flowing waters.

> . . . ; mean while murmuring waters fall
> Down the slope hills, dispersed, or in a lake,
> That to the fringed bank with myrtle crowned,
> Her crystal mirror holds, unite their streams. (IV.260–3)

The concluding mirroring action of the lake clarifies the self-sufficiency of the pastoral space, containing the cycle of nourishment in a mirrored reproduction of the process. As the river runs, the garden flourishes. Having once been set in motion by the Creator, the creational imperative within the garden is presented as self-stimulated and self-regenerating, a model of a self-sustaining ecosystem. Flowers bloom, fruits ripen and animals graze. One presumes that within a natural cycle that precludes decay, fruit that falls to the ground is to be eaten by the animals. Gaining nourishment in this fashion, the animals themselves will go on to manure the ground, replenishing the earth for further production within the ongoing round of natural harmony.

The garden does not need any external force to encourage its growth but its equilibrium is nonetheless vulnerable to invasive activity. Although Diane McColley finds a marital metaphor in the description of the myrtle fringing the lake, there are other more ominous referents. Louis Martz, for example, traces an Ovidian resonance from the crown of myrtle to the tale of Dryope in Book IX of *Metamorphoses*. Dryope is cruelly punished for plucking the sacred water-lotus that grows by the banks of a myrtle-fringed pool, 'a fatal act innocently perpetrated'.[8] It is easy to position Satan as an alien force of disruption within Eden but perhaps there is a more insidious anxiety centred on the very perfection of the place. The interdependent description of the garden's unity seems to exclude all human involvement as a potentially violatory threat to the sacred space. The postlapsarian narrative needs to be wary over conceptualizing mankind as native to Paradise. How can the fallen mind set humanity in such a pastoral cycle without spoiling it, without plucking the water-lotus? Indeed on reconsidering the Miltonic concept of prelapsarian existence one finds an emphasis on the georgic arts of gardening ordained by the Creator as meet work for the first couple. Such husbandry is intended to function as a form of rational activity, a form of self-governance of benefit both to man and to the garden, but the doctrine of human maintenance also disturbs the descriptions of an absolute natural design. Despite the spontaneity of the Edenic descriptions, the garden must now conform to human expectations. It is not to be considered as existing for its own sake but rather as a functional gift from God to man, there to be utilized and manipulated in the exercise of temperance and rational thanksgiving. The arts of gardening are of training, pruning and cultivating plants, activities which control growth and aim to ensure that the natural impulse for expansion in the garden will be measured by the hand of man.[9] The poetic aspirations to describe Eden as the ultimate, inviolate, self-sustaining system of monist creation have been surrendered in favour of the lesson of judicious moderation.

Comparable circumscriptions can be traced throughout the central books of the epic in the lengthy exchange between the archangel Raphael and the human pair. Raphael's visit is intended to sanction prelapsarian mankind's place within the Edenic system, but within his supervisory discourse the need for man to regulate his own conduct will repeatedly accompany the angel's awed admiration for the infinite invention of divine creativity. The nature of creation is explained to our first parents by Raphael in a supreme articulation of a monist theology,

> O Adam, one almighty is, from whom
> All things proceed, and up to him return,
> If not depraved from good, created all
> Such to perfection, one first matter all,
> Indued with various forms, various degrees
> Of substance, and in things that live, of life; (V.469–74)

The Almighty is the one source for all creation, the cause of 'one first matter all'. Despite the profusion of created forms, there is a fundamental point of source and return, a core identity beneath all diversity. To exemplify the theory, Raphael chooses the metaphor of the plant (V.479–90) – an organic model for creaturely comprehension of the Creator's beneficence and the potential in matter for evolution and reconstitution within the original source. The model is perfectly decorous and controlled but it is apparent that the angel's theoretical explanation based on a generic 'plant' is tidier than the discomforting multiplicity of the Eden that surrounds his discourse. The metaphor of the plant works well emblematically but the experience of the profusion of delights in a monist Paradise is necessarily restrained by the abstracted, singular, and essentially hierarchical model.

Although the philosophical model of the plant is skilfully crafted, the lesson on monist living is taught as much by the comportment of the archangel within the garden as by his oral directives. Sent to assist man's understanding of the nature of Edenic existence, the sociable angel comes not to preach but to converse with mankind. Such rational communication suggests a close relationship between earthly and heavenly bodies but the communing of these created forms goes beyond an intellectual understanding of their place in God's creation. The context for Raphael's discourse on monist philosophy is a meal shared by man and angel, and, as an angel who lunches, Raphael stands as a vital exemplar of the likening of spiritual and corporeal forms. The philosophical theory of monism is embodied and proven by the messenger who has undertaken the active transfer of a heavenly body to the earth. The angel emphasizes at some length the fact that he will eat and gain nourishment from the same Edenic fruits that sustain the corporeal frame of man. The physical action is employed by Raphael as metaphor – he theorizes, he eats, he explains the interrelations of the created universe as a cycle of digestion, and then finally he employs the plant as spiritual metaphor for God's plan. This meal offers nourishment for both body and intellect, reminding us perhaps of the New Testament text, 'man shall not live by bread alone, but by every word that proceedeth out of the mouth of God'.[10] Surprisingly, however, it is the material presence of the angel Raphael within the domestic economy of Eden that is conceptually liberating rather than the doctrinal discretion of his words.

It is clear that Raphael's formal message is one of prudence, a somewhat contradictory lesson of continuous thanksgiving for God's limitless bounty linked to a repeated admonishment of creaturely speculation as potentially transgressive. His authorized version of the Genesis creation story told in Book VII of *Paradise Lost* is intended both to stimulate wonder and to check any potential for undisciplined free-thinking on the part of mankind, while also giving pride of place to the creation of man as climax of the hexameron. The first man, Adam, comes from the earth and the fact that he is named for this origination, *ha'adam*, presents Raphael with a perfect opportunity to enforce his message of divine creational monism.

> This said, he formed thee, Adam, thee O man
> Dust of the ground, and in thy nostrils breathed
> The breath of life; in his own image he
> Created thee, in the image of God
> Express, and thou becamest a living soul.
> Male he created thee, but thy consort
> Female for race; ... (VII.524–30)

Like the extended metaphor of the plant in Book V, this narration is intended to reinforce Adam's awareness of the material base for all divine creation. Adam, the first man, was dust but is now a living corporeal thing, raised to the status of *imago dei* through the power and goodness of the Creator. The concept of man as a 'living soul' is crucial to an understanding of the monist implications of Creation: this is the Hebraic concept of man's holistic creation, body and soul inseparably united.[11]

In *De Doctrina Christiana*, Milton argues against the traditional Neoplatonic division of spirit from corporeality in his exegesis of Genesis 2:7 and for just such compositional vitality in the created form of man.

> When man had been created in this way, it is said, finally: *thus man became a living soul.* Unless we prefer to be instructed about the nature of the soul by heathen authors, we must interpret this as meaning that the man is a living being, intrinsically and properly one and individual. He is not double or separable: not, as is commonly thought, produced from and composed of two different and distinct elements, soul and body. On the contrary, the whole man is the soul, and the soul the man: a body, in other words, or individual substance, animated, sensitive, and rational.[12]

This theory is put into practice in the genesis of man. Raphael's retelling of the event allows Adam insight into the full mystery of his name and status but it offers little by way of exploration of Eve's existence beyond a glance at the reproductive potential of heterosexual relations.[13] However, Adam in Book VIII will have a controversial story to tell and it seems a disconcerting revision of Raphael's authorized statement. For Adam, woman is crucial to mankind's understanding of the concept of a 'living soul' and, if the aetiology of his name defines Adam as dust inspired, the story he has to tell of the birth of Eve furthers the implications of the divine creative practice. Once again the actuality of life in Eden is much more profuse than any abstracted model.

The story of Eve's birth echoes the second chapter of Genesis in outline and so may seem at first glance to conform to the familiar patriarchal subordination of woman implicit in the 'rib story' but when evaluated more closely the narration overturns convention. The creation of Eve as related by Adam (VIII.452–89) is an integral part of Adam's story of his first memories and divine colloquy as revealed in Book VIII of *Paradise Lost*. This book is the story of man's education, of a coming to knowledge of the self. That education starts with the exercise of motor skills, man's intense joy in physical movement is a part of his learning process. Awareness of his own created form then prompts a desire for contact with the creating force (VIII.267–82). The debate with the Godhead acts as a trial of man's reasoning powers and an expression of his growing self-awareness. It concludes with man's comprehension of his need for companionship and a mate. The gift to man of woman is the reward for that exercise. This creation is the culmination of the creational experiences but it is also a *new* lesson in human self-knowledge.

Adam's narrative of the birth of woman is worth considering in some detail. This moment recalls the originating point not just of one woman but of womankind. The as-yet-unnamed being is described as formed within Adam's imagination, his 'cell / Of fancy' (VIII.460–1). The very Idea of woman begins as a conceit within man's dream, 'authored' in collaboration with the Creator in that the form shaped within that dream state corresponds to the deity's promise to produce 'Thy wish exactly to thy heart's desire' (VIII.451). The creation of one 'Manlike, but different sex' (VIII.471) opens up a narratorial space to describe the literal generation of woman and also the psychological depths channelled in the generation of erotic other. Adam's dream acts as a crucial transitional space, for, just as the rib metamorphoses into a new being, so the dream state of fancy must be transferred to a physical reality, thereby transforming the conceit of woman as an embodiment of desire into a realized entity. Creating woman in this way allows for the divine authorization of man's erotic desire, at least within heterosexual monogamous relations, but this Miltonic version of the Pygmalion myth also actualizes the philosophical premise of monism and of the elemental energy inherent in matter. The rib as material base shows the making of a new form from extant materials and is a glorification of substance. This means that the birth of Eve works as a living example of animist materialist creation. Her creation is a climax to the genesis formations in the poem and guarantees the promise of secondary reproduction through procreation by the human couple. With the birth of Eve, we are entering a new phase in the ongoing creative process, whereby the miracle of creation is transferred to creaturely creativity under the divine imperative of 'increase and multiply'. For humanity, however, procreation is not just a creaturely necessity but a further way for man to become like the Maker. By allowing Adam such intimate knowledge of monism, the Creator eroticizes human reason, giving the act of love a philosophical dimension.

The description of Eve's birth relies on a spatial movement from the internal or private dream state to more public fields of consciousness. To describe his dream and the emotional verity of his experience, Adam draws on past events, reworking his extant knowledge to create a language of lyric intensity. Close consideration of the narrative suggests that man teaches himself to express his emotional state through accessing his accumulated knowledge of his own physical states of being. As Adam explains himself to Raphael, a new language develops: a vocabulary fitted to articulate human desire. Metaphors of love are produced from physical phenomena. The rib extracted from man's side comes dripping with blood. The 'cordial spirits' (VIII.466) extracted are reformed to bring 'Sweetness into my heart' (VIII.475), while the 'life-blood streaming fresh' (VIII.467) that is to be used to animate the new creation is reinvested as that new form becomes a vitalizing force in its own right, able to inspire all things with 'The spirit of love and amorous delight' (VIII.477). The unspoken metaphor throughout the narration is of ecstasy, of the individual taken outside of himself by overwhelming joy and erotic rapture. That sense of ecstasy is known to Adam from his initial encounter with the divine and his transferral into Paradise, events narrated to Raphael as Adam's first dream in Book VIII (292–311). That experience of dreaming that one can stand outside of oneself and watch oneself physically transported from one locale to another is the context for man's understanding of the creation of woman from his side. This creation offers him a new self, apart from his own being and yet a part of his being.[14] Later in his discourse with Raphael, Adam will use the term 'transported' (VIII.529, 530), the final transition of ecstasy from a physical memory to an erotic metaphor.

That infamous description of passion (VIII.528–59) is corrected by Raphael as potentially carnal and idolatrous but Adam's impression of the absolute completeness of this last creation and his joy at physical contact with his 'other self' (VIII.450) have more to do with his understanding of monist creation than Raphael allows. It is easy to see how the unbarred intensity of the union of the human couple alongside the unrestrained vitalism of Eve's created form could appear subversions of the moral order rather than extensions of the divine plan. The final act of creation is self-vitalizing. There is no need for the Creator to breathe life into this form as it is based in living matter. In Adam's description, the focus transfers seamlessly from the shaping powers of the Father to the vitality of the form. With the phrase 'a creature grew' (VIII.470), the agency of the creation takes control, monopolizing Adam's attention and erasing God from the narration.

The Genesis rib story should position male creativity as prior to, and authorization for, female procreative potential, but this has been reversed in Adam's narrative as the newly created form re-invigorates her surroundings, and in particular the male 'author', with an erotic force,

> That what seemed fair in all the world, seemed now
> Mean, or in her summed up, in her contained
> And in her looks, which from that time infused
> Sweetness into my heart, unfelt before,
> And into all things from her air inspired
> The spirit of love and amorous delight. (VIII.472–7)

Woman embodies the Edenic erotic of an eternal spring, a harmony of the senses first described in the 'vernal airs' of Book IV (264–8), and Adam delights in her being, her bearing, or what might be termed the ambience of Eve. Even so, his lexical choice is highly irregular. Adam is inspired with the divine breath of life at the moment of his creation but now he claims a new source of inspiration in the presence of Eve. The displacement of the term 'inspired' onto Adam as author rather than as might be expected heralding the critical moment of vital animation for the created object is telling. Adam claims to be 'from her air inspired' at the very point when woman is transferred from Adam's imagination to a separate corporeal vitality. The Idea of woman is to function primarily as a physical beloved as well as the more traditional (Neoplatonic) literary conceit of an ideal muse. The implications of such animist materialism are unorthodox in the extreme and Raphael for one is unwilling to contemplate such radicalism. His 'knee-jerk' reaction, 'For what admir'st thou, what transports thee so, / An outside?' (VIII.567–8), is not in keeping with his earlier expounding of the theory of monism. Here, woman is limited to a role as procreator, matter/*mater* controlled by her husband. Any other conception of the intimacies of the human couple is censured. The angel will undertake no examination of the recreative erotic we see licensed in Eden.

The Idea of Edenic woman as both mistress and muse has far-reaching implications for poetic composition; for Adam himself it links to his sense of their being soul partners. The lesson taught of man's existence as a 'living soul' is extended by Adam to cover the concept of the human couple as 'one soul'. The relationship is regularized in the speech of the marriage covenant, closing on the flourish 'And they shall be one flesh, one heart, one soul' (VIII.499), and renewed in Adam's attempts to explain his feelings to Raphael, specifically the climactic definition of his emotional estate, 'Union of mind or in us both one soul' (VIII.604). For Adam, the base of his union with Eve remains their common material base, but, with the knowledge of flesh-animated-by-spirit gained by his dream of her creation, it is a monist definition of humanity that shapes his understanding of matrimony. It is because of this insight that he is willing to gamble linguistically and conceptually in his discussion with Raphael, exploring topics in a spirit of Edenic enthusiasm.

The creation of Eve can be seen as a crux within the monist epic of genesis, a radical endorsement of human potential and the ultimate figuration of animist materialism within the creation story. In the wake of this conceptual achievement come the anxieties voiced by Adam and particularly Raphael, but the remainder of this chapter will focus on the ways in which this forming of the ideal woman functions as a poetic statement and personal validation of Milton's Edenic composition. As we have seen, Adam's story in Book VIII gives an insight into the psychological make-up of man – dealing with man's loneliness, the formation of woman, man's love for her, his loss of her, his search for her and his reunion with her – and it has further been shown that the creation of woman extends the potential for further human reproduction as one turns from the hexameron to future creaturely multiplication. It is significant then that both the quest for love and the first human authorship within the devolving creational process should be so closely linked to poetic composition.

In the late 1650s Milton wrote his last known sonnet, 'Methought I saw my late espoused saint', a sophisticated poem that engages with the traditions of Petrarchanism in its elegy for a departed wife.[15]

> Methought I saw my late espoused saint
> Brought to me like Alcestis from the grave,
> Whom Jove's great son to her glad husband gave,
> Rescued from death by force though pale and faint.
> Mine as whom washed from spot of childbed taint,
> Purification in the old Law did save,
> And such, as yet once more I trust to have
> Full sight of her in heaven without restraint,
> Came vested all in white, pure as her mind:
> Her face was veiled, yet to my fancied sight,
> Love, sweetness, goodness in her person shined
> So clear, as in no face with more delight.
> But O as to embrace me she inclined
> I waked, she fled, and day brought back my night.

Within the poem, the loved one is tantalizingly rediscovered through sleep but reunion in this medium must ultimately be denied. In order to maintain the chaste hope for a final apocalyptic union, the poem demands asceticism. The theme of confinement initiated

by the references to the grave, childbirth and 'churching' are realized in the formal restraints placed upon the poem's rhyme scheme.
The imposed semantic and aural restrictions mirror the tonal suppression of hope, while the limited span of the sonnet form is
exploited in the terminal rhyme where 'sight' and 'delight' lead
only to the bleak living exile of the final word, darkest 'night'. The
poem relates how the beloved was snatched away at the very
moment of arousal and response. With the embrace denied, seemingly by the narrator rather than the vision, the speaker wakes to
take advantage of his memory and to commemorate the loss of the
beloved within this poetic construction. Such employment of the
female figure as an unobtainable goal, a figure whose physical
absence makes her representable in poetic form, is a commonplace
of the Petrarchan tradition: Laura metamorphosed into laurel. Elizabeth Harvey's daring feminist reading of the gender issues within
such Renaissance texts in her book *Ventriloquized Voices* includes
a brief but stimulating discussion of this Milton sonnet. She argues
for an intentional alignment of the maternal figure with the threat
of death within the sonnet in order to free space for the male poetic
voice. The procreative potential of the maternal figure is to be
sacrificed for the sake of the pure form of male poetic creativity.[16]

Critics have established that within the epic text of *Paradise
Lost* can be found 'embedded' a number of sonnet formations,
both reworkings of earlier Miltonic texts and new compositions
(e.g. Eve's sonnet, IV.641–56). Nardo argues that the sonnets contained within *Paradise Lost* are a means of exploring the lyric
possibilities of the epic, an argument that would complement the
reading of Adam's narrative given above, but equally rewarding is
Peggy Samuels's argument that the embedding of sonnet structures
within the epic format radically subverts the sonnet form because
there can be no closure in the text of the epic equivalent to that of
the compact sonnet. She claims that the finality of closure necessitated by the sonnet is denied in the epic perspective, allowing only
what she terms a 'false pause'.[17] Neither Nardo nor Samuels would
introduce Adam's dream of Eve as a possible sonnet as, strictly
speaking, it does not adhere to the formal rules of sonneteering,
but it is remarkable that the body of this sonnet should be so
closely involved in the text of Eve's birth in Eden. A number of
specific verbal parallels to the sonnet of loss and grief occur within
Adam's narrative of his joy at Eve's birth. The phrase 'methought

I saw' (VIII.462) is of course also to be found in the opening line of the sonnet. Line ten of the sonnet has 'my fancied sight', while VIII.461 has 'Of fancy my internal sight'. Moreover, there are similarities between 'Love, sweetness, goodness in her person shined / So clear, as in no face with more delight' (Sonnet 11–12) and 'Sweetness into my heart, unfelt before, / And into all things from her air inspired / The spirit of love and amorous delight' (VIII.475–7).[18] In addition, there is the allusive quality of the sonnet's 'espoused' relationship and its recognition of Orphic motifs to be considered with regard to the epic recontextualization within Adamic narration. In short, it does seem significant that the Edenic high point of erotic desire fulfilled should prove a reworking of this sonnet text, refashioning its themes for a distinctive context where the interaction of human desire, inspiration and material creativity identifies the poetic process directly with the dynamic of monist creation.

From sonnet to epic, the birth motif shifts significantly. The veiled liminal figure threatening death contrasts with the animate and animating Edenic body. But, within the celebration of Edenic union, the sonnet's core expression of loss is retained. As Adam relates the moment when he wakes from his dream, he recalls a fear for the loss of the new form that is unprecedented. Rather than having Eve brought directly to Adam by the Father, Milton's Adam must endure intense anxiety in his search for her. Reading his experience against the sonnet form is helpful. The final lines of the sonnet, 'But O as to embrace me she inclined / I waked, she fled, and day brought back my night', are re-presented within the epic text as

> She disappeared, and left me dark, I waked
> To find her, or for ever to deplore
> Her loss, and other pleasures all abjure: . . . (VIII.478–80)

The inclusion of privation in the hiatus between dream state and sensory reality gives an unexpected psychological depth to this presentation of Edenic love. Waking to a solitary state, Adam is intent solely on reunion or despair. One brief phrase, 'She disappeared, and left me dark', encapsulates the entire tradition of Orphic and Petrarchan lament. The pain of loss experienced by Adam means that he can voice the poignant verities of the lyric

mode within Eden. Unlike the impenetrable state of darkness at
the close of the sonnet, the threat of desolation is momentary for
Adam but nonetheless, by means of the sonnet's emphasis on
frailty and mourning, an aestheticizing of fear is framed within
Adam's narrative. His experience of loss admits an emotional comprehension of mortality within the prelapsarian state. This interval
comes exactly at the moment of the 'false pause' at the close of an
embedded sonnet and the composition thereby offers a skilled
manipulation of both epic and sonnet structural forms. Where the
sonnet closed, the epic text continues charting Adam's search for,
sight of and ultimate union with Eve. The vision of Eve in the
garden can be read as a fulfilment of the prayer for 'Full sight'
(Sonnet 8) beyond the confines of the sonnet form: a prelapsarian
rather than an apocalyptic conclusion.[19]

Regaining Eve in this fashion may have personal motivation but
it is also a conscious literary manoeuvre and I wish to close this
chapter by suggesting that the Miltonic construction of the ideal
woman claims primacy over all other poets' championing of their
mistresses. Milton's sonnet counters many of the secular influences
of Petrarchan sonneteering but it is by no means an a-Petrarchan
text. It is compared by Jonathan Goldberg to Sir Walter Raleigh's
sonnet 'A Vision vpon this conceipt of the Faery Queene', and the
common link between the opening lines of these two poems does
suggest an intentional echo on Milton's part.[20] This prefatory text
by Raleigh discusses poetic succession and rivalry through a consideration of the fate of the female subject. The displacement of
Laura as the ideal by the new beloved, the 'Faerie Queene', exposes the transience of poetic fame and human relations by highlighting the mortality of the beloved. Once Laura is dead, it will
only be a matter of time before the laurel is passed on. As Spenser
displaces Petrarch, so presumably Raleigh quietly appropriates
Spenser's 'Faerie Queene' and indeed the main theme of Raleigh's
meditation is mutability. His sonnet concentrates on the moment
of the transferral of allegiance from one woman as beloved to
another, focusing on the disruptive and disconsolate nature of this
action.

Milton's epic renewal of his own sonnet within the context of
Edenic perfection is intended to play off such Petrarchan literary
conceits. The competition between poets, vying to present elaborate compliments to their respective mistresses, is a futile struggle

against mortality but Milton's presentation of the ideal woman
has the opportunity to trump all such attempts: 'Woman' in this
prelapsarian conception is not subject to death and no future poet
could hope to oust a mistress that has been divinely formed and
sanctioned. The lyric presentation of the Edenic creation of Eve
achieves, by means of Adamic reminiscence, what has never been
said of any woman. There can be no comparison to the Miltonic
reconstruction of the divine creation of the first beloved and its
conclusive twist on the poetic conceit of the personal mistress-as-
muse. The text is not a secular dream fantasy such as Donne,
Jonson or Herrick might employ but a radical ideal of creational
perfection and monist practice.[21] The first woman is not representable only by her absence, for, challenging Petrarchan standards,
the Edenic dream sequence liberates its poetic material, creating a
lyric voice that articulates desire and also experiences fulfilment
and physical union. Such an unrestricted ideal will not survive beyond the garden state but the Edenic opportunity for such poetic
consummation has been grasped. This means that the Miltonic
text has licensed itself to achieve what other poets can only dream
about – it adequately controls the poetic medium both to have and
to hold the girl.

Notes

1. All references to John Milton's poetry are to the Longman edition,
   The Poems of John Milton, ed. John Carey and Alastair Fowler
   (Harlow, 1968).
2. For Milton's theory of monism, see William Kerrigan, *The Sacred
   Complex: On the Psychogenesis of Paradise Lost* (Cambridge, Mass.,
   1983), pp. 193–262; Stephen Fallon, *Milton among the Philosophers:
   Poetry and Materialism in Seventeenth-Century England* (Ithaca, 1991),
   pp. 79–110; John P. Rumrich, *Matter of Glory: A New Preface to
   Paradise Lost* (Pittsburg, 1987), pp. 53–69 and *passim*; John Rogers,
   *The Matter of Revolution: Science, Poetry, and Politics in the Age of
   Milton* (Ithaca, 1996), pp. 103–143.
3. Milton's theological thesis, *De Doctrina Christiana*, was written in
   Latin. The manuscript was discovered in 1823 and was first published
   in 1825. All references here are to the Yale translation, *Christian
   Doctrine*, vol. 6 in the *Complete Prose Works of John Milton*, ed.
   D.M. Wolfe *et al.*, 8 vols (New Haven, 1953–82). Hereafter, *Yale
   Prose*.

4. *Yale Prose.* VI 308.

5. *Yale Prose.* VI 309.

6. For the 'fluidity' of the syntax in the descriptions of Eden, see Christopher Ricks, *Milton's Grand Style* (Oxford, 1963), p. 101.

7. One might say that, as a vitalist metaphor, the circuit of the waters function as a blood supply for the organism that is 'Eden'. John Rogers's exploration of animist materialist theories in England in the 1650s, and particularly his argument concerning the work of William Harvey, is pertinent. See Rogers, *Matter of Revolution*, pp. 16–27.

8. Diane McColley, *Milton's Eve* (Urbana, 1983), p. 79; Louis Martz, *Poet of Exile* (New York, 1980), p. 229.

9. See Barbara K. Lewalski, *Paradise Lost and the Rhetoric of Literary Forms* (New Jersey, 1985), p. 187. On human anxieties over the potential for excessive growth in Eden, see John Guillory, 'From the superfluous to the supernumerary: reading gender into *Paradise Lost*', in Elizabeth D. Harvey and Katherine E. Maus, eds, *Soliciting Interpretation: Literary Theory and Seventeenth-Century English Poetry* (Chicago, 1990).

10. Matthew 4:4. All biblical references are to the Authorized Version. For the metaphor of 'digestion' in Milton's texts, see Fallon, *Milton among the Philosophers*, pp. 102–7; Rogers, *Matter of Revolution*, pp. 133–5.

11. J.A.T. Robinson calls it 'flesh-animated-by-soul, the whole conceived as a psycho-physical unit'. See J.A.T. Robinson, *The Body: A Study in Pauline Theology* (London, 1952), p. 14. For more on the Hebraic existence of Adam and Eve before the Fall, see the excellent discussion by Jason P. Rosenblatt, *Torah and Law in Paradise Lost* (Princeton, 1994).

12. *Yale Prose.* VI 317–18.

13. For an alternative, feminist reading of the marginalization of woman in Raphael's account of the creation, see Mary Nyquist, 'The genesis of gendered subjectivity in the divorce tracts and in *Paradise Lost*', in Mary Nyquist and Margaret Ferguson, eds, *Re-membering Milton: Essays on the Texts and Traditions* (London, 1988), pp. 116–17.

14. Adam's first recorded words in the epic are an address to Eve, 'Sole partner and sole part of all these joys, / Dearer thy self than all; ...' (IV.411–12). For more on the 'partnership' of Adam and Eve, see R.A. Shoaf, *Milton, Poet of Duality: A Study of Semiosis in the Poetry and the Prose* (New Haven, 1985), pp. 15–17.

15. The dream vision is often presumed to refer to Katherine Woodcock, Milton's second wife, who died in 1658, but the text is non-specific. There are numerous readings of this sonnet, e.g. Kurt Heinzelman, ' "Cold consolation": the art of Milton's last sonnet', *Milton Studies* 10 (1977).

16. Elizabeth Harvey, *Ventriloquized Voices: Feminist Theory and English Renaissance Texts* (London, 1992), pp. 99–101. Gerald Hammond, *Fleeting Things: English Poets and Poems 1616–1660* (Cambridge, Mass., 1990), p. 216, attempts to link this sonnet to the story of the nightly visits from the muse said to have inspired Milton's composition of *Paradise Lost*.

17. See A.K. Nardo, 'The submerged sonnet as lyric moment in Milton's epic', *Genre* 9 (1976) and Peggy Samuels, 'Milton's use of sonnet form in *Paradise Lost*', *Milton Studies* 24 (1988). The term 'embedded' is used by Samuels.

18. E. Le Comte, *Milton and Sex* (London, 1978), p. 42, notes two of these parallels, i.e. Sonnet 13–14 / VIII.478–80, and Sonnet 11–12 / VIII.474–7.

19. In an Edenic rather than an apocalyptic context, even physical contact is sanctioned and no threat of suffering is attached to procreative activities. One might compare Louis Schwartz's argument in ' "Spot of child-bed taint": seventeenth-century obstetrics in Milton's Sonnet 23 and *Paradise Lost* 8. 462–78', *Milton Quarterly* 27 (1993), on the emotional guilt underwriting the sonnet. 'Men do not give birth. Milton, therefore, finds himself not only helpless in the face of his wife's suffering but forced to recognize that this suffering is caused by his own desires to express love and to procreate' (p. 100). Schwartz argues that the Edenic birth is 'an idealising projection' driven in part by Milton's personal pain (p. 104).

20. Jonathan Goldberg, *Voice Terminal Echo* (New York, 1986), pp. 147–9. See also Harvey, *Ventriloquized Voices*, p. 101. For Raleigh's poem, see *The Poems of Walter Ralegh*, ed. A. Latham (London, 1951), p. 13.

21. See, for example, Elegy X, 'The Dreame', in *The Poems of John Donne*, ed. Herbert J.C. Grierson, 2 vols (Oxford, 1953), vol. 1, p. 95; 'The Dreame' in *The Complete Works of Ben Jonson*, ed. C.H. Herford, Percy and Evelyn Simson, 11 vols (Oxford, 1925–52), vol. 8, pp. 150–1; 'The Vision to Electra' in *The Poetical Works of Robert Herrick*, ed. L.C. Martin (Oxford, 1956), p. 20.

6 Jonson, the antimasque and the literary fantastic: The Vision of Delight

Lesley Mickel

In this chapter I wish to pay close attention to Ben Jonson's court masque for the New Year celebrations of 1617, *The Vision of Delight*. This will involve analysis of the masque's rhetorical structures as well as its formal display in an attempt to understand Jonson's deployment of fantasy in this most illusionist of literary and theatrical creations. I intend to show that, for Jonson, fantasy and literary creativity are closely allied. While this masque exploits some of the more outlandish trappings of fantasy (or fants'y), including surreal dream visions, it is deeply materialist as Jonson demonstrates the creative artist's ability to examine and question the nature of monarchical rule. It is the translation of Stuart courtiers from the real world to a fantastic context that allows for a playful, yet didactic, examination of their apparent corruption and ignorance. Moreover, in displaying the deficiencies of the corrupt courtier, Jonson also proclaims his elevated status as a creative artist and moral arbiter. The antimasque and masque of this entertainment partly constitute a meta-narrative investigating the ideological function of masque, and fantasy itself is a vital component of this analysis, both as a literary mode and as a symbolic character appearing in the masque presented to the court. Jonsonian fantasy is in no way escapist, as earlier critics of masque have implied, but rather seeks to comment on court-sponsored culture and on the experienced effects of literature itself.[1] In what follows, I intend to summarize briefly certain aspects of fantasy theory and their Jonsonian applications before going on to put theory into practice with an analysis of that most fantastic of court entertainments,

The Vision of Delight. Jonson roots literary wonder and fantasy in the body, siting them in the antimasque, and deflates the lofty, intellectual claims of the masque by bringing our attention back to the body and its effects. This partial appropriation of the masque is done by the imposition of rhetorical devices and visual representations that more usually inhabit the antimasque, and *vice versa.* Jonson questions the meaning of the court entertainment as a whole and even its audience's ability to decode and profit from it, as he mixes forms and themes from one part of the masque into the other.

The court masque developed as a combination of early ballet, opera, and visual display in costumes and setting, with Jonson's most important contribution to the form being the addition of dramatic dialogue. These elements were melded together into an extravagant, and often mystifying, celebration of the monarchy, which was presented as a divine extension of God's authority. As an elaboration of this entertainment Jonson introduced the antimasque, initially a minor prelude to the main masque, where discord and strife were staged to offset and enlarge the representation of royal power in the following masque proper. As the masque entertainment evolved, Jonson expanded the antimasque, to the point where it interrogates the proclamations of the main masque. Many important analysts of the form, such as Stephen Orgel and Martin Butler, believe that any dissent raised by the antimasque is incontrovertibly contained and dispelled by the masque proper.[2] Nevertheless, the claim that the antimasque is subversive can be supported by the materialist basis of fantasy asserted by later critics.[3] George Puttenham's *Arte of English Poesie* (1589) explicitly associates 'phantasy' and literary creativity, and descries the fact that these linked modes of writing and thinking are so misunderstood and undervalued by gentlemen with 'grosse heads'. Jonson possessed a copy of Puttenham's work which he annotated, indicating that he paid close attention to Puttenham's views on literature and creativity.[4]

Any student of the fantastic will be aware of its often confusing terminology, and in order to circumvent any such confusion I have chosen to follow the precedent set by Neil Cornwell, who distinguishes between 'fantasy' functioning as a behavioural or mental pattern, which is the subject of psychoanalysis or psychology, and the 'literary fantastic', which is a literary mode or genre (perhaps subgenre) made recognizable by certain formal and narrative characteristics. Cornwell cites a definition of the fantastic from Jorge Luis Borges, 'that the basic devices of all fantastic literature are only four in number: the work within the work, the contamination of reality by dream, the voyage in time and the double', but then he dismisses this analysis as 'useful, but inadequate'.[5] However, in the face of the confusion and contradiction that appears intrinsic to much theorizing of the fantastic, Borges's definition has a pleasing clarity and seems particularly pertinent to the Jonsonian antimasque. Borges's notion of 'the work within the work' strikingly correlates with the antimasque's evolution as a component which questioned the assumptions of the main masque, although it experienced a contraction and trivialization after the death of James I (1625). The mature antimasque operates as a kind of inverse mirroring of the masque, its satirical double where chaos reigns instead of harmony, and mob rule is substituted for monarchy. The antimasque often combines a gritty, low mimetic realism with astonishing illusory effects, particularly when it gives way to the masque proper; this intermingling of realism, fantasy and transformation involves a distortion of orthodox notions of time and space.[6]

Jonson's tendency to examine structures of authority is not merely limited to his masques, but can also be detected in his plays and poems. While 'To Sir Robert Wroth' is often viewed as pastoral panegyric, it also incorporates a subtle subtextual criticism of Wroth and aristocratic attitudes to the country, giving rise to a certain ambiguity regarding authorial tone and point of view. Careful attention to rhetorical structures within the poem and its historical context has led Gary Waller to counter the standard view of this poem as a hymn to aristocratic hospitality rooted in the heart of the country with the suggestion that Jonson deploys a sly irony at the expense of Robert Wroth, attempting to please multiple audiences rather than Wroth alone.[7] Such a strategy allows him to meet his own standards as a poet of integrity as well as those of his patrons, thereby linking with much fantasy writing where ambiguity is often deliberately deployed, enabling greater authorial freedom with regard to both literary content and form.

Ambiguity arises when the chaotic antimasque is apparently contained and dissolved by the following masque, a grand expression of royal propaganda. Although the antimasque does disappear so suddenly with the appearance of the masque, its effects remain to disturb the complacent discourse of the masque. This ambiguity is akin to what Amaryll Chanady has described as 'antinomy', a defining characteristic of the literary fantastic, 'the simultaneous presence of two conflicting codes in the text'.[8] Ambiguity is not a subsidiary effect of the text but a deliberate rhetorical strategy on the part of the writer. Rather than signalling its artistic failure or lack of integrity, the masque's ambiguity operates as dialectic, exploring the nature of the political *status quo* and demonstrating the relationship between politics and poetics as the poet seeks to comment on the operations of power – in this case, the ambiguity of the entertainment acts as shield protecting Jonson from accusations of inappropriate criticism. Recent critics have highlighted the political and materialist aspects of the literary fantastic.[9] Rather than being a self-enclosed genre that does not require any reference to the outside world, the fantastic always rests on a fundamental basis of reality; no matter how wonderful its narrative apparatus, it refers to the contemporary social formation, to the here and now, in an attempt to address topical issues. Nowhere is this more true than in Jonson's court entertainments, where the antimasque tackles issues such as the abuse of monopolies or the foibles of aristocratic behaviour, thereby disproving twentieth-century criticism of the form as theatrical or literary escapism.

The Vision of Delight was composed and performed as part of the New Year celebrations of 1617. While it was doubtless a sumptuous performance (unfortunately there are no extant designs by Inigo Jones that can be precisely linked to this masque), it is also verbally rich; its interest lies largely in the speeches of its emblematic characters, who conjure up a cornucopia of images. These images are often disjunctive, but they are shaped into fertile associations, where incongruous elements are melded together for the purposes of satire. At the outset Delight enters and urges all to 'play, dance and sing', but is interrupted by the first antimasque when a she-monster gives birth to six burratines and six pantaloons (young and old men, grotesques or caricatures taken from the Italian *commedia dell'arte*) who dance together. Delight introduces Night, whose 'phantoms' of sleep 'make delight more deep'. In turn, Night conjures Fants'y, who then begins a long speech full of incongruous verbal images and allusions, echoing the way in which disjunctive images cross-fertilize in dreams. As in dreams, there is often a kind of truth lurking behind such visions, and

Fants'y's speech gestures towards concepts of relativism and, particularly, the way in which appearance and reality are not always in tune (a typically Jonsonian preoccupation). Fants'y's speech is punctuated by a second antimasque of dancing 'phantasms'; shortly after, the masque proper begins with the appearance of Peace and the displacement of Night's phantoms by a pastoral paradise. Fants'y recognizes that these overwhelming sights are directly attributable to the King, 'Behold a King / Whose presence makes this perpetual spring', and in what remains of the masque the Choir hymn the King's power and the beauty of his creation. The entertainment would have continued with dancing and revels for many hours.

The Vision of Delight is a remarkable masque, although it has received so little comment from major critics of the form.[10] In his edition of the masques Orgel hints at the reason for this silence when he notes that, 'Fantasy's speech is a verbal antimasque . . . the general sense is clear, and the speech is not, as all commentators have assumed, either nonsensical or entirely incoherent'.[11] *The Vision of Delight* may have perplexed those critics who view the court entertainment as a primarily panegyrical and eulogistic mode.

At its outset, the entertainment betrays no sign of its unusual nature and opens with the 'perspective of a fair building discovered'. *The Vision of Delight* moves from a 'fair building', probably neoclassical in style, to the wonder of a pastoral fantasy, thereby typifying the court entertainment's latter phase where urban gives way to pastoral. Orgel argues that the court masque began as a transition from pastoral to the neo-classically urban, a movement which was reversed after 1616. This was politically motivated: the mature masque's movement from city to country may be read as part of a larger attempt to emphasize the king's elevated position in a natural, divinely sanctioned hierarchy.[12] The monarch thus attempted to resolve some of the political disquiet of the period, caused by clashes between his assertion of royal prerogative and the ancient rights claimed by the House of Commons. As with much of Jonson's work, the separation of these categories (urban and pastoral, antimasque and masque) is not easily sustained. The 'fair building' functions as an impressive symbol of the achievements of architectural science, a rational exercise demonstrating the sublime nature of mankind. Thus the setting and perspective of this entertainment herald the values we usually associate with the neo-classical masque. Yet by this stage in the development of the masque there was an expectation that an antimasque would precede the masque, and indeed *The Vision of Delight* is structured in this way. The pastoral masque itself is so hyperbolic and fantastic that it becomes a very strange royal paradise, one where hyperbole risks collapsing into irony. One of Jonson's prime strategies in this entertainment is to frustrate our expectations – disorienting the reader/spectator – signalled by the masque's emphasis on wonder. Wonder, like Fant'sy, is a personification within the antimasque as well as a response attributed to the audience; the rhetoric of the antimasque reinforces the splendours of its setting as Jonson literally tells us how wonderful it is, and informs us that we should not expect to penetrate in any rational manner the mysteries of this spectacle, rather we should give ourselves up to our senses:

> Yet let it [Fant'sy] like an odor rise
>   To all the senses here,
> And fall like sleep upon their eyes,
>   Or music in their ear. (ll. 44–7)

It is difficult to judge just how the original audience responded to this riddling masque as it seems to have elicited very little comment from contemporary observers, although this fact in itself may indicate that viewers did not know what to make of it, as Jonson predicts in the masque itself. John Chamberlain reported to Dudley Carleton that the newly made Earl of Buckingham and the Earl of Montgomery danced with the Queen, although it is not clear at which stage of the entertainment this dancing took place. He adds laconically, 'I have heard no great speach nor commendations of the masque neither before nor since'. A further, more exotic detail provided by Chamberlain is that 'the Virginian woman Pocahuntas, wth her father counsaillor have ben wth the king and graciously vsed, and both she and her assistant well placed at the maske'.[13]

The masque's celebration of the sensual and physical at the expense of the rational is typical of Jonsonian grotesque, and the antimasque as a whole exuberantly parades its fantastic apparatus:

> From air, from cloud, from dreams, from toys,
>   To sounds, to sense, to love, to joys;
> Let your shows be new, as strange,
>   Let them oft and sweetly vary; (ll. 9–12)

Moreover, as Delight tells us, much of the impact of the fantastic relies on the immediacy of its quick changing visions: 'Too long t'expect the pleasing'st sight / Doth take away from the delight' (ll. 15–16); fantasy is a trope for creative transformation, and is thereby a powerful metaphor for the literary imagination. It is closely associated with night, as sleep is displaced by the imaginings of the fertile brain. This is a traditional image for inspired composition, when the fantasist or creator is liberated from the mundane minutiae of everyday life and possessed by a poetic fury: 'This night in dew she [Night] will not steep / The brain nor lock the sense in sleep, / But all awake with phantoms keep' (ll. 30–2). Indeed, we might say that this masque is largely concerned with analysing the nature of literary composition through the metaphorical deployment of fantasy. Jonson partly propagates the liberal humanist notion of the artist commanded or possessed by his inspiring muse, and to this end fantasy is borne on 'purple wings', an image both celestial and imperial. Fantasy is a powerful imaginative force, with its rewards and dangers, and, as Jonson tells us, fantasy can enlarge the creative spirit, as well as curtail it:

> Wherefore I would know what dreams would delight 'em,
> For never was Fant'sy more loath to affright 'em.
> And Fant'sy, I tell you, has dreams that have wings,
> And dreams that have honey, and dreams that have stings.
> (ll. 51–4)[14]

The text of this masque declares that after an introductory speech by Delight, sung in *stilo recitativo*, 'Here the first antimasque entered, a she-monster delivered of six burratines that dance with six pantaloons'.[15] These are elements reminiscent of earlier and later masques, for example the dancing she-fool appearing in *Love Freed From Ignorance And Folly* (1611), and *pantomimi* in the 'habits of the four prime European nations' in *Love's Triumph Through Callipolis* (1631). The she-fool or the she-monster is clearly a figure of social and physical excess, while the burrantines and pantaloons patently belong to the Italian tradition of *commedia dell'arte* and pantomime. In fact, Jonson takes great pains with his masque text to signal its continental influences. For example, although the exact nature of *stilo recitativo* is obscure, we can be certain that it was a continental import. Anne Lake Prescott, one of the few critics to have analysed this masque, has demonstrated that one of its major influences was a French text, *Les Songes Drolatiques*, featuring illustrations of grotesque characters.[16] In Jonson's day it was widely believed that this book was by Rabelais, a belief probably shared by Jonson as he combines it with other Rabelaisian images and motifs in this masque. Although the book was not, in fact, by Rabelais, Jonson and his colleague, the designer Inigo Jones, must have had access to a copy of it, as many of the verbal and visual images in the masque reproduce its grotesque illustrations. This European influence extends even further with an unmistakable allusion to the opening of Rabelais's *Gargantua*, where the giant's mother gives birth to him casually, almost incidentally, amid a scene of feasting and grotesque carnival excess; that grand opening is recalled by Jonson when his 'she-monster' (significantly, her size is indicated by this term, relating her to Rabelais's family of giants) is 'delivered' of the six pantaloons and six burrantines. These pointed references to a European tradition of the grotesque and the fantastic are aimed at Jonson's educated and literary readers and spectators. Jonson wished to be viewed as part of this satirical and didactic tradition. Yet Jonson's approach to source material was a decorous *imitatio*, a shaping and adapting of material to suit the situation.[17] In *The Vision of Delight* the grotesque and the fantastic are linked with the humours. Jonson had already exploited the humours in his earlier dramatic comedies, where a single characteristic in an individual becomes so exaggerated that it defines the person. Within the philosophical framework of the bodily humours, *The Vision of Delight*'s antimasque is essentially sanguine, and Delight informs us that 'Our sports are of the humorous night' (l. 22); shortly after, Night calls on Fant'sy to 'Create of airy forms a stream; / It must have blood and nought of phlegm' (ll. 41–2). As Orgel notes, 'blood and phlegm are two of the bodily humours, producing temperaments that are respectively hot and lively (sanguine), and moist and dull (phlegmatic)'. While Jonsonian fantastic is firmly located in the body and the antimasque, it threatens to spill into the philosophical world of masque at any time.

Yet if the antimasque is essentially sanguine, giddy and heated, do Night's words imply that the masque must be phlegmatic? This is an acutely ironic interpretation of the masque's harmony and order as dull apathy. The intensely physical and sensual nature of the fantastic antimasque presses against the intellectual pretensions

of the masque in an attempt to reduce it to its physical manifestation
– dull apathy. It seems that Jonson might well be questioning the
value of the masque proper here (as opposed to the antimasque), a
form that rehearses year after year the pieties of the Stuart court,
while failing to address some of the more pressing issues of the day.

Fant'sy's long speech about the nature of dreams has perplexed
critics; it is a visual and verbal cornucopia of the fantastic. Jonson
exploits a discursive strategy similar to his early dramatic comedies where individuals are reduced to single physical characteristics and temperamental impulses. Once we appreciate that this is
how Fant'sy's reductive discourse works, the speech makes some
kind of sense. We need to pay close attention to the semantics
of the speech to appreciate the metonymy underlying Jonsonian
fantastic, where an inanimate object commonly associated with a
character type comes to represent it in its entirety. For example,
in *The Vision of Delight* an aristocratic courtier acting as judge in
a riddling debate becomes no more than his cod piece or feather:
'it were an odd piece / To see the conclusion peep forth at a
codpiece' (ll. 65–6). It seems appropriate that he wears the feathers
of the ostrich, as the bird is a freakish work of nature, sharing
important characteristics, Jonson hints, with the typical male
courtier. The ostrich hides its head in the sand, content in its
ignorance. Fant'sy's exposition on the nature and variety of dreams
suggests that vice and physical appetite can consume the rational
human being:

> For say the French farthingale and the French hood
> Were here to dispute; must it be understood
> A feather, for a wisp, were a fit moderator? (ll. 61–3)

The farthingale was a hooped skirt, outmoded by the date of
this masque, while the hood had become fashionable; the feather
alludes to the male courtier who wore it in his hat. So we may
decode these lines to read, somewhat mundanely, thus, 'if a
mature female courtier and a young female courtier were to be in
a dispute, would a male courtier be a fit judge?'. While these lines
playfully question the ability of an aristocrat to judge anything,
they also address the rival claims of lechery and gluttony to be the
prime source of delight, drawing on the suggestive symbolism of
the farthingale, covering the sexual region of the body, and the
hood, emphasizing the face and mouth. Thus Jonson's fantastic

discourse works at several levels incorporating multiple puns: it is three dimensional and dynamic, or, in its own terms, it is 'sanguine' indeed. This speech self-consciously and overtly draws on the fantastic, the self-consciousness being perhaps most salient in the lines, 'Your ostrich, believe it, 's [sic] no faithful translator / Of perfect Utopian; and then it were an odd piece / To see the conclusion peep forth at a codpiece' (ll. 64–6). The blatant allusion to Sir Thomas More's fantastic masterpiece, *Utopia* (More coined the term 'utopia', of course, which then entered the vernacular), places this antimasque within the European and scholarly tradition of the fantastic, which Jonson roguishly declares may not be fully understood by an 'ostrich'. As I have suggested, the courtier is meant by the ostrich as he wears its feathers, and, somewhat appropriately, in the iconology of the day the ostrich was held to symbolize both gluttony and justice.[18] The playful irony of these lines acknowledges that the judgement of the masque audience will probably be flawed, and that they will be unable to decode fully the fantastic semiotics of this occasion. If the courtier is reduced to his feather and his codpiece, it is indeed ironic that such a base individual should be in a position to judge a sophisticated work of art, and yet, paradoxically, it is also wholly appropriate as he represents the physical appetite that characterizes the grotesque and fantastic literary mode. We might say, then, that this entire court entertainment operates as a huge joke at its own expense, laughing at the fact that while the profound implications of the antimasque may be misread or misunderstood, the masque itself has ossified into a meaningless ritual. The limits of pastoral and panegyric in the masque proper are revealed in the way that its images are exaggerated and distorted into fantastic and ironic versions of themselves; as Wonder exclaims,

> How comes it winter is so quite forced hence,
> And locked up under ground? that every sense
> Hath several objects? trees have got their heads,
> The fields their coats? . . . (ll. 171–4)

We are accustomed to the wonder generated in masque by the powers of the pastoral 'Sun-King', but this wonder is not the eulogistic or even spiritual kind that we are familiar with from the panegyrical masque, rather it is related to the wonder and fantasy of the riddling and comically ironic antimasque. For example, in these lines the masque proper also involves a suspension of rational faculties and the prominence of the physical senses, while inanimate objects (trees and fields) take on the kind of human personification that was at work in the antimasque, where human images were conjured up out of a collection of disparate inanimate objects such as a windmill, bells, spurs, a mousetrap etc.: in the antimasque the human was rendered inhuman, whereas in the masque this process is reversed with the animation of the natural world. Thus not only does the fantastic reign in the antimasque, it has colonized the masque proper. In an apparently risky rhetorical strategy Jonson goes to the extreme of plainly linking the monarch and the fantastic world conjured up by the court entertainment: ''Tis he, 'tis he, and no power else, / That makes all this what Fant'sy tells' (ll. 194–5).[19] As we have seen, the fantastic is firmly located in the body and repudiates the claims of rationalism; its giddy humour ironically undermines those who are intellectually and socially aspiring, revealing them to be base hypocrites, such as the shallow, plumed courtier who presumes to judge works of art from a position of ignorance. The implications of associating this fantastic discourse with the monarch are potentially overwhelming, as the traditional masque image of Stuart Britain slides from Platonic peace and order to a land where appetite is allowed to rage unchecked. Jonson's mastery of the fantastic mode and its ironic laughter is directed into a dialectic, questioning the orthodox assumptions of royal propaganda. However, some may accuse him of a self-defeating laughter if we remember Jonson's earlier hints that his audience would not understand this fantastic and ultimately didactic court entertainment properly; but to make such an assumption is to misunderstand the power of the masque's laughter, as its most raucous laughter is reserved for itself in a profoundly self-reflexive dialectic. Moreover, Jonson was always prepared to put up with the ignorant multitude in the belief that he would be understood by the discerning few.

Notes

1. In this respect, many of my comments in this chapter chime with Julie Sander's emphasis on the material nature of literary fantasy in her chapter on Jonson and Richard Brome, included in this volume. For Jonson's poems, *Discoveries*, and *Conversations with Drummond*,

see *Ben Jonson*, ed. Ian Donaldson (Oxford, 1985); for masques, see *Ben Jonson: The Complete Masques*, ed. Stephen Orgel (New Haven, 1969). Elsewhere I refer to *The Complete Works of Ben Jonson*, ed. C.H. Herford, Percy and Evelyn Simpson, 11 vols (Oxford, 1925–52).

2. Stephen Orgel, *The Jonsonian Masque* (New York, 1967) and *The Illusion of Power* (Berkeley, 1975); Martin Butler; 'Reform or reverence?: The politics of the Caroline masque', in J.R. Mulryne and Margaret Shewring, eds, *Theatre and Government Under the Early Stuarts* (Cambridge 1993), pp. 118–56. For a more materialist approach, Butler and David Lindley, 'Restoring Astrea: Jonson's masque for the fall of Somerset', *English Literary History* 61:4 (1994), pp. 807–27.

3. Christine Brooke-Rose, *A Rhetoric of the Unreal: Studies in Narrative and Structure, Especially of the Fantastic* (Cambridge, 1981), *Stories, Theories and Things* (Cambridge, 1991); Rosemary Jackson, *Fantasy: The Literature of Subversion*, (London, 1981).

4. George Puttenham, *The Arte of English Poesie* (1589; Menston, 1968), p. 14. Unfortunately, Jonson's hand-written notes here are limited to asterisks, underlining and the sketch of a hand pointing to passages of interest.

5. For definitions of fantasy/fantastic, see Neil Cornwell, *The Literary Fantastic: From Gothic to Postmodernism* (Hemel Hempstead, 1990), pp. 1–34.

6. On Bakhtin's 'chronotope' see Cornwell, *The Literary Fantastic*, pp. 9–10. The term 'chronotope' refers to the idiosyncratic use of time and space in fantastic literary works.

7. Gary Waller, *The Sidney Family Romance: Mary Wroth, William Herbert, and the Early Modern Construction of Gender* (Detroit, 1993), p. 117.

8. Amaryll Chanady, *Magical Realism and the Fantastic: Resolved Versus Unresolved Antimony* (New York, 1985).

9. Brooke-Rose, *Rhetoric of the Unreal*; Jackson, *Fantasy*.

10. Stephen Orgel, *The Jonsonian Masque* (1967; New York, 1981); John C. Meagher, *Method and Meaning in Jonson's Masques* (Notre Dame, 1966); *The Complete Works* vol. 10, pp. 568–71. Elsewhere the editors of *The Complete Works* remark that, 'beautiful as it is, *The Vision of Delight* bears the marks of decadence', yet they fail to elaborate on this conclusion (vol. 2, p. 304). They further note that in her seminal study, *The Court Masque* (Cambridge, 1927), Enid Welsford argues that *The Vision of Delight* is directly descended from the Italian and French entertainments, *Notte d'Amore* (Florence, 1608) and the *Ballet de la Foire St Germain* (Paris, 1606). Welsford's argument rests on the fact that these earlier entertainments feature

monstrous births like that in Jonson's masque, yet Herford and Simpson conclude that these are assumptions on Welsford's part and not substantiated claims (vol. 10, p. 568). This essay argues that it is more appropriate to look for Jonson's inspiration for *The Vision of Delight* in the works of Rabelais.

11. *Ben Jonson: The Complete Masques*, p. 486.
12. Orgel, *The Illusion of Power*, pp. 49–50.
13. *The Complete Works*, vol. 10, p. 568.
14. Jonson may have been following Puttenham's cue in distinguishing between good and bad fantasy. Puttenham writes that, 'even so is the phantasticall part of man (if it be not disordered) a representer of the best, most comely and bewtifull images or apparences of thinges to the soule and according to their very truth. If otherwise, then doth it breed *Chimeres* & monsters in mans imaginations, & not onely in his imaginations, but also in his ordinarie actions and life which ensues' (*Arte of English Poesie*, p. 15).
15. It is apparently impossible to ascertain definitely what Jonson means by '*stilo recitativo*'. In his notes on *Lovers Made Men*, Orgel suggests the remote possibility that the term *stilo recitativo* indicates that the entertainment was set to music, and the parts sung by professional performers, while the aristocratic participants mimed their roles. However, he concludes that all we can be sure of is that the work was set to music. He also notes that these *recitativo* entertainments are generally regarded as the first English operas; see *Ben Jonson: The Complete Masques*, p. 257. On the general subject of the music composed and performed as part of the Jonsonian masque, and on recitative in particular, see Mary Chan, *Music in the Theatre of Ben Jonson* (Oxford, 1980), pp. 44, 156, 273. Chan describes recitative as a 'declamatory' style.
16. Anne Lake Prescott, 'The Stuart masque and Pantagruel's dreams', *English Literary History* 51 (1984), pp. 407–30.
17. Jonson's own definition of *imitatio* is highly instructive, 'Not, to imitate servilely, as Horace saith, and catch at vices, for virtue: but, to draw forth out of the best, and choicest flowers, with the bee, and turn all into honey, work it into one relish, and savour', *Discoveries*, ll. 3068–72.
18. In his notes to the masque Orgel writes on the ostrich figure: 'See C. Ripa, *Iconologia* (Padua, 1625), pp. 284 and 320 on the ostrich as garrulousness and gluttony, and p. 179 on the bird as justice. Ripa also cites Alciati's emblem 'In Garrulum et Gulosum' (Leyden, 1608, no. 95, p. 100) in an Italian version that translates Alciati's 'truo' as 'struzzo' (ostrich), though the bird depicted is swimming and resembles a dodo' (*Ben Jonson: The Complete Masques*, p. 486). I am

grateful to Dr Michael Bath of Strathclyde University for pointing out to me that Alciati's sixteenth-century editors translated 'truo' variously as either 'pelican' or 'ostrich', while modern editors opt for the 'pelican' translation. Clearly Jonson is playing here with a complex emblematic tradition; in *The Vision of Delight* Jonson appears to draw on the figure of the ostrich as an oxymoronic symbol of both justice and gluttony. Moreover the ostrich typically hides its head in the sand, an image suggesting the courtier's ignorant self-oblivion to the real meaning of Jonson's critique.

19. In his influential book, *James I and the Politics of Literature: Jonson, Shakespeare, Donne, and their Contemporaries* (Baltimore, 1983), Jonathan Goldberg suggests that *The Vision of Delight* represents the monarch's transcendent powers of vision and creation: 'seen properly, it gives the monarch the creative powers it claims for itself' (p. 62). This is a valid yet partial analysis, and Goldberg concludes that Jonson equates royal absolutism and poetic power. Goldberg's view here may be modified by recent historical work that challenges the traditional view of James I as an entrenched absolutist (see for example Paul Christianson, 'Royal and parliamentary voices on the ancient constitution *c*.1604–1621', in Linda Levy Peck, ed., *The Mental World of the Jacobean Court* (Cambridge, 1991), pp. 71–95). Jonson connects the creations and visions of the masque and the king's power, yet this is at least an ambivalent association, because fantasy is part of creativity. Furthermore, fantasy is located in the body and the antimasque, and threatens to contaminate the rational certainties of masque. By linking the king's creativity and the fantastic creations of this entertainment, Jonson challenges the traditional image of monarchical rule, replacing it with the suggestion that royal creativity is also irrational, and royal subjects are often characterized by ignorance and greed.

7 Writing sexual fantasy in the English Renaissance: potency, power and poetry

Danielle Clarke

Fantasy is a multivalent category which often fragments into a set of *moral* judgements, masquerading as aesthetic judgements. This is particularly marked when the subject of fantasy is sex. Sexual fantasy is seen to reside in two main types of text, the pornographic and the erotic, which are notoriously difficult to separate. The different moral positions articulated in relation to them are often the result of anxieties about the class composition of the readership and the mode of circulation, rather than any absolute quality of the texts themselves.[1] When the term 'pornographic' is applied to texts which deal with sexual fantasy, it implies a set of prior judgements about literary value; that the content is unmitigatedly sexual, the language is crudely direct, and that there is little in the way of narrative sophistication.

Thomas Nashe's poem 'The Choice of Valentines', written in the early 1590s, has been placed on the sidelines of the literary canon. This has been explained by characterizing 'The Choice of Valentines' as pornographic in style and subject matter. Such judgements depend upon a retrospective imposition of categories on texts and on suppositions regarding the 'proper' content of poetry rather than upon stylistic assessments. The affiliation of Nashe's poem with pornography has also affected its critical reception, as Ian Moulton suggests, leading 'it either to be dismissed out of hand or presented to the reader as something distressingly self-evident'.[2] This forms an underlying thread of the argument, as I suggest that critics and editors of Nashe have constructed their own fantasy of the Renaissance, imposing concepts and judgements in a way which obscures our understanding of sexual fantasy and its expression in this period. In reducing meaning to sex, critics have been blind to the ways in which this poem encodes fantasies of poetic, economic and social power through the medium of sexuality. The fantasy element of Nashe's poem also resides in its relationship to a social and historical context, not simply in what the poem *says* or the acts it represents. Meaning is also a matter of audience and circulation: the ways and means and reasons why a poet should choose to represent himself to a reader through the framework of sex, and the criss-crossing of the flexible boundary between private fantasy and the public expression of it.

'The Choice of Valentines' is a difficult text to categorize, not only because of its tangential relationship to a canon of less explicitly sexual poetry, but because Nashe's poem itself refuses to align itself neatly with any clear-cut strand of convention.[3] It is parodically indebted to Petrarchanism, to Aretinian 'pornography', to the bodily openness of the medieval period, and to the poetic treatment of the sexually explicit found in the Roman elegists, Ovid in particular. The poem itself is an account of the narrator's visit to a prostitute named Frances, his need for stimulation, his belated arousal and brief sexual conquest of her, followed by Frances's articulation of her own dissatisfaction. Frances then uses a dildo to reach sexual climax, observed by the narrator. There are many anomalies and conflicts in the poem: why, for example, in the context of an economic exchange, is Frances's sexual pleasure so important? What, apart from the deliberate echo of Ovid's *Amores* 3.7, is at stake in the display of the male member and its impotence?[4] While the eroticized female body is a constant focus for male poetic fantasy, it is rare to find explicitly sexual representations of the male body, and this substitution within the Petrarchan convention creates troubling disruptions in the hierarchy which asserts male sexual power over women.[5] The erect penis here is an object of desire both for Frances and for the narrator: given the poem's similarities to bawdy and obscene verse circulated among the young and sexually inexperienced men of the Inns of Court, the scenario also fuels and reflects a fantasy of long-lived male potency for its readership as well.[6] The narrator's sexual failure does not ultimately diminish the phallic economy of the poem, but replaces the fallible male penis with the artificial power of the dildo, thus maintaining the double fiction of woman's desire for the erect penis, and the constructed fantasy of the potentiality of undiminished potency. The narrator's impotence therefore becomes an occasion for humour, for a parodic *bricolage* of poetic discourses on time, immortality and beauty, and for the reinscription of phallic power mediated by the observation of a scene of female self-pleasuring. The figure of Frances is both given and denied authority in 'The Choice of Valentines', as the articulation of her desire and her status as a prostitute justify her display, and reinforce Renaissance notions of woman as sexually voracious: the narrator here simply cannot satisfy, and is symbolically castrated by the excess of her desire, much as the discourse of Petrarchanism renders the male poet/lover immobile and static. At the same time, Frances's apparently subversive assertion of sexual need is redacted into the poet's narrative frame, made subject to his will and whim, and 'The Choice of Valentines' is therefore as much a fantasy of poetic as of sexual control. The rhetorical control of discourse comes to function as a metonymy for a fantasized sexual power.

Nashe's poem 'The Choice of Valentines' has been interpreted in terms of the (im)morality of its sexual content. However, the poem can also be read as an exercise in imitation, where the fantasy is that of poetic self-display, the desire to expose Nashe's 'originality' through breach of decorum, parody and satire, and a projected, aggressive wish to burst the bubble of disguise surrounding the expression of eroticism by more readily patronized courtly and Petrarchan poets.[7] It also repeatedly displaces Petrarchan motifs into contexts dominated by sexual satisfaction and economic exchange, relocating the fantasy of masculine power as a joke or an obfuscation: the woman is a prostitute paid for her ability to dispense sexual pleasure, not the passive recipient of an ennobling desire. Yet unlike the silent mistress of sonnet sequences, her sexual needs are placed centrally and vocally and the chasm between the poet's words and his deeds are cruelly exposed. At the same time as Nashe allies his descriptions of Frances with dominant literary discourses, he raises the spectre of an emasculating female who threatens to escape from his control, symbolically enacted in his own inability to will his penis into action. Paradigms are reversed on the level of both sexuality and poetics. Firstly, in the context of the brothel, her job is to satisfy him, not to seek her own pleasure, but we cannot rule out the possibility that Frances's actions with the dildo finally provide this pleasure. Secondly, as Nashe culls and rewrites his dual literary heritage, English and classical, he runs the risk either of losing his own authority, or of such radical transformation that his predecessors become unrecognizable.

'The Choice of Valentines' is an attempt by Nashe to assert his own poetic authority by marrying Ovidian subject matter and Chaucerian diction in a way which is reminiscent of Spenser's Virgilian-Chaucerian project in *The Shepheardes Calender* (1579). Nashe's careful dismissal of the poem as the necessary purgation of 'lascivious witt' preceding 'purifide word's, and hallowed verse' which will praise his patron, appears to be a false and perhaps judicious *apologia* which attempts to inflate the status of his poem by the promise of greater things to come and the downplaying of a poem which Nashe, at least, endows with serious purpose.[8] The poetic fantasy *does* operate via the sexual, putting the act of sex on display textually for the consumption of the reader, but the fact that the poem circulated exclusively in manuscript suggests that however titillating Nashe's text may be, his intended readership was expected to recognize his literary references and the poetic targets of his satire.[9] Given Nashe's struggle for recognition, it seems reasonable to see 'The Choice of Valentines' as the projection of unsatisfied desire, particularly in terms of poetic achievement, coded as a narrative of sexual failure which nevertheless inscribes the primacy, potency and productiveness of male sexuality.

This framework seems to have provided a mask and a legitimation for his uncompromising satire upon the conventions of Petrarchan poetry.[10] This impulse is evident from the dedicatory sonnet, a parody of the conventional dedication of a serious work to a noble patron, underlined by its similarity to Spenser's sonnet to the Earl of Oxford prefacing the 1590 *Faerie Queene*.[11] The sonnet inverts the usual terms of praise (ll. 1–2) as it relocates them in relation to a self-consciously innovatory form of writing, which derives from the poem's relationship to its context. Nashe's 'wanton Elegie' (l. 4) is represented not in terms of its power to arouse, but in a purely poetic context:

> Complaints and praises everie one can write,
> And passion-out their pangu's in statelie rimes,
> But of loves pleasure's none did ever write
> That hath succeeded in theis latter times. (ll. 9–12)

This is a veiled critique of the deceptions of courtly amorous verse, and an indirect evocation of Ovid, for the Renaissance the poet of 'loves pleasure's' *par excellence*, and for Nashe clearly a model that he wished to adopt, 'the fountaine whence my streames doe flowe' (Epilogue, l. 5). Notably, while bawdy and obscene poetry exists in significant amounts in the Renaissance, it is rarely framed in terms of a specifically poetic project.[12]

This professed desire for an innovatory return to a classical model of erotic verse seems to be motivated by several things. The first is alluded to in the dedicatory sonnet, 'Ne blame my verse of loose unchastitie / For painting forth the things that hidden are' (ll. 5–6), where his undertaking tallies with his critique of the hypocrisies of the Petrarchan mode.[13] This critique is partly poetic, partly professional, as Nashe clearly resents the success of poets who use eloquence which overwhelms matter and who justify their veiled immorality by 'a pretence of profit mixt with pleasure'.[14] He suggests that the underlying aim of such poetry is to corrupt:

> there is scarce to be found one precept pertaining to vertue, but whole quires fraught with amorous discourses, kindling *Venus* flame in *Vulcans* forge, carrying *Cupid* in tryumph, alluring even vowed *Vestals* to treade awry, inchaunting chaste mindes and corrupting the continenst.[15]

He suggests a move away from the veiled expression of sexuality in poetry, from the dangerous deception and misguided reading that such metaphoricity promotes:

> I would there were not any, as there be many, who in Poets and Historiographers, reade no more then serveth to the feeding of their filthy lust, applying those things to the pampering of their private *Venus*, which were purposely published to the suppressing of that common wandering *Cupid*.[16]

This critique involves Nashe presenting himself rather oddly as the reformer of poetic models through the direct imitation of Ovid, as he attempts to drive a wedge between his poetry and his morality:

> I woulde not have any man imagine that . . . I endevour to approove . . . *Ovids* obscenitie; I commende [his] witte, not [his] wantonnes, [his] learning, not [his] lust.[17]

In 'The Choice of Valentines' the return to Ovidian form and Chaucerian diction is an inverted parody of the 'fabulous follie'

and 'painted shewe' of contemporary poetry: hence, by the dis-
lodgement of convention, Nashe indulges his own particular poetic
fantasy of being England's Ovid.[18]

Closely related to this desire is Nashe's attempt to fashion himself as the 'true English Aretine'.[19] Nashe's works are peppered
with references to Aretino (1492–1556), most of which allude to
his power as a satirist and his capacity for wit, *not* his reputation for bawdy: 'We want an *Aretine* here among us, that might
strip these golden asses out of their gaie trappings.'[20] As David
McPherson has argued, opinion on Aretino was deeply divided in
the Renaissance; some praising him for his inventive power, and
others condemning him for his immorality.[21] While Aretino was
widely known as a pornographer, it is not this which underwrites
Nashe's project in 'The Choice of Valentines', although Aretino
would have provided a precedent (as would Ovid) of a poet who
wrote both lascivious and moral works, without apparent contradiction, as long as a clear division between the life and the work
is insisted upon, as Nashe always does, in relation to Aretino.
Significantly, he does this by citing Ovid:

> If lascivious he were, he may answere with *Ovid* . . . My life is chast
> though wanton be my verse . . . what good poet is, or ever was,
> who hath not hadde a lyttle spice of wantonnesse in his dayes?[22]

Although it might be argued that the poem is indebted to Aretino's
Ragionomenti, notably in its adaptation of the dialogue form and
its description of Frances's dildo (ll. 269–79), this could be viewed
as part of the poem's overall investment in imitation and the satire
of poetic convention and morality, a precedent that Nashe would
have found in Aretino. Like Nashe, Aretino was a social climber
who hoped to gain advancement through his wit and originality,
and most of Nashe's references to him are made in the context of
imitation and justification.[23] His influence on Nashe is both moral
and stylistic:

> of all stiles I most affect & strive to imitate *Aretines*, not caring for
> this demure soft *mediocre genus*, that is like water and wine mixt
> together; but give me pure wine of it self, & that begets good
> bloud, and heates the brain thorowly.[24]

Aretino bequeaths a useful model of a satiric poet close to the
centres of power, who wrote both salacious poetry and serious,

pornography and Psalm translations. Hence, he allows Nashe to indulge the fantasy that a poem such as 'The Choice of Valentines' will not damage his career, but enhance it.

The poem's framework, the choosing of sweethearts on St Valentine's Day, is indebted to Chaucer, who treats the subject in the *Parlement of Foules*. Chaucer's narrator repeatedly and disingenuously stresses his lack of experience in love ('For al be that I knowe nat Love in dede'), while Nashe's poem depends upon the author's profession of *sexual* inexperience, as well as his self-identification with the diminutively named narrator, 'Tomalin', if his poetic originality and humour is to be attributed to him and appreciated by his readers.[25] Given that Chaucer's poem has as one of its primary concerns the issue of how to write about love, and the relationship between reading and the experience of love, it seems a particularly appropriate model for Nashe to have used. It too is a spoof of Petrarchan conventions.[26] The dichotomy between Chaucer's narrative of birds choosing mates for life, and Nashe's use of the language of love as self-advancing rhetoric used for financial gain ('but thy self, true lover have I none' [l. 92] says the prostitute to her client) rather than truth, is an additional jibe at the language of eternity and permanence so prevalent in Elizabethan love poetry. The poem is full of implicit and explicit references to Chaucer: as G.R. Hibbard has noted, the medieval poet seems to have been Nashe's main model, and this is evident in Nashe's attempt to recreate both Chaucer's metre and his alliterative style.[27] The opening of the poem, as M.L. Stapleton suggests, recalls that of the General Prologue, and the description of sex in ll. 145–6 has strong echoes of *The Reeve's Tale*.[28] Specific items of vocabulary may also have been culled from Chaucer, such as 'flockmeale' (l. 13), found in *The Clerk's Tale*; the use of horses as indicative of sexual status (ll. 25–8);[29] 'siccarlie' (l. 37) is a common word in Chaucer; the complaint beginning at l. 191 is an echo of the Wife of Bath and so on.[30] The application of a Chaucerian formula to alert the reader to Nashe's simultaneous dependence on and departure from his sources, reveals a playful mimicry which is strongly indebted to the Chaucerian tradition. Like Chaucer, the statement 'as my Aucthor saies' (l. 46) occurs at the point where the narrator invokes Ovid, fails to name his source directly and signals that he is about to depart from him.[31] Such allusions could be multiplied, but the point is that Nashe seems to see in Chaucer a textually playful precedent, who enables him to treat his bawdy subject matter in a poetically innovative way, whose authority prevents the compromise of morality.

Nashe's references to Ovid in this poem have been well documented, but little has been said about his *use* of Ovid.[32] The use of the trope of impotence in ll. 123f. is taken directly from Ovid's *Amores* 3.7, but is framed in terms which are far more colloquial and direct than those of, say, Marlowe's translation. Nashe combines several elements of Ovidian discourse, blending, imitating and reworking in order to shore up his desire to be the English Ovid. As well as referring directly to l. 13 of Ovid's poem, he brings in the common Ovidian comparison between love and war, punning as he goes:

> Hir arme's are spread, and I am all unarm'd
> Lyke one with Ovids cursed hemlock charm'd (ll. 123–4)

Rather than the poet asserting his usual potency in compensation as Ovid does, Nashe concentrates upon Frances's attempts to stimulate him, drawing strongly upon native English words to do so:

> I kisse, I clap, I feele, I view at will,
>   Yett dead he lyes not thinking good or ill.
> Unhappie me, quoth shee, and wilt' not stand?
>   Com, lett me rubb and chafe it with my hand. (ll. 129–32)

While Nashe's use of directly sexual vocabulary is a breach with decorum as far as the general run of love poetry is concerned, it is in line with the dictates of decorum in as far as it is fitting for the baseness of his subject matter, and the social status of his speaker. It is also an attempt to recreate the effect of Ovid in English. The sexualizing of Ovidian imagery is calculated to reinstate Ovid as the poet of direct sexuality, or at least to assert Nashe's ribaldry in relation to his chosen authorities. When Danae is invoked,

> Hould wyde thy lap, my lovelie Danae,
>   And entretaine the golden shoure so free,
> That trilling falles into thy treasurie (ll. 193–5)

the 'golden shoure' of Zeus is equated directly with the poet's ejaculation, both literalizing Ovid and elevating the poet/narrator.

Nashe's use of vocabulary is the key to his poetic and parodic undertaking. The pastiche of styles, run together, undercuts the authority of any one of them, and Nashe asserts his own poetic authority by the appropriation and parody of powerful discourses, that of religion in particular, replacing the structure of religious pilgrimage with the search for sexual love. This refers us back to Nashe's repeated implication that underlying love poetry is sex. The presentation of the poet as 'poore pilgrim' (l. 17), the brothel as the 'Sanctuarie' (l. 23) and 'Oratorie' (l. 37), and the payment for sex as 'offertorie' (l. 39) is deeply ironic: it not only lends power to Nashe's bawdy undertaking by association, but it deliberately debases the use of the language of religious devotion in Petrarchan poetry. It is a spoof which works by hyperbole, by drawing a direct comparison between the baseness of the act and the elevation of the language in which it is conventionally described. Further evidence of this deflation of Petrarchan discourse can be found in Nashe's deployment of an inverted *blason* in his description of Frances. Contravening convention, it works upwards from the feet, rather than downwards from the face (ll. 99f.), and once again parodies the abstractions of Petrarchanism by placing them in the context of urgent sexual desire, polished off neatly by the bathos added by Nashe's use of the popular euphemism 'To dye ere it hath seene Jerusalem' (l. 120), meaning to be drunk, and hence, impotent. Something similar happens in lines 169–76, where Nashe uses Petrarchan convention very self-consciously, but plays with it sardonically as a device to delay orgasm, and to assert his sexual power in literally keeping going. It is significant that one of the few genuinely metaphorical passages in the poem bridges his penetration of Frances, and her plea for his delay, 'Oh not so fast, my ravisht Mistriss cryes' (l. 179). In other words, the power of poetic invention and imitation is, on the one hand, equated with sexual potency, and on the other, it is implied that this kind of poetic discourse is merely a device which stands in for sexual pleasure.

This two-way substitution of words and sex enables us to view sexual power as a metaphor for poetic prowess. It wittily literalizes the image of the powerful, chaste and cruel mistress of the sonnet sequences by representing Frances in opposition to them, highlighting the vacancy of such forms of expression. Secondly, it provides the occasion for a satire on the dildo, a satire which alludes indirectly to the process of poetic invention. 'The Choice of Valentines' is not a fantasy about acts *tout court*, but about the erotics of writing them. Nashe elevates the power of artifice over the natural, precisely by inferring that the 'artificial' dildo can provide pleasure where the 'natural' penis fails, but this is a success created by his own poetic skill, a skill disseminated and circulated by means of the uncompromisingly sexualized female body. Nashe's poem is concerned with sexual failure, and uses this as a means to explore other kinds of fantasies, not only poetic, but sexual and economic. The poet's self-presentation is in terms of his financial power, a power which is sexualized by means of puns and innuendoes: 'he that will eate quaile's must lavish croune's;' (l. 63) is not only an assertion of spending power (and recall the frequent Renaissance pun on *spend* to mean ejaculation) but of sexual desire (a 'quaile' is not only a delicacy, but also a harlot).[33] The validity of male sexual power is asserted also by the fact that the poet's is only a temporary failure, and that the dildo, whilst capable of pleasure, cannot reproduce, it can only repeat and imitate:

> If anie wight a cruell mistris serve's,
>   Or in dispaire (unhappie) pine's and sterv's
> Curse Eunuke dilldo, senceless, counterfet,
>   Who sooth maie fill, but never can begett: (ll. 262–5)

The echoes of Petrarchan vocabulary are unmistakable here, especially given that 'dilldo' 'wayte's on Courtlie Nimphs, that be so coye, / And bids them skorne the blynd-alluring boye' (ll. 255–6). The concluding lines of the poem, as well as underplaying the seriousness of the text, also reassert male sexual power as the primary term, as 'dilldo' is seen to be denying men their sexual pleasure with women. Once again, sexual pleasure is directly linked to expenditure, as the poet bewails the fact that

> Druggs and Electuaries of new devise
>   Doe shunne my purse; that trembles at the price (ll. 305–6)

The failed expenditure on a prostitute is also equated with poetic failure, as Nashe attempts, disingenuously, to dismiss his poem as a trifle, written only for his own pleasure:

> Regard not Dames, what Cupids Poete writes.
> I pennd this storie onelie for my self,

Who giving suck unto a childish Elfe,
And quite discourag'd in my nursurie,
   Since all my store seemes to hir, penurie. (ll. 296–300)

This appears to be a humility *topos* calculated to draw attention to the collocation of authors and predecessors used in the poem, as his double claim to sexual and poetic success at the end seems to imply. The vocabulary here brings together the sexual and the poetic, as Nashe's 'I pennd this storie onelie for my self' hints at its function as a masturbatory fantasy, which ends only in wasteful expenditure. On the poetic level, it implies the failed project of poetic *copia*, and the impotence of poetry itself to bring recognition and reward.

The labelling of 'The Choice of Valentines' as pornography has been made on the assumption that such a category is distinct from fantasy, and this has fundamentally affected the way it has been read, or rather, not read.[34] It has been assumed that the poem is a description of experience, and that its directness precludes it from being 'poetic'. For Robert Merrix it is this 'realistic' aspect which elicits the label of pornography, rather than recognizing the poem simply as a differently nuanced interpretation of the Ovidian elegaic mode.[35] Standing alone among the critics, G.R. Hibbard takes a pragmatic view of the poem's sexual content: 'its bawdry is of the elementary, direct, indecent kind'.[36] His problem is with the poem's poetic failure, but for most critics poetic failure proceeds from its purportedly pornographic status.

The fantasy of authorship that 'The Choice of Valentines' represents is multiple, and is mediated through Nashe's adaptation and disruption of his chosen models: Aretino, Ovid and Chaucer. The model of authorship is Aretinian, the form Ovidian, and the diction Chaucerian. It is an attempt to recreate Ovid's 'wanton elegie' without the careful reorientation of his directly sexual vocabulary found in most Renaissance translations and imitations. It is an emphatic rejection of the obfuscations of Petrarchanism and a deliberately recalled attempt to provide the blend of Latinate and English models which was central to the creation of an authoritative English poetic diction in the Renaissance. Sexual fantasy in literature is never autonomous, but always part of a complex network of discourses. Sex is not an act, but part of a larger economy, social, financial and poetic.

Notes

1. Ian Hunter, David Saunders and Dugald Williamson, *On Pornography: Literature, Sexuality and Obscenity Law* (Basingstoke, 1993), pp. 12–56, and Rachel Bowlby, *Shopping with Freud* (London, 1993), pp. 25–45. I am grateful to Margaret Kean for her incisive comments.

2. Ian Frederick Moulton, 'Transmuted into a woman or worse: masculine gender identity and Thomas Nashe's "Choice of Valentines"', *English Literary Renaissance* 27 (1997), p. 61. See also Daniel Carey's essay in this volume pp. 151–65, where generic expectations, more than the experience of travel, divide the erotic, pornographic, the utopian and the commercial.

3. Moulton, 'Transmuted into a woman', p. 59.

4. Bod. Rawlinson. Ms. Poet 216 contains a translation of Ovid's *Ars Amatoria* as well as Nashe's poem. See Nashe, *Works*, ed. R.B. McKerrow, 5 vols (Oxford, 1966), vol. 3, p. 397.

5. Male sexual identity is the focus of Moulton, 'Transmuted into a woman'.

6. Moulton, 'Transmuted into a woman', p. 58.

7. Ibid., pp. 64–5.

8. Ll. 9–10. Quotations are taken from *The Penguin Book of Renaissance Verse 1509–1659*, selected and introduced by David Norbrook, ed. H.R. Woudhuysen, 95 (Harmondsworth, 1992), and included in the text.

9. See Arthur F. Marotti, *Manuscript, Print, and the English Renaissance Lyric* (Ithaca, 1995), p. 76.

10. See Dorothy Jones, 'An example of anti-Petrarchan satire in Nashe's "The Unfortunate Traveller"', *Yearbook of English Studies* 1 (1971), pp. 48–54.

11. G.R. Hibbard, *Thomas Nashe: A Critical Introduction* (London, 1962), p. 56.

12. See R.H. Miller, 'Unpublished poems by Sir John Harington', *English Literary Renaissance* 14 (1984), pp. 148–58.

13. See 'If I must die', *Works*, vol. 2, pp. 262–3, which Jones notes in 'Anti-Petrarchan satire' is 'an expression of savage and violent sexuality', p. 49.

14. *Works*, vol. 1, p. 10.

15. *Works*, vol. 1, p. 10.

16. *Works*, vol. 1, p. 30.

17. *Works*, vol. 1, pp. 29–30.

18. *Works*, vol. 1, p. 10.

19. Thomas Lodge, *Wit's Misery* (1596), quoted in *Works*, vol. 5, p. 147.

20. *Works*, vol. 1, p. 242. See also vol. 1, pp. 282, 259–60.

21. David C. McPherson, 'Aretino and the Harvey–Nashe quarrel', *Publications of the Modern Language Association* (1969), pp. 1551–8.
22. *Works*, vol. 2, p. 266.
23. *Works*, vol. 1, p. 324; vol. 2, pp. 264–6.
24. *Works*, vol. 3, p. 152. Harvey's earlier statements about Aretino's originality are also relevant: 'Aretines glory, to be himself: to speake, & write like himself: to imitate none, but him selfe & ever to maintaine his owne singularity', quoted in McPherson, 'Aretino', pp. 1552–3.
25. *The Complete Works of Geoffrey Chaucer*, ed. F.N. Robinson (Oxford, 1974), p. 310, l. 8. This may also account for the fact that in most extant copies of the poem, Nashe is identified as its author, unlike most bawdy verse, and in one case asserts his authorship by means of his signature. See the listing in *Index of English Literary Manuscripts*, compiled by Peter Beal (London, 1980), vol. 1, and *Works*, vol. 5, p. 141.
26. See Moulton, 'Transmuted into a woman', p. 64.
27. Hibbard, *Thomas Nashe*, pp. 58–9.
28. M.L. Stapleton, 'Nashe and the poetics of obscenity: *The Choise of Valentines*', *Classical and Modern Literature Quarterly* 12 (1991), pp. 36–8.
29. The word 'hackneis' can be found in *The Canon's Yeoman's Tale*, l. 559.
30. See Nashe's comment, *Works*, vol. 1, p. 299: '*Chaucer*, and *Spencer*, the *Homer* and *Virgil* of England'.
31. The reference is to Ovid's *Metamorphoses* 8.161.
32. See Stapleton, 'Nashe and the poetics of obscenity', for the best account.
33. Eric Partridge, *The Penguin Dictionary of Historical Slang* (Harmondsworth, 1972).
34. See Stephen Hilliard, *The Singularity of Thomas Nashe* (Lincoln, 1986), p. 199.
35. Robert P. Merrix, 'The vale of lillies and the bower of bliss: soft-core pornography in Elizabethan poetry', *Journal of Popular Culture* 19 (1986), pp. 3–4.
36. Hibbard, *Thomas Nashe*, p. 57.

8 *Silly money, fantastic credit*

Ceri Sullivan

Discussions on the concept of credit changed direction in the six-teenth century. Credit became a new form of property: a social product rather than evidence of a moral quality. It was divorced from the private person of the borrower and attached to his public character, his market value measured by the interest rate granted him. Literary and mercantile texts began to explain the accumula-tion of credit – then capital – as the result of the success of the merchant's rhetoric about himself. Unease over the production of this unreal estate was foregrounded in the fantastic figures of mon-strous usurers and irrepressible tricksters, of sermons, chapbooks and plays. This chapter sketches the developments in the credit market of the second half of the sixteenth century. It describes how merchant handbooks published in this period provide methods to protect and to trade in that most volatile of assets, business credit. It goes on to argue that city comedies, exemplified here by Ben Jonson's *The Alchemist* of 1610, profit from the riskiness involved in the fantasy of value which is credit.

Credit was fundamental to consumption expenditure in the late sixteenth century. The smallest practicable units of the gold and silver currency were not small enough to measure much domestic spending – the Elizabethan halfpence was about the size of a drawing-pin head. Thus purchases on credit were usual until the tally reached a level where it could be paid for in coin. The coin-age itself was no surer a method of payment than credit, since debasement, clipping, coining, washing and sweating could reduce the acceptance of a coin to well below its face value. In the area of trade England's metropolitan market, where goods made in the provinces were brought to London for distribution to other parts of the country, or abroad, worked on the basis of credit. Since the supplier was not paid until his factor returned with the sale proceeds, it was usual when selling goods to expect payment in one, three or six months' time; payment on the nail often earned a discount. Consumption and trade expenditure used simple forms of credit as an effect of the market organization and of the unit size and quality of the currency. Central to this organization, however, was the intention of converting the credit to cash as soon as possible.[1]

The market in money itself had a different aim, and the late sixteenth century saw a vastly increased range of debt packaging develop, more of which could be negotiated or assigned as an object of value without the intention of recourse to the original borrower. Robert Ashton warns that 'the absence of institutionalized finance and the prevalence of individual and personal financial relationships precludes systematic historical treatment' of the money markets.[2] Nonetheless, historians of the English economy can delineate two main changes in the terms of credit. Personal brokers, from simple scriveners to merchant brokers such as Thomas Gresham, matched the demand and supply of credit and arbitraged between the different interest rates which were charged in response to the credit ratings of different borrowers. It was not usual for brokers to act as parties to the debt themselves. Rather, they used a variety of new instruments for short-term borrowing, the simplest being the bill obligatory, a personal acknowledgement of debt like the modern IOU. Bills of exchange, essentially a tripartite arrangement which involved a borrower making promises of repayment on behalf of a third party, began to be used for domestic as well as foreign trade. These bills could be indorsed over to a third party and were thus technically negotiable, though their use was limited by the fact that the bill was drawn for a specific sum, and there were legal difficulties put in the way of an indorsee suing on a dishonoured bill. For financing needs of over six months, the most common methods which emerged included borrowing on a bond, and mortgaging land and other assets. Such instruments could represent an investment by the lender into a desired default by the borrower, since the penalty for failure was that the ownership of the assets securing the debt was assumed to have changed hands.

The second development in the money market came in the development of commercial banking in England in the early part of the seventeenth century. Deposit takers lent out on a fractional reserve basis, where a deposit made was lent out again with only a small amount reserved, on the assumption that it would not be called on suddenly. While English banking originated in domestic trade, English merchants were familiar with continental banking facilities: the first retail bank opened in 1609 in Amsterdam, giving customers accounts and requiring them to settle all bills of more than 600 florins in bank money, thus allowing the bank to operate a fractional reserve lending policy. Commercial banking moved the credit system further towards the impersonal, since the bank was the counterparty to both borrower and lender. It also increased the money supply, an effect remarked on by Gerald Malynes in *Lex mercatoria* (1622): banks 'can easily please men at particular, in giving them some credit of that great credit which they have obtained in generall'.[3]

The production of this new form of unreal property, through the increasing sophistication of instruments of credit and the introduction of commercial banking, ensured that credit had become a subject of intense *secular* interest for trade handbooks of the period. Credit was discussed for the first time as a product in itself, a part of the money supply which could be traded and not merely as an aid to efficient retailing. For R.W. Gordon, such 'contractual property required heroic acts of reification to make it fit into the picture of the proprietor standing majestically alone upon his thing, in defiance of the outside world'.[4] This unreal estate – impersonal, negotiable and endlessly expandable – was understood by merchants to be a social product of rhetoric, a fantasy of value which could be made real. Uncoupling it from its links with the ethics of credit-worthiness, merchants connected credit to the methods by which they described themselves and their activities.

About sixty handbooks in English on trading and accounting are extant from the century following the first redaction, in 1547, of the section of Luca Pacioli's *Summa Arithmetica* on double-entry book-keeping.[5] The handbooks provide a range of techniques to secure the gold standard of the merchant's word, yet they bank on the possibility that this asset could be debased. They insist that incurring and managing risk is the essence of business. Profit in trade – and, in particular, interest from the trade in money – is the reward for risking one's assets, including one's credit. The merchant is pictured by the handbooks as a guarantor of meaning, someone who can speak and discern the truth amid the flux of value. Gerard Malynes's *Lex mercatoria* is typical of the handbooks in devoting a chapter to the importance of merchants' promises, since 'faith or trust is to be kept betweene merchants, and that also must be done without quillets or titles of the law, to avoid interruption of trafficke', for 'the Credit of Merchants is so delicate and tender, that it must bee cared for as the apple of a mans eye'.[6]

For the handbooks, the words 'I promise to pay the bearer' are an illocutionary speech act, which create an asset, the promise, in saying them. Auditing the conditions which would make such promises valid demands skill, pains and moral perspicuity.[7] Each handbook concentrates on two mechanical aids which will guarantee that the merchant can keep faith: controls on the numbers of events recorded, and on whether the information is captured accurately. Intervening in the diverse flows of trade, merchants were advised to compartmentalize each transaction, describe it formally, and ensure each one is recorded, though only once. Richard Dafforne's *Apprentices Time-Entertainer* (1640) insists that transactions must be accounted for individually, not netted off as some do:

> (Charitably) I rather conjecture, that long sitting at the Pen is Tedious to them. I have seen it (in my four and twenty years Accomptantship) that some (yea many) have paid full dearly for their Paper-penuriousness, and nimble hast from their countinghouse ... for our former Paper-sparing, we must also spare our sweet sleep; and spend the sable Night in Melancholy Merits.[8]

Furthermore, the transaction must be recorded in a recognized mercantile form; John Browne's *Merchants Avizo* (1589), for instance, gives sample descriptions to be used. In order to control the flow of transactions, Dafforne suggests that the waste book (a list of transactions as they occur) is entered up with every matter

> in plain sincerity, as it was acted; every parcel close under each other, without leaving of any empty place between them, for the avoiding of suspicion of entring forged parcels.[9]

Every event must be recorded immediately, and, as Lewes Robert says in the *Mappe of Commerce* (1638), every entry should be just, true, and perfect, and not to falsifie any parcell, matter, or thing, or yet interline or shuffle one matter with another, but to set every thing ... plainly, directly, and orderly downe.[10]

The books stress the necessity of painfully detailed hard work. Even after the tyro merchant learns to compile the general ledger, the cash book, petty cash book, letters book, memorial or waste book, and factors book, Richard Dafforne warns sternly against believing that 'having well understood the former instructions, you may (through Selfe-conceit) suppose that you are able to manage the Booking of all Trafficking affaires, and so to leave your Study'.[11] Jan Christoffels Ympyn's *Boke of Accomptes* (1547) concurs: 'it is more painful to become a merchant than to be a Master of Art, or a doctor'.[12]

The handbooks were equally as concerned to advise merchants to be cautious about believing others' words. The *Avizo* urges them to 'be not hastie in giving credit to every man; but take heed to a man that is ful of words, that hath red eyes, that goeth much to law, and that is suspected to live unchast'.[13] Peele's *How to keepe a perfecte reconyng* (1553) breaks into verse on the importance of this:

Thus in thy callinge if warely thou walke,
Of promises be just confirminge thy taulke,
Wainge before hand with whom thou doest deale,
Let diligence seke all doubtes to reveale:
For Credit once crackt that maintaines the state
Then dame repentaunce will come verie late.[14]

The texts understand the ethical imperative of being an honest trader; as Ympyn says,

the marchant man ought more diligently serve and praie to God, then other ecclesiasticall persons or laie people, that get not their livings and charges with such perilles and dangers as merchants do.[15]

Indeed the *Avizo* recommends that the first action a trader takes on entering port is to fall to his knees, 'for to feare God and to bee thankefull unto him, is the beginning of all happines & prosperitie in our affaires'.[16] The majority of English sample ledgers open each account with a prayer and a cross. Moreover, the texts also understand the profitability of seeming virtuous. The *Avizo*'s young trader must eschew the aristocratic habits of wine, dice, women and feasts, 'for all these things are especially noted, and doe bring any young beginner to utter discredit and undoing'.[17] Books, as well as merchants, have a credit-worthy ethos to maintain. Malynes insists that

> in the Journall and Leidger Booke, there may not be any alteration of cyphers, blotting (nor places left blanke in the Journall) ... otherwise the bookes are of no credit in law, or before any Magistrat; whereas otherwise much credit is given to bookes well and orderly kept.[18]

Two figures – 'cannibal' usurers and deliberate bankrupts – discussed by the mercantile texts show how far the new ideas about credit had moved away from the Aristotelian and Thomist positions on 'biting usury'. The texts work hard to reinforce the implication of credit, that it will eventually be reversed from its conditional form into hard cash, and then into goods. These two figures threaten their efforts, and both are vilified and envied for not providing a final physical referent. Thomas Powell's *Art of Thriving* (1635) turns deliberate default into an art. The debtor sends his wife to her mother's, shuts up shop, makes a catalogue of all his debts, and waits for his creditors to hear that he has broken.

> The newes reaches to the Exchange by noone, where they that have given credit to him, looke so prettily and pittifully one upon another, as you might know and challenge them by their faces.
> Then they gather together, and conferre their notes, cast up the whole sum what all their credits may come unto, onely some of the more pragmaticall sort, who feare to publish their losses lest their owne estates should come likewise into question, doe dissemble the matter.[19]

Creditors here are caught in a chain of credit which must not be seen to break, even if it means that they must conceal their losses for their own credit. This multiplier effect also lies at the heart of the texts' fascination and unease with usury, partly distinguished from righteous credit by the absence of risk to the money: 'it is a Rule in Law: To whom the hazard appertaineth, to Him the fruit and profit belongeth'.[20] *Usurie Araigned* (1625) notes that 'the estate of usurers consist not in money but in Bills and Bonds for debts upon use' which can be withdrawn without notice, ruining the credit system:

> it pleaseth Usurers to lend to one Debtor to pay another usurer ... and though one usurer take but ten pounds for his use, will not those twentie usurers enforce their severall Debtors to gather from the ordained use twentie severall ten pounds.[21]

Credit, based on market confidence rather than a physical thing, can expand and contract endlessly. Miles Mosse bears witness to its flexibility:

> there are thirteene hundred, yea thirteene thousand devices, which men of evill conscience have invented to avoyde the shew and danger of usurie ... sometimes it semeth to be buying, sometimes selling, sometimes letting, sometimes pawning, sometimes one thing, sometimes another. And therefore whereas it cannot be rightly saide of usurie, that it is an Arte, or Trade, or Occupation, or Science: to the ende that it may have a name whereby to be knowne in Lawe, I suppose that we may ... fitly call it a mysterie.[22]

Recent analysis of credit has often focused on the hypothesis of Max Weber, developed by R.H. Tawney, that the emergence of early modern capitalism was fuelled by Protestant ethics. Usury is seen as an example of economic individualism, which repudiates the charitable duty to lend to a poorer neighbour.[23] In the realm of literature Richard Halpern has suggested that

> the ideological work carried out by the [literary] myth or narrative of social mobility was to reduce a complex social phenomenon to a discourse of capacities which explained vertical movement exclusively by means of quasi-ethical powers within the individual.[24]

It appears, however, that merchant handbooks from the period link ethos to profit as a saleable product, and not to moral worth. They suggest that creating credit in, and so for, the self, is an art that can be learned, not an occasion for an analysis of avarice. The distinction is important when we turn to literary criticism of city comedies.

Postmodern studies of accounting draw parallels between twentieth-century credit and artistic representation. K. Hoskin and R.H. Macve describe both as

similar fictions, for each generates further rewritings which decon-
struct the apparent unities . . . within the world of value, constant
re-writing of instruments into new forms (cheques, stocks, bond
issues, credit cards) . . . which works only because it is guaranteed
and controlled by other writings.[25]

Yet the comparison had already been anticipated and criticized
by Roberts's *Mappe of Commerce*: the merchant's art is like the
poet's in needing to have skill in all knowledges,

whose excellency must consist in a coursory judgement in all sciences, and to be learned in all professions, [the] difference being
that the Merchants skill, must be real, solid and substantiall, and
the Poets may be fained and poeticall.[26]

Both produce rewritings, but the merchant can – indeed must, for
his credit – be attached ultimately to a good solid signified.

Ben Jonson's *The Alchemist* was published at the point at which
the English money market had developed considerably in scope
and sophistication. The city comedy is variously viewed as a response to anxieties over the new urban commerce, or as a satire
on greed, with the caveat that the satirist is fascinated by the sin
he can mock so energetically.[27] Most recently, critics regret with
Jean-Christophe Agnew the development of 'a commodity self:
a mercurial exchange value or "bubble" floating on the tides of
what attention others were disposed to invest'.[28] Rather more cheer-
fully, however, the play's energy could be read as stemming from
the production of a rhetoric of credit. *The Alchemist* explores how
a fantasy of value, credit, is created and maintained. The interest
of the play, for both the gulls and the audience, arises from the
risk that there is nothing substantial behind the credit.[29]

The play opens by establishing a joint stock enterprise in countenance, with equal profit shares for Subtle, Face and Dol. From
being a trio 'whom not a puritan, in Blackfriars, will trust / So
much, as for a feather' (I.i.129–30), they move to creating and
trading on a reputation for realizing dreams: Kastril's wish to
quarrel in fashion, Pliant's desire for a good husband, Mammon's
consumption complex, Ananias and Tribulation's need for gold for
the saints, Surly's play for the widow, Drugger's trading success,
or Dapper's haut ton gambling. This alchemy is not unearned profit:
getting and maintaining these customers' belief in them is hard
work, as Face grumbles:

> Why, now, you smoky persecutor of nature!
> Now, do you see, that something's to be done,
> Beside your beech-coal, and your corsive waters . . .
> You must have stuff, brought home to you, to work on?
>
> (I.iii.100-4)

Each 'account' of the customers is set aside from the others; it is compartmentalized so that the appropriate – spurious – rhetoric may be applied to it. The 'heathen language' which Ananais rebukes is a vocabulary of precision which persuades because of its arcane detail. Dapper is told to prepare himself fasting before he meets the Fairy Queen with three drops of vinegar in at his nose, two at his mouth, one at either ear, to bathe his fingers' ends and cry 'hum and buzz' (I.ii.165–70); Drugger must put his shopboard on the west, his door on the south, and bury a loadstone under the threshold (I.iii.61–70); Kastril must move from the simple 'you lie' as grounds for a quarrel to an infinite sophistication of insult, before he can even begin to take up his rapier, as Subtle informs him:

> You must render causes, child,
> Your first, and second intentions, know your canons,
> And your divisions, moods, degrees, and differences,
> Your predicaments, substance, and accident,
> Series extern, and intern, with their causes
> Efficient, material, formal, final . . . (IV.ii.22–7)

Moreover, the cony-catchers insist that their prescriptions are carried out exactly:

Subtle: Is yet her Grace's cousin come?
Face: He is come.
Subtle: And is he fasting?
Face: Yes.
Subtle: And hath he cried 'hum'?
Face: Thrice, you must answer.
Dapper: Thrice.
Subtle: And as oft 'buz'?

(III.v.1–3)

The details are endlessly improvised, a copia which maintains the customers in a state of desire, since there is never any end to what should be done next to put them into a fit condition to fulfil their dreams. Such copia also then keeps them in a state of disappointment, consuming the dreams produced by the rhetoric. The fact that the cozeners produce a series of deferred satisfactions increases the desires of the dreamers, and the credit of the three. Alas for Epicure Mammon: the nobleman's sister hears rabbinical words and goes mad, while Mammon's lascivious thoughts fracture the alembic; Dapper can only see her Grace after vinegar, or after fasting, or after pinching, or after 'fumigation'; Drugger has to beg repeatedly for Subtle's help; Ananias and Tribulation are chastised as 'froward' while Subtle threatens to bring down the whole still: 'Your threescore minutes / Were at the last thread, you see; and down had gone / *Furnus acediae, turris circulatorius*' (III.ii.1–3). The customers are kept perpetually in the realm of the conditional, of desire. Only if they do this or that deed will the unreal estate of credit be converted to solid success.

Yet the visionaries could be said to get what they pay for. Lovewit's house has become an alembic which is farced with gold to be converted into endless plausible language. The philosopher's stone in *The Alchemist* is all face: if it is believed, it is true. The gulls pay in physical goods (gold, tobacco, a sister) which are abstracted into the dreams they are venturing for. There is no force used; the gulls cooperate with the cozeners, as Surly notes about Mammon:

> Heart! Can it be,
> That a grave sir, a rich, that has no need,
> A wise sir, too, at other times, should thus
> With his own oaths, and arguments, make hard means
> To gull himself? (II.iii.278–82)

The audience shares in the customers' pleasure in such dreams: the 'perpetuity of lust and life' which each is promised, from the magnanimous man's harem of succubi in silk, down to a quick cure for worms. This is a cornucopian understanding of credit, whose capacity is dependent only on the extent of each gull's imagination. The cozeners are there to refine and extend the latter. Even Drugger dares to gaze amorously on the widow, while Mammon repeatedly corrects his own hyperbole as litotes: beds, for instance, are to be blown up, not stuffed; down is too hard (II.ii.41–2). Yet while taking pleasure in the magical fulfilment of these desires, the audience is also required to see how such dreams are the product of a system manipulated by Subtle, Face and Dol.

The multiplier effect is an important feature of the gulls' trust in what Subtle knows: putting themselves into his hands means each one becomes a means to incite another gull to belief. Dame Pliant gets circulated by Subtle on a fractional reserve basis! Yet certain characters challenge the state of happy hyperbole which the other characters live in. Ananias and Surly's refusals to participate in the distillation are not simply dull, they contribute to a comedy of risk. Fantasy characteristically – indeed by definition – employs tropes of excess. Such tropes must gain their effect from the perception that a more mediocre reality exists. The deflation of the gulls' desires is as important as their arousal. Surly and, to a lesser extent, Ananias are there to be sceptical, to keep alive the risk that the tricksters will be discovered. Surly is habitually employed in a duet with Mammon for this purpose:

Mammon:	I'll purchase Devonshire, and Cornwall,
	And make them perfect Indies! You admire now?
Surly:	No faith.
Mammon:	But when you see th'effects of the great medicine!
	Of which one part projected on a hundred
	Of Mercury, or Venus, or the moon,
	Shall turn it, to as many of the sun;
	Nay, to a thousand, so *ad infinitum*:
	You will believe me.
Surly:	Yes, when I see't, I will.
	But, if my eyes do cozen me so (and I
	Giving 'em no occasion) sure, I'll have
	A whore, shall piss 'em out, next day.
Mammon:	Ha! Why?
	Do you think, I fable with you?

(II.i.35–46)

As the production of desire and belief continues so the risk of bankruptcy grows, of not being able to produce the goods.

This is why the play compels the audience's interest. In such an overheated economy the comedy depends on keeping up formal barriers – but only just. The multiple-plotted nature of the farce can work if each gull is kept privy to himself. The fragile structure then comes to depend on a speed of transfer by the cozeners between one rhetoric of credit and another, as there is yet another knock on the door. The play is deliberately limited – just the three cozeners, squeezed into a small house, with only six hours to do their alchemy – so the velocity of their circulation must increase as an increasing number of gulls are involved. The audience is put into the split position of desiring the fictions to inflate and the gulls to continue to believe, but enjoying, minute-by-minute, the mounting risk of a sudden deflationary spiral, of the realization that there are too many words chasing too little meaning. The discovery by Lovewit of

> The empty walls, worse than I left 'em, smoked,
> A few cracked pots, and glasses, and a furnace,
> The ceiling filled with poesies of the candle:
> And madam, with a dildo, writ o'the walls

provides the crash (V.v.39–42). The audience is returned to an unsatisfactory reality: Subtle and Dol sneak over the wall, the gulls sidle away with embarrassment (apart from Ananias, contentious to the last), and the quick marriage of Pliant and Lovewit ties up the loose ends of the plot. Jonson chooses to present an ending that makes the audience nostalgic for the past dreams, not one which celebrates the return of moral rectitude or of gritty reality.

In both trade and art, it would seem, the risk which a merchant takes with his credit produces his profit. Far from being unearned, such interest is the product of hard work, careful artistry and a shrewd understanding of people. Credit is no longer associated with credit-worthiness, or damned as usurious dealing in unreal estate. Critics of the literary and mercantile markets tend to overlook the excitement that this fantasy product arouses, in their discussions of the moral implications of economic individualism. Yet Jonson, just as the merchant handbooks do, profits from playing on risk: here, that the hyperinflation of the farce could tip over into satiric deflation, where the gap between the reality and the fantasy would be foregrounded.

Notes

1. Eric Kerridge, *Trade and Banking in Early Modern England* (Manchester, 1988), pp. 5–75, provides a clear description of the credit market.

2. Robert Ashton, *The Crown and the Money Market 1603–1640*, (Oxford, 1960), p. xvi.

3. Gerard Malynes, *Consuetudo: vel, Lex mercatoria, or The Ancient Law-Merchant* (London, 1622), p. 133.

4. Robert W. Gordon, 'Paradoxical property', in John Brewer and Susan Staves, eds, *Early Modern Concepts of Property* (London, 1995), p. 99.

5. The principal manuals run in a self-referencing line from the first redaction of Pacioli's *Summa Arithmetica*, Jan Christoffels Ympyn's *How to Kepe a Boke of Accomptes* (London, 1547), through James Peele's *How to keepe a perfecte reconyng* (London, 1553) and *The Pathewaye to perfectnes, in th'accomptes of Debitour and Creditour* (London, 1569), John Mellis's *Briefe instruction and maner how to keepe bookes of accompts* (London, 1588), John Browne's *The Merchants Avizo* (1607; London, 1589), Nicolaus Petri's *Pathway to knowledge* (London, 1596), to Richard Dafforne's *The Merchants Mirrour* (London, 1635) and *Apprentices Time-Entertainer* (London, 1640). While concerned to discuss theories of trade, Malynes's *Lex mercatoria* and Lewes Roberts's *Merchants Mappe of Commerce* (London, 1638) also provide advice on book-keeping and credit. Peter Ramsey provides evidence on how English merchants actually accounted, 'Some Tudor merchants' accounts', in A.C. Littleton and B.S. Yamey, eds, *Studies in the History of Accounting* (London, 1956).

6. Malynes, *Lex mercatoria*, pp. 93, 104.

7. J. L. Austin, *How to Do Things with Words* (Oxford, 1962), pp. 94–108.

8. Dafforne, *Time-Entertainer*, pp. 78–9.

9. Ibid., sig. A5 v.

10. Roberts, *Mappe*, p. 36.

11. Dafforne, *Merchants Mirrour*, sig. Ii v.

12. Ympyn, *Accomptes*, sig. A5 v.

13. Browne, *Avizo*, p. 62.

14. Peele, *Pathewaye*, sig. *ii v.

15. Ympyn, *Accomptes*, sig. A5 r.

16. Browne, *Avizo*, p. 2.

17. Ibid., p. 4.

18. Malynes, *Lex mercatoria*, p. 363.

19. Thomas Powell, *The Art of Thriving* (London, 1635), pp. 229–30.

20. Robert Bolton, *A Short and Private Discourse . . . Concerning Usury* (London, 1637), p. 28.

21. *Usurie Araigned and Condemned* (London, 1625), p. 10.

22. Miles Mosse, *The Arraignment and Conviction of Usurie* (London, 1595), signs. K2 v–r.

23. M.J. Kitch excerpts and summarizes arguments over this topic, in *Capitalism and the Reformation* (London, 1967); this suspicion of credit has been challenged, most recently by Craig Muldrew, who suggests that credit promoted social cohesion, 'Interpreting the market: the ethics of credit and community relations in early modern England', *Social History* 18 (1993), pp. 163–83.

24. Richard Halpern, *The Poetics of Primitive Accumulation: English Renaissance Culture and the Genealogy of Capital* (Ithaca, 1991), p. 88.

25. Keith W. Hoskin and Richard H. Macve, 'Accounting and the examination: a genealogy of disciplinary power', *Accounting, Organizations and Society* 11 (1986), p. 118. A similar imbrication of literature and credit can be seen in the dream of Caesellius Bassus related in Christopher Pelling's essay in this volume on pp. 22–4, where poets' praise of Nero as the producer of wealth helps sustain the rumours that affect real spending.

26. Roberts, *Lex mercatoria*, p. 42.

27. There have been three major directions to the analysis of city comedy. The first, initiated by L.C. Knights's *Drama and Society in the Age of Jonson* (London, 1937), ch. 5, sees them as a response to a changing British society, and in particular to the growth of London's middle class. Alexander Leggatt, *Citizen Comedy in the Age of Shakespeare* (Toronto, 1973) looks at reiterated topoi in city comedy, such as the prodigal gallant, the citizen hero, shrewish wife, the whore to be married on, and the heiress-virgin; see also Leggatt's *English Drama: Shakespeare to the Restoration, 1590–1660* (London, 1988), ch. 6, and, more recently, essays by Leonard Tennenhouse, Peggy Knapp and Stephen Mullaney, in David Scott Kastan and Peter Stallybrass, eds, *Staging the Renaissance: Reinterpretations of Elizabethan and Jacobean Drama* (London, 1991). Laura Stevenson's ground-breaking discussion of the figure of the merchant in plays of the period, *Praise and Paradox: Merchants and Craftsmen in Elizabethan Popular Literature* (Cambridge, 1984), opposes elite and bourgeois culture; see also Theodore B. Leinwand, *The City Staged: Jacobean Comedy 1603–1613* (Madison, 1986). The second line of analysis has looked at the comedies in terms of their generic background; Brian Gibbons, *Jacobean City Comedy* (London, 1968), looks at a range of materials such as the jest book, satire and didactic drama to analyse the plays as belonging to a stylized subgenre of corrective moral comedy on greed. Recently, a third line of analysis places the comedies as rewritings of anxieties over capitalism: Richard Halpern's *Poetics of Primitive Accumulation* (Ithaca, 1991) and Jean-Christophe Agnew's *Worlds Apart: The Market and the Theater in Anglo-American*

Thought, 1550–1750 (Cambridge, 1986) take a cultural materialist stance on the plays.

28. Agnew, *Worlds Apart*, p. 13.
29. Ben Jonson, *The Alchemist*, ed. Douglas Brown (London, 1966). All quotations are from this edition. Richard Dutton sums up critical descriptions of the play as a suppression of moral judgement in favour of comedy, in *Ben Jonson: To the First Folio* (Cambridge, 1983), pp. 113–24.

9 The politics of escapism: fantasies of travel and power in Richard Brome's The Antipodes and Ben Jonson's The Alchemist

Julie Sanders

The English early modern stage had an endless fascination with notions of travel. Marlowe's drama famously tested and exploited the limits and the possibilities of stage space via the geographical wanderings of Tamburlaine and Dr Faustus.[1] There are obvious links between the experience of watching a play and that of travel, and not surprisingly many sixteenth- and seventeenth-century playwrights chose for their subject matter travel and exploration, mirroring the colonial and expansionist interests of their age.[2]

What these plays invariably tell us most about, however, are not the locations of travel, the exotic far-off lands, actual or fictional, to which their characters journey, but the fantasies of those doing the travelling and therefore of the theatre audience that shares the experience.[3] Anthony Parr has indicated the extent to which commercial theatre plays in this period provided an imaginative substitute for real travel and adventure.[4] He cites an account by the Swiss traveller Thomas Platter of a visit to London in 1599 and the diverse entertainment he found in the capital: 'with these [plays and bearbaitings] and many more amusements the English pass their time, learning at the play what is happening abroad ... since the English for the most part do not travel much, but prefer to learn foreign matters and take their pleasures at home'.[5] Stephen Greenblatt has suggested that the 'utopian moment of travel' occurs 'when you realize that what seems most unattainably marvelous, most desirable, is what you almost already have, what you could have – if only you could strip away the banality and corruption of the everyday – at home'.[6] What happens to the experience of travel when it is travel in the mind only? Is the final reckoning still with understandings of home? Are those same desires for the marvellous, the exotic and the fantastic answered or frustrated?

The early modern period witnessed many colonial expeditions and displayed great interest in the literature of travel, actual and fictional, for political, commercial and scientific reasons – but also as a source of aesthetic pleasure.[7] One particular text, the fourteenth-century literary production known as *The Travels of Sir John Mandeville*, proved particularly popular: the book was supposedly the account of the travels of an English knight to, amongst other places, the Holy Land and the Orient, and of the manifold encounters he had *en route*. Even though it was no longer held to be a true account as early as the fifteenth century, it remained an important text of imaginative literature throughout the early modern period, one that engaged with the romance, the fantasy, of travel. The *Travels* was the subject of a 1599 play, *Sir John Mandeville* (now lost), of several verse satires, and was reprinted five times between 1612 and 1639 alone.[8] A heady mix of genuine travellers' accounts and more fantastic materials, all passed off by the narrative persona as eyewitness truth, this text had a profound effect on the period's imagination. In 1638 Richard Brome wrote a play about a young man, Peregrine, who has become mentally unhinged by his readings of the *Travels* and his inability to imitate the narrator's wanderings due to parental prohibition. Brome's play, *The Antipodes*, refers to this as 'Mandeville madness' (IV.i.466). In this chapter, I want to consider the potency of fantasies of travel, their complicity in the colonial desires for power and possession, and the politics of fantasies of this nature in the period. The plays that form the focus of that discussion, Ben Jonson's *The Alchemist* and Brome's *The Antipodes*, are in many respects intricately related: Jonson was Brome's theatrical mentor and directly influenced many of his plays. In a dedicatory poem attached to the printed version of *The Antipodes*, 'C.G.' observes that 'Jonson's alive!' (l. 1) and 'sojourns in Brome's *Antipodes*' (l. 22). *The Antipodes* looks back to Jonson's own 1610 play about impossible desires in its dealings with fantasy and theatre, and it is both Jonson's influence and the related politics of these two plays that this chapter explores.[9]

Greenblatt has accounted for the motives of Columbus, Raleigh and other New World explorers as the concomitant desires for gold and possession.[10] These are also the structuring desires in the lives of the gulled clients in Subtle and Face's alchemical laboratory in *The Alchemist*. These clients come to find the secret of the philosopher's stone, the elixir that will turn base metals into gold.[11] The monomaniac knight Sir Epicure Mammon is consumed by such desires. When we first see him onstage, Mammon is already fantasizing about the possibilities that possession of the stone will open up for him.

> Come on, sir: Now, you set your foot on shore
> In *novo orbe*; here's the rich Peru:
> And there within, sir, are the golden mines,
> Great Solomon's Ophir! He was sailing to't,
> Three years, but we have reached it in ten months. (II.i.1–5)

Mammon envisages himself as a second Pizarro, taking possession of this new Peru. What is intriguing about his fantasy of colonialism is that it is not located in the far-off locale of the Americas or the Indies but at home in the London of 1610, in which the play is so emphatically staged and set. The laboratory is in truth Lovewit's London house, transformed by the fraudsters Subtle, Face and Dol during his absence in plague-time into an alternative theatre. Mammon's transformations will all take place at home: 'I'll purchase Devonshire and Cornwall, / And make them perfect Indies!' (II.i.35–6). He will, in his utopian fantasy, make the sick well again, the old young, and enjoy extravagant luxuries himself into the bargain. There is a philanthropic aspect to this, but essentially Mammon is aping the way in which colonial imperialists dressed their actions in the language of education and enlightenment. At heart he desires to experience the spoils of colonial travel for himself: 'My meat shall all come in, in Indian shells, / Dishes of agate, set in gold, and studded, / With emeralds, sapphires, hyacinths, and rubies' (II.i.72–4).

Mammon's dreams quite literally go up in smoke, in the staged explosion of the laboratory furnace. When Lovewit describes his house on his return, the theatre audience is shocked to realize how

active its own imaginations have been in filling the bare space of
the stage with fantastic projections.

> Here I find
> The empty walls, worse than I left 'em, smoked,
> A few cracked pots, and glasses, and a furnace,
> The ceiling filled with poesies of the candle;
> And madam, with a dildo, writ o'the walls. (V.v.38–42)

Home is reinterpreted by the fantasies of travel and power in *The
Alchemist*.[12]

Metatheatrical staged fantasies are at the heart of Brome's *The
Antipodes* as well. In order to cure Peregrine of his Mandeville-
inspired melancholy, Dr Hughball and Lord Letoy stage a play to
persuade the young man that he has travelled to the Antipodean
lands described in Mandeville's text – a world of Amazons, and
one-footed peoples, of woolly hens, and women with stings in
their hymens who would slay their husbands on their wedding
nights were other men not hired.[13] The latter account is what stays
Peregrine from sleeping with his own wife of three years, so potent
is the effect of Mandeville's story-telling on his psyche:

> Mandeville writes
> Of people near the Antipodes called Gadlibriens,
> Where on the wedding night the husband hires
> Another man to couple with his bride. (IV.i.461–5)

In Brome's version Mandeville's *Travels* has a powerful impact
on the fantasy life of its readers. In the seventeenth century,
Mandeville's name was a signifier for travel and diverse experience: in Jonson's *The New Inn* (1629) Lord Frampul talks of his
errant lifestyle and how his wife became a 'she-Mandeville' in his
wake (V.iv.101).[14] In *The Antipodes* Peregrine regards Mandeville
as the most authoritative of travel writers:

> *Doctor*:   Mandeville went far.
> *Peregrine*: Beyond all English legs that I can read of.
> *Doctor*:   What think you, sir, of Drake, our famous countryman?
> *Peregrine*: Drake was a didapper to Mandeville. (I.iii.27–30)

There is considerable irony here. By 1638, when Brome's play was
staged at the Salisbury Court theatre, Mandeville's text had long

been a byword for the fraudulent or inauthentic. Admittedly Raleigh had travelled to the New World with a copy of the *Travels* in his possession, but he never endorsed the truth of its material; Richard Hakluyt included a Latin text of the *Travels* in his first edition of *The Principal Navigations* but removed both it and his defence of its authenticity from the second issue.[15] Josephine Bennett suggests that Mandeville's *Travels* held a paradoxical status as both fantasy and fact in the seventeenth century; increasing navigation of the world revealed many of the text's claimed truths to be fantastic fabrications, an artistically ambitious gathering, under the persona of Mandeville, of the writings of numerous other authors such as William of Boldensele, Oderic of Pordenone, Giovanni de Pian Carpini and Albert of Aix.[16] To quote Greenblatt, 'Mandeville is radically empty; his name is a textual effect, signalling only the absence of an authentic traveler'.[17]

Brome's play too is characterized by the absence of authentic travellers. Peregrine never actually leaves home despite his belief that he has undertaken a lengthy journey to the other side of the world (he regrets his failure to record that experience in writing, in II.iv). As a consequence, identity and authenticity are radically destabilized in *The Antipodes*. By the end Peregrine has emerged in a new guise as a happy and loving husband, having also played the Antipodean king for a time, seizing power in this imaginary land, but he is not the only one affected by his fantastic journey. Letoy, the play-within-a-play's director, and not Truelock, proves to be father to Diana, young wife to Peregrine's father Joyless, and that revelation plays its part in testing Joyless's possessive attitude to his wife. The sojourn in the Antipodes, although feigned, has radically altered perceptions of the social space the 'travellers' usually inhabit.

As with Jonsonian masques, however, the resolution of the fifth act in *The Antipodes* is incomplete. The masque at the end that witnesses the banishment of the antimasque of Discord by Harmony appears both to acknowledge the performative power of masque fantasies and yet also their limits, their questionable fixity.[18] Peregrine remains confused as to the status of his recent experience: 'For I have had (if now I wake) such dreams, / And been so far transported in a long / And tedious voyage of a sleep' (V.ii.322–5). Brome explicitly opposes diverse experiences such as folly, dreams, madness, masque and travel in this way, enacting Todorov's theory of the 'ambiguity of adventure', its problematic status as both reality and dream, truth and illusion.[19] Fantasy contains within it the etymological sense of 'madness', but there is never one sole interpretation of fantasy in this play: at various times it is linked to psychological illness, to travel or the lack of it, to domestic restrictions, and to theatre itself.

Such is the power of dreams that they can unsettle any stable sense of reality. The voyage into fantasy is not over until the audience decides it is so with their applause:

> And from our travels in th'Antipodes
> We are not yet arrived from off the seas;
> But on the waves of desp'rate fears we roam
> Until your gentler hands do waft us home. (V.ii.385–8)

The last word of this play is 'home'. The fantasy of travel is in the end a means of reinterpreting one's own place and space. The Anti-London of Letoy's play, where men are subjected to the ducking stool as scolds, where lawyers are honest, and where women are seen on top, is a vibrant depiction of the world turned upside down. This Antipodean city-state, as its name suggests, performs the function of critiquing some of the social realities of contemporary 1630s Caroline society by reflecting them back to its inhabitants. The focus is on home rather than abroad. As Doctor Hughball claims,

> This, sir, is Anti-London. That's the antipodes
> To the grand city of our nation:
> Just the same people, language, and religion,
> But contrary in manners, as I ha' told you. (II.ii.38–41)

Greenblatt has made similar observations with regard to Mandeville's *Travels*:

> In place of a world in which all paths lead to the perfect center, Mandeville comes to imagine a world in which every point has an equal and opposite point . . . Each point in the world is balanced by an antipodean point to which it is at once structurally linked and structurally disjoined.[20]

Brome appears to have recognized this in his Mandevillian source material some three centuries earlier, although by including desirable elements in his staged Antipodes (such as female autonomy, a mode of living that the watching Diana admires) as well as more negative images, he deliberately complicates audience responses to the place.

The Antipodes, in an intriguing mirror of the narrative composition of Mandeville's *Travels*, blend reality and fantasy – and the meeting point is home. In the play-within-a-play we receive a microcosmography of the bawds, usurers, sedanmen, projectors, courtiers and lawyers one would expect to find in London. As Martin Butler has evidenced, there are images in the Antipodes that are mere reflections rather than straight inversions of the truth of seventeenth-century London: 'Anti-London is not always an inversion of normality but a revelation of what normality ordinarily hides; inversion – sickness – is a part of "normal" life'.[21] Butler hits on the significance of sickness, disease and the unsettling to this drama. Almost the entire stage community has some troubling obsession or concern. The London that Joyless comes to is one recently wracked by plague (another important parallel with the London of *The Alchemist*); fantasy as madness may be alluded to in the text, but it is the sickness of contemporary society that proves to be the real threat. Travel and even the fantasy of travel prove restorative, homeopathic even, in their impact upon society. Butler detects subversive political commentary within this play. The world turned upside down, he argues, is being proffered as a dramatic lesson to the monarch of the time. When the play was first performed, Charles I had been governing for almost a decade without summoning a parliament, the so-called period of 'Personal Rule' of 1629–40.[22] Brome, Butler suggests, is offering the counsel that Charles should turn his autocratic style of government 'upside down', and by implication summon a parliament and listen to those subjects who were opposing unparliamentary innovations in the period such as Ship Money, raised as its name suggests to maintain the navy, and other extraordinary taxations which had been levied on the population.[23] In the parodies of the legal world contained within Letoy's play, Butler identifies allusions to specific cases such as the drawn-out hearings over Ship Money in the late 1630s. The play is seen to hit home despite its mode of high fantasy.

That precise political context for the play is one possible reading of Brome's multi-faceted text; more generally the fantasy of travel is employed as a trope for many different social needs and desires. Barbara, wife to the Joyless family's London host Blaze, describes Peregrine as being 'in travail' (I.i.175): this puns on the etymological roots of the term 'travel' in 'travail', meaning to labour, toil, or suffer. Peregrine (and even his name contains the sense of travel) is suffering *from* the lack of journeying in his life.[24] Such is the young man's inner despair that his parents now regret forbidding him to travel.

> When he grew up towards twenty,
> His mind was all on fire to be abroad.
> Nothing but travel still was all his aim;
>   . . . all prevailed not,
> Nor stayed him – though at home – from travelling
> So far beyond himself that now, too late,
> I wish he had gone abroad to meet his fate. (I.i.138–40; 147–50)

Peregrine's unsatisfied adolescent desires have a detrimental effect upon those around him, especially his wife, Martha. She is portrayed as mentally destabilized by his behaviour, pathetically obsessed with the unattainable desire of childgetting:

> I am past a child
> Myself to think they are found in parsley beds,
> Strawberry banks, or rosemary bushes, though
> I must confess I have sought and searched such places,
> Because I would fain have had one. (I.i.241–5)

Martha's searching provides an intriguing parallel with Peregrine's own mental wanderings and the labour of travel functions as one element of Brome's exploration of social yearning.

The Antipodes is concerned with obsessional desires of many kinds. Letoy's play reveals his monomania for power in controlling the acting company. There is something dangerously self-contained about his theatrical stagings. If theatre and travel are linked experiences then Letoy is also confined to and by home:

> Stage plays and masques are nightly my pastimes,
> And all within myself: my own men are
> My music and my actors. I keep not
> A man or boy but is of quality. (I.ii.56–9)

Letoy's play exacerbates Joyless's obsessive jealousy of his young wife Diana, whose interjections throughout the performance help to stress the relevance of the play-within-a-play to Brome's home audience. Joyless suspects her of alternative wanderings, and subjects her to the same oppressive patriarchal control under which his son languishes. Joyless's desire is for sexual possession, a drive akin to that in Mammon in *The Alchemist*. The relationship of travel with open and unrestrained sexuality underpins *The Antipodes* at various moments: in Letoy's drama, a world of greater sexual freedom, not least for women, is glimpsed through dramatic fantasy; the oppressions of home for women, as well as for young men such as Peregrine, are highlighted. Like Mammon's, Joyless's quest fails, consequently the multifarious journeys of the play may be seen as liberating rather than containing in their effects.

Fantasies function as agents of release (in Peregrine's case enabling a fantasy of power and autonomy clearly disallowed him in his parental home), yet also, in certain manifestations, as potentially self-consuming. Rosemary Jackson has observed how fantasy can function simultaneously as both a positive and negative presence in society: 'in expressing desire, fantasy can operate in two ways . . . it can *tell of*, manifest or show desire . . . or it can *expel* desire, when this desire is a disturbing element which threatens cultural order'.[25] Ian Donaldson reads the carnivalesque elements of *The Antipodes* as being in a constrained and conservative mode, suggesting that Peregrine is allowed temporary access to the topsy-turvy world of the Antipodes merely to aid him in future conformity. In that respect Donaldson interprets the end masque 'straight' as a confirming fantasy of harmony.[26] Yet it remains surely just that, a fantasy – as staged and inauthentic and ephemeral as anything else we have witnessed in Letoy's theatrical household.

Lucie Armitt has suggested that the utopian mode is necessarily open-ended, with fantasy operating as a site of 'hesitancy, uncertainty, and disquieting ambivalence'.[27] Jonson and Brome similarly see in the fantastic mode an unsettling of social fixities. In *The Alchemist* the role-play of the cozeners subverts social hierarchies, with Subtle and Face adopting the titles of General and Captain for their alternative personae; in *The Antipodes* it is patriarchal law and, in particular, family hierarchy that is most directly challenged, both by a son's gaining of maturity through the experience, albeit fantastic, of travel and through the damaging fantasy of jealousy that pervades Joyless's thinking on his marriage. If, to appropriate a sub-Freudian paradigm, fantasy is to some extent always tied up with family relationships and romances, then Brome here resists the endorsement of the traditional role of the father as the head of the household. By the end of the play Joyless's decisions about his marriage and his son are proved to have been mistaken.

Travel is seen to focus the mind in Peregrine's case, and in many respects the play is an account of his rite of passage into adulthood. The infantilizing prohibitions of his family are swept away in the assertive role he assumes as a romance hero in his attack on the stage properties of the actors' tiring house. Brome, like Jonson, employs metadrama to keep the audience alert to its own complicity in the stage fantasy. Peregrine goes backstage and takes survey of the properties there – a materialist catalogue of the theatrical mode of making fantasy manifest that Armitt has identified as the central paradox of the form. Byplay observes that Peregrine has noticed,

> Our statues and our images of gods,
> Our planets and our constellations,
> Our giants, monsters, furies, beasts, and bugbears,
> Our helmets, shields, and vizors, hairs, and beards,
> Our pasteboard marchpanes, and our wooden pies. (III.i.290–4)

Believing them to be genuine, Peregrine pulls down a sword and shield used to perform the role of Sir Bevis of Hampton – a romantic fantasy hero of the sixteenth century who was regularly reworked by seventeenth-century dramatists in ironic fashion – and

> Rusheth amongst the foresaid properties,
> Kills monster after monster, takes the puppets
> Prisoners, knocks down the Cyclops, tumbles all
> Our jigambobs, and trinkets to the wall.
> Spying at last the crown and royal robes
> I'th'upper wardrobe, next to which by chance
> The devils' vizors hung, and their flame-painted
> Skin coats, those he removed with greater fury;
> And having cut the infernal ugly faces
> All into mammocks, with a reverend hand
> He takes the imperial diadem and crowns
> Himself King of the Antipodes, and believes
> He has justly gained the kingdom by his conquest. (III.i.305–17)

It is significant that Peregrine, like Mammon, cannot envisage a nation other than his own without seeking to conquer and possess it; the colonialist impulse of travel is clearly re-enacted here. There is humour in Peregrine's belief that the props room is an enchanted castle in the sub-Spenserian mode, but there is also a genuine sense of release from boyhood into maturity. Peregrine's actions have been remarked upon as evoking the actions of the apprentice boys of London on their regular Shrove Tuesday city riots when they would attack the commercial theatre houses.[28] What I have recounted here, however, is a working through of a personality disorder: Peregrine's stage trajectory is to enter into masculinity by slaying monsters and rejecting his father's rule, albeit within a purely theatrical context.

There is then an understanding that travel, and indeed theatrical journeys of the imagination, can provide a release to otherwise dangerous energies and emotions. The fantasy of travel operates not as some transcendental act of escapism but constitutes the act of coming home. But to return does not mean to be unchanged; this is where containment readings of fantasy display their limits.[29] The experience of travel, a dynamic imaginative action, if static in terms of physical location, enables the fantasist to see anew their everyday world and in the case of Jonson's and Brome's plays this impact extends to watching or participating audiences.[30]

Fantasies of travel and power as they operate in *The Alchemist* and *The Antipodes* are by no means escapist in the sense of being devoid of political or social relevance. While the political context of Jonson's playwriting is beginning to emerge with force, Caroline drama has too often been dismissed as an escape into aestheticism which blinded itself to the tense political situation in the period of Personal Rule.[31] Fantasy, like travel, has productive links with drama; the theatrical medium relies on the participating imaginations of the audience – even more so in the pre-realist theatre of the seventeenth century – but this does not mean that fantastic literatures seek to escape or evade realities. In locating their travel plays so self-consciously 'at home', Jonson and Brome recognize the potential for fantasy to contain social critique and potentially subversive or radical messages – to demonstrate the possibilities of the everyday, to indicate what their society 'almost already' had, or 'could have'. Escapism for them and for their characters, like the writing and the staging of theatre, was a distinctly political act.

Notes

1. The editions of primary texts used are as follows: Richard Brome, *The Antipodes*, in *Three Renaissance Travel Plays*, ed. Anthony Parr (Manchester, 1995); Ben Jonson, *The Alchemist*, ed. Douglas Brown (London, 1966); and *The Travels of Sir John Mandeville*, ed. C.W.R.D. Moseley (Harmondsworth, 1983). See Stephen Greenblatt, *Renaissance Self-Fashioning: From More to Shakespeare* (Chicago, 1980), pp. 193–221.

2. Peter Holland, ' "Travelling hopefully": the dramatic form of journeys in English Renaissance drama', in Jean-Pierre Maquerlot and Michèle Willems, eds, *Travel and Drama in Shakespeare's Time* (Cambridge, 1996), p. 160.

3. For the significance of fantasy in the experience of travel in this period, see Daniel Carey's essay in this volume, pp. 151–65.

4. See Parr's introductory essay to his edition of *Three Renaissance Travel Plays*.

5. From *Thomas Platter's Travels in England 1599*, trans. Clare Williams (London, 1937), cited by Parr, *Three Renaissance Travel Plays*, p. 1.

6. Stephen Greenblatt, *Marvelous Possessions: The Wonders of the New World* (Oxford, 1991), p. 25.

7. For a useful introduction to the impact of travel upon literature and social understanding in this period, see Jeffrey Knapp, *An Empire Nowhere: England, America, and Literature from 'Utopia' to 'The Tempest'* (Berkeley, 1992); Stephen Greenblatt, ed., *New World Encounters* (Berkeley, 1993); Margo Hendricks and Patricia Parker, eds, *Women, 'Race', and Writing in the Early Modern Period* (London, 1994).

8. A detailed study of the various manuscript and printed editions of Mandeville can be found in Josephine Waters Bennett, *The Rediscovery of Sir John Mandeville* (New York, 1954). On seventeenth-century editions, see pp. 251–3. See also Mary B. Campbell, *The Witness and the Other World: Exotic European Travel Writings, 400–1600* (Ithaca, 1988).

9. As if to anticipate the theatrical future, the Stagekeeper in the Induction to Jonson's *Bartholomew Fair* (1614) talks about 'Master Brome behind the arras' (l. 8).

10. See Greenblatt, *Marvelous Possessions*, especially ch. 3.

11. See Ceri Sullivan's discussion of the elixir as constituting the fantasy of ever-expanding credit, in her essay in this volume, pp. 122–36.

12. See Lucie Armitt's essay in this volume discussing utopian desires for originary spaces, pp. 185–96.

13. Parr suggests that many of these details were depicted in woodcuts that accompanied the 1625 edition of Mandeville's *Travels*, which he suggests is the edition used throughout by Brome, p. 230 (n. 196); Ann Haaker's introduction to her edition of *The Antipodes* (London, 1966), p. 27. Since Jonson mentions Mandeville in *The New Inn* within four years, it does seem that this publication renewed popular interest in the text in the Caroline period. For Mandeville's account of the 'stinging women', see *The Travels of Sir John Mandeville*, p. 175. On the gender politics of Renaissance travel writings, see Louis Montrose, 'The work of gender in the discourse of discovery,' in Greenblatt, ed., *New World Encounters*, pp. 177–217.

14. Along with *Bartholomew Fair* and the collaborative production of *Eastward Ho*, Rebecca Ann Bach investigates the intersection of theatrical and colonial tropes in *The New Inn* in 'Ben Jonson's "civill savages"', *Studies in English Literature* 37 (1997), pp. 277–93.

15. See Bennett, *The Rediscovery of Sir John Mandeville*, pp. 245–6.

16. Ibid., p. 246.

17. Greenblatt, *Marvelous Possessions*, p. 34.

18. For a related politicized, non-escapist reading of the Jonsonian masque and antimasque see Lesley Mickel's essay in this volume, pp. 95–108.

19. See Tzvetan Todorov, *The Fantastic: A Structural Approach to a Literary Genre*, trans. Richard Howard (Ithaca, 1973), p. 25.

20. Greenblatt, *Marvelous Possessions*, pp. 42–3.

21. Martin Butler, *Theatre and Crisis, 1632–42* (Cambridge, 1984), p. 215.

22. See Butler, *Theatre and Crisis*, p. 218. For a detailed study of the decade of 'Personal Rule', see Kevin Sharpe, *The Personal Rule of Charles I* (New Haven, Conn., 1992).

23. Ship Money became a particular focus of grievances and by 1637 was subject to non-payment in certain areas. See Ann Hughes, *The Causes of the English Civil War* (Basingstoke, 1991), pp. 162–3.

24. And indeed gestures towards another of Jonson's theatrical travellers: Peregrine, the scourge of the Politic Would-Bes in *Volpone* (1606). See Jonathan Bate, 'The Elizabethans in Italy', in Maquerlot and Willems, eds, *Travel and Drama in Shakespeare's Time*, pp. 55–74.

25. Rosemary Jackson, *Fantasy: The Literature of Subversion* (London, 1981), p. 3.

26. Ian Donaldson, '"Living backward": *The Antipodes*', in his *The World Upside Down: Comedy from Jonson to Fielding* (Oxford, 1970), pp. 78–98.

27. Lucie Armitt, *Theorising the Fantastic* (London, 1996), p. 32. For a related discussion of borders and frontiers in the genre of the fantastic, see Todorov, *The Fantastic*, p. 117.

28. See Ira Clark, *Professional Playwrights: Massinger, Ford, Shirley, and Brome* (Lexington, 1992), p. 183. He compares the play communities' operations on the May–December Joyless marriage as comparable to the actions of the Charivari. For accounts of the apprentice boy riots, see Andrew Gurr, *The Shakespearean Stage, 1574–1642* (1970; Cambridge, 1980), pp. 18–19.
29. For an astute formulation of the way in which fantasy's mobility as a literary mode allows the contravention of quotidian norms, see Barbara White's essay in this volume, pp. 166–81.
30. Armitt identifies this tension between the static and the dynamic as a defining feature of the fantastic, *Theorising the Fantastic*, p. 6.
31. Butler, *Theatre and Crisis*, has altered the critical landscape in this respect. Accounts of Caroline drama that come in his wake include James Bulman, 'Caroline drama', in A.R. Braunmuller and Michael Hattaway, eds, *The Cambridge Companion to English Renaissance Drama* (Cambridge, 1990), pp. 353–79, although Simon Shepherd and Peter Womack's recent overview *English Drama: A Cultural History* (Oxford, 1996) simply omits Caroline drama from its account.

This article is dedicated to Stephen Greenblatt and the postgraduate seminar on Travel and Literature at the University of California at Berkeley, 1994.

10 *Travel and sexual fantasy in the early modern period*

Daniel Carey

Fantasy played an integral part in the experience of travel in the early modern period. The promise of gold and silver from Indian mines or argosies of spice from Eastern shores evoked fantasies of untold wealth. The enterprise of conquest, occupation and possession depended, in turn, on Renaissance fantasies of self-aggrandizement, glory and renown, a vision troubled, once settlement occurred, by fantasies of Indian reprisal and annihilation. Although these occasions of fantasy could be acknowledged publicly, sometimes in lurid detail, the matter of *sexual* fantasy proved more difficult to signal and describe.[1] Travel clearly facilitated the circulation of sexual desire, but open expression of this dimension of the experience remained problematic. In fact, although sexual matters came under discussion in accounts of travel they rarely did so in a way that exposed the position of the author, whether by describing actual or imagined participation in the first person. In this chapter I explore the dynamics of sexual fantasy in early modern travel, both the disciplining of fantasy and desire, and those occasions in which they flourished in a less inhibited way.

To discuss this theme we need to explore an array of printed sources but we also need to remain sensitive to differences of rhetorical occasion. Questions of sexual practice surfaced in travel writing in its anthropological moment, ordinarily as a means of deploring a lack of due restraint among native peoples and occasionally among their European visitors. Reportage of this kind served not to stimulate fantasy but rather to encourage dismay and disdain, emphasizing the author's moral integrity. By contrast, in promotional tracts which invited exploration and settlement such decorum often disappeared as they linked the prospect of sexual conquest with the occupation of foreign land. However, the fullest opportunity to explore the possibilities for sexual fantasy emerged in the genre of the imaginary voyage. By studying Henry Neville's *The Isle of Pines* (1668), an elaborate fantasy of sexual congress on a deserted South Sea island, I will show one of the major incentives for the composition of imaginary voyages, namely to venture into the terrain of fantasy, beyond the more constricting conventions of 'authentic' narrations of individual experience.

In the eyes of contemporary observers, travel brought with it an association with various forms of illicit sexual adventure. Commentators recognized that departure from the mother country, even in journeys no farther than the Continent, marked an escape from the demands of established sexual mores. The traveller Fynes Moryson expressed the view in 1617 that 'women for suspicion of chastity' proved unfit for travel, a point that reminds us both of the sexual threat posed by these departures, as well as the fact that the discourse of travel in the sixteenth and seventeenth centuries remained, predominantly, a male one.[2] Moryson went on to remark that shame disappeared during travel among strangers, leading corrupt individuals to exploit the opportunity for sensual pleasure. Later in the century, the Puritan divine Richard Baxter lamented the activities of those inspired by carnal ends, whose waywardness made them seek out 'Penthouses of pomp and lust' in the midst of their journeys.[3] Travel afforded freedom from the check of inherited standards and expectations, while also providing a useful measure of anonymity.

At one level, travel constituted a danger because of its inherently liberating effect. This problem was compounded by the fact that foreign countries occasionally sanctioned customs that English observers regarded with suspicion. Francis Osborne, writing in 1656, offered guidance to travellers which included the issue of sexual conduct. He countenanced the possibility of romantic liaisons abroad as long as youths avoided marriage, for the simple reason that by marrying they risked being taken in by bawds who coveted their property. More worrying still was Italy where, he averred, 'handsom, young and beardless' travellers needed to proceed with caution to protect themselves as much from 'the *Lust of Men*, as the *Charms of Women*'. Various debauched individuals sent

Emissaries abroad, to entice men of delicate complexions, to the Houses of these decrepit Lechers; under pretence of an Assignation made by some Feminine Beauty; and thus ensnared, the poor uncircumspect young Man cannot with Conscience do, or safely refuse this base Office.[4]

The rival demands of courtesy and safety came into conflict with conscience, placing naive youths in a tense and awkward social situation.

In the light of these warnings, those who published accounts of their travels adopted a distinctive set of strategies for discussing sexual issues. Rather than declare their own subject position, they customarily avoided exploring individual desire, other than within sanctioned limits, and they frequently made an active effort to disparage sexual abuses they observed among foreign peoples. For example, travellers took note of sexual depravity in the countries they traversed, condemning it in similar terms to those used by orthodox moralists like Osborne. In 1670 John Burbury reported on a sect of Turkish holy men addicted to sodomy, 'yet many of the Turks are so senseless and blind, to hold them for saints', he pointed out in disbelief, while among the 'grandees', given over to a life of luxury, idleness, feasting and debauchery, no abuse was more common, which, 'when 'tis not forced, 'tis hardly look'd upon as a Vice'.[5] In an otherwise sympathetic account of the Chinese, Domingo Navarrete, a Jesuit missionary, thought the vice so common among them that their authorities could never implement the punishment of sending offenders to the Great Wall. If enforced, China would be 'unpeopled, and the Wall overgarison'd'.[6] Men did not have a monopoly on same-sex liaisons, however. George Sandys, a classical scholar who later translated Ovid's *Metamorphoses*, made this clear in his observations on Turkey during a tour of the country that began in 1610. After describing the rituals associated with Turkish baths, he noted that 'Much unnatural and filthie lust is said to bee committed in the remote closets of these darksome Bannias: yea, women with women'. Sandys based his remark, characteristically, on rumour not personal witness, but he cautioned against a sceptical response to the story by noting obliquely that 'former times' had provided prior instances both of 'detection and punishment'.[7]

The loose habits of women in exotic countries did not end there. In 1671 Pierre Martin de La Martiniere recorded his conviction that Lapland and Russian women would have volunteered themselves for sexual intercourse at a moment's notice if unhindered by the jealous vigilance of their husbands. Women in Ceylon had the same disposition according to Abraham Duquesne, a French sea-captain sent to defend French trading interests in Siam in the 1690s, the only difference being that their husbands neglected to restrain them. They not only smoked perpetually but indulged without scruple in 'the vilest lusts', readily prostituting their bodies.[8] Along the Gold Coast of Africa, the female denizens proved equally lacking in chastity according to Nicolas Villault, who journeyed there in 1666 as part of slave-trading activity by the French West India Company. He remarked of the women that 'their lasciviousness is above all, which they suck as it were with their milk, playing hoyty-toyty amongst the young fellows starke naked'.[9] Regarding American Indians, some travellers noted with a degree of puzzlement that young girls were allowed to engaged in sexual activities unhindered, but once they married they became strictly chaste.

In certain contexts, travel writers mentioned with evident pride that local women developed a taste for foreign visitors, as in Madagascar where one author reported the preferences of female residents, claiming 'the *Europeans* are a singular good ragoust to them'.[10] Others noted the custom, practised in a number of countries, of men making their wives available to visitors. Although these cases hinted at European participation in a field of exotic sexual adventure, authors rarely remarked on their own involvements while abroad, preferring to cultivate the stance of distanced observers.

Travel accounts veered from offering anthropological testimony in a neutral mode to generating outrage that served to discredit the people they described, underlining the implied superiority of European custom as well as the right to occupy such morally barren ground. But it was not all dismay and disparagement. If fantasy (as an expression of desire rather than fear) emerged at any point in this literature it did so in praise for the modesty, chastity and submissiveness of native women. George Warren, who resided in Surinam for a period of three years shortly before the colony passed from English to Dutch possession, pressed the boundaries of this convention in 1667. His unusual frankness stands out boldly

against the familiar tendency towards restraint in the genre. Warren described the female residents of the territory as lascivious but
also 'truly handsom, as to Features and Proportion'. His enthusiasm became more marked when he described the young virgins he
encountered. He commended their 'pretty Bashfulness' in the presence of strangers which added 'such a Charming grace to their
perfections too nakedly expos'd to every wanton Eye', and he
went on to confess more openly 'that who ever lives amongst them
had need to be owner of no less than Joseph's Continency, not at
least to Covet their embraces'. In short, Warren hinted at an
urgent sexual response to their beauty which would only restrain
itself miraculously, registered at the very minimum in the desire
for embrace, but extending to the need for far greater intimacy.
He then played ironically on the established representation of
Indian peoples:

> They have been yet so unfortunately ignorant, not to enrich their
> amorous Caresses with that innocent delight of Kissing, but con-
> versing so frequently with Christians, and being naturally docile
> and ingenious, we have Reason to believe, they will in time be
> taught it.[11]

Warren wryly confirms their primitive status, untutored in the
finer points of the *ars amatoria*. But this unfortunate condition
will soon be remedied by English instruction, availing of the distinctive mixture of qualities that characterizes local women, namely
their gentle passivity as well as their ingenuity. Doubtless he played
on the inclusion of sexual intercourse within the semantic range of
the term 'conversation'.

If travellers remained conventionally circumspect in their reporting of custom and physical appearance, excluding their own
desires and sexual history from the record of their authentic voyages, then the promotional literature of the period exhibited rather
different priorities. The vast development of colonial projects, ranging from huge tracts in North America to the Caribbean, South
America and Madagascar, necessitated capital investment on a
prodigious scale as well as sustained emigration to populate these
different territories. Projectors competed with one another in
advertising the benefits of the location they sought to exploit.
Accordingly, they portrayed any prospective colony as a land of
milk and honey. This powerful fantasy also contained a sexual

component. Writers figured the land itself in sexual terms, and described the act of settlement as a form of union with virgin terrain. Perhaps the most famous example is the colony of Virginia, named not only to compliment the Queen but also to highlight the innocence and availability of the land itself.[12] Even more striking is Walter Raleigh's description of Guiana. Raleigh sailed there in search of El Dorado, a city of fabled wealth hidden somewhere in the vast interior of the country. The mission, sanctioned by the Queen, promised the discovery of a state as rich as the Aztec and Incan empires which the Spanish had exploited to such advantage. Raleigh's mission famously ended in failure. The ore he returned with proved valueless, and the project as a whole became a personal embarrassment. Raleigh saved face by writing a heroic account of his adventures in 1596 which contained an appeal for further exploration through the twisted branches of the Orinoco river. In this context he made the famous remark that '*Guiana* is a Countrey that hath yet her Maydenhead'.[13] Here he not only sexualized the landscape, stressing its virginity, but he also invited a form of sexual conquest in the act of settlement.[14]

Raleigh introduced a metaphorical connection between travel and sexual adventure that heightened the element of fantasy. Others who encouraged settlement made a similar appeal, even if they did so less explicitly. An intriguing example of this approach appears in an account of the province of New York by Daniel Denton, published in 1670 shortly after the English acquired the territory from the Dutch. Among the staple items of virtually all promotional literature, unsurprisingly, was the inclusion of long lists of the natural productions of the territory. As prospective planters, readers needed to know what commodities would sustain life there whether at a basic level or for the purposes of trade and the accumulation of wealth. In this context, Denton noted an array of fruits that flourished in New York in June: mulberries, persimmons, grapes, huckleberries, cranberries, plums, raspberries and strawberries grew in such abundance, he announced, 'that the Fields and Woods are died red'. He then inserted a narrative that elaborated on the life settlers enjoyed there during this ripe season. Denton reported that the country people, on witnessing the sight,

> instantly arm themselves with bottles of Wine, Cream, and Sugar, and in stead of a Coat of Male, every one takes a Female upon his

Horse behind him, and so rushing violently into the fields never leave till they have disrob'd them of their red colours and turned them into the old habit.[15]

Occupying an expressly male perspective, Denton drew on a series of associations, predominantly sexual in nature, to strengthen the appeal of the province. The male colonists, abandoning knightly armour, and laden with food and drink rather than the implements of war, take hold of their women, evidently without resistance. They enter the fields with the haste of urgent sexual desire and leave the terrain, once clad in the colours of red fruit, denuded, as they satisfy their appetite for the fruit, in a scene that mirrors sexual consumption as well as the moment of undressing to perform the act.

The literature of travel, whether of 'authentic' accounts of particular journeys or consciously rhetorical promotional tracts, gave a certain play to sexual fantasy, but this was not always explored in an expansive fashion. The potency of the connection between travel and sexual fantasy arrived at a fuller expression in the context of the imaginary voyage.[16] In this domain, greater scope existed for heightening the element of sexual desire contained within conquest and possession. One example among many will suffice to introduce this theme, the striking case of Donne's elegy 'To his Mistress Going to Bed' (rejected by the censor when his verse appeared in print posthumously in 1633). The poet issues a series of imperatives to his lover, insisting that she undress and unlace herself, entering 'love's hallowed temple, this soft bed'. In a metaphor of travel he asks her to license his hands to rove 'and let them go / Before, behind, between, above, below'. Donne plays on the notion of licentiousness as well as the particular licence required by travellers to depart their country. This leads to a famous exclamation:

> O my America, my new found land,
> My kingdom, safeliest when with one man manned,
> My mine of precious stones, my empery,
> How blessed am I in this discovering thee![17]

For Donne, in typical fashion, the pleasures of the bed compensate for public disappointment by *becoming* public themselves, by being figured in the grandest terms of states, princes, empires. Licensed to travel, he embarks on a journey of discovery where the body is represented as America, a continent he possesses for himself alone as monarch.

Donne's metaphorical connection between travel and sexual adventure became literal in Henry Neville's *The Isle of Pines*, one of the most remarkable works of prose fiction in the seventeenth century. The remainder of this chapter will focus on Neville's anonymous text, which spanned only nine pages of print when its first edition appeared in 1668. Neville exploited the strong potential for fantasy in travel which was side-stepped in 'authentic' relations for the most part. But instead of presenting the piece as an obvious fantasy, the invention by an armchair traveller musing at the possibility of erotic activity, he achieved even greater impact by alleging the authenticity of his fictional island in the South Sea.

The Isle of Pines tells the story of an English book-keeper, George Pine, who travelled to India at the age of twenty in order to establish a factory there with his master in 1569. The title page of the pamphlet summarizes the fantastic nature of the story:

> The Isle of Pines, or A late Discovery of a fourth Island in Terra Australis, Incognita. Being a true Relation of certain English persons, Who in the dayes of Queen Elizabeth, making a Voyage to the East India, were cast away, and wracked upon the Island near to the Coast of Terra Australis, Incognita, and all drowned, except one Man and four Women, whereof one was a Negro. And now lately Anno Dom. 1667. a Dutch Ship driven by foul weather there, by chance have found their Posterity (speaking good English) to amount to ten or twelve thousand persons, as they suppose. The whole relation follows, written, and left by the Man himself a little before his death, and declared to the Dutch by his Grandchild.

The piece itself consisted in the first edition solely of Pine's first-person account of his experience, so the title page provided important historical detail which gave it verisimilitude.[18] At the same time, Neville carefully tucked his imaginary island away in 'Terra Australis, Incognita', the unknown fourth quarter of the world. He also stressed the veracity of the story which focused on the fate of four women and one man who, in the space of a century, managed to instigate a spectacular population of the island.

While *The Isle of Pines* marks a high point in the imaginary voyage's exploitation of fantasies of sexual freedom, it should be viewed initially against the background of earlier contributions to the genre of travel fiction. In fact, sexual themes occupied a relatively modest part of utopian literature. More's *Utopia* (1516) touched on the theme by describing the curious custom of allowing prospective marital partners to inspect one another naked before entering the pact, but his purpose seems to be comic and satirical rather than licentious. Bacon expanded on this proposal in the *New Atlantis* (1627), with the suggestion that the couple's best friends should perform this signal office of inspection, presumably to avoid any impropriety. Again his tone is far from amorous when describing this novel custom. Matters of gender arose in other contexts of imaginary travel, but the representation of femininity was usually far from libertine in inspiration.[19] On the contrary, the romance element in such works of prose fiction and drama frequently emphasized the ideality of the female figure, whose constancy, virtue and chastity marked a contrast with more imperfect mortals. In *The Tempest* (*c*.1611), Shakespeare presents us, in Miranda, with an ideal daughter who submits readily to patriarchal authority, thus naturalizing deference to the father in the midst of the play's other prospective inversions of power relations.

This brief sketch highlights the unusual nature of Neville's text. On reading the sensational narrative, contemporaries learned, ostensibly from Pine himself, what transpired on the journey. The voyage out proved unexpectedly eventful. After a series of storms, the fateful ship, the *India Merchant*, rounded Madagascar, but again blew off course in the midst of an extended gale. The vessel neared the rocky shore of an island which threatened to destroy it. The captain, several crewmen, and Pine's master all departed in the long boat, while the rest of the crew jumped overboard in a vain attempt to save themselves. Only Pine remained, along with the four women, who, like himself, were unable to swim. The ship hit the rocks, but they escaped injury by huddling in the bow which broke off and settled in a small stream. No one else survived, as they soon discovered.

Pine proceeded to relate how they lived on the deserted island. Apart from himself, the party consisted his late master's fourteen-year-old daughter, two maids, and a black woman, presumably a slave. They managed to recover much of the ship's contents to set up house, forming a tent out of the rigging and sail cloth before they removed to a makeshift hut of their own contrivance, complete with hammocks. A local creature, a bird the size of a swan, proved easy to catch for food. Hens and cocks that escaped from the ship also bred there. In due course Pine and his companions settled in comfortably, finding the island a pleasant place, 'never colder then *England* in *September*', abundant in fruit, nuts, birds' eggs, fish, game and fowl.[20]

However, where a conventional account might have ended at this point, Neville continued with an extended report on the sexual history that ensued. Having lived on the island for six months, Pine reported that 'Idleness and Fulness of every thing begot in me a desire of enjoying the women' (p. 66). Far from meeting any resistance, he found the two maids ready for his embrace. At first they coupled in private, 'but after', he stated, 'custome taking away shame (there being none but us) we did it more openly, as our Lusts gave us liberty' (p. 66). Seeing this open intercourse, his master's daughter also expressed a desire to join him. At this point Pine acknowledged that they 'were all handsome Women, when they had Cloathes, and well shaped, feeding well' (p. 66). He explained that their decision to heed the impulses of nature stemmed from their idleness, the availability of ample food, from liberty itself, and finally the fact that they had no hope of returning home. Travel had indeed released them from the bonds of conventional morality. But the unanswered question, at this stage, was whether Pine would sleep with the negro servant. He went on to relate how the event occurred. One night, she crept beside him while he slept, with – he noted – the consent of the others. In the darkness she hoped to beguile him, but Pine awoke and perceived who she was. Once again, he overcame any hesitation: 'yet willing to try the difference, [I] satisfied my self with her' (p. 67).[21] Stimulated by the experience he went on to have sex that night with another of the women as well.

After documenting these occasions of sexual intimacy, Pine began to describe the birth-rate of his companions. Essentially he kept each of his wives in production, so much so that he found himself with forty-seven children by the time they ceased bearing. In this fertile country they lived a life of ease, without rancour. Pine completed the fantasy by sketching out a portrait of their situation:

> we were now well satisfied with our condition, our Family beginning to grow large, there being nothing to hurt us, we many times

lay abroad on Mossey Banks, under the shelter of some Trees, or such like (for having nothing else to do) I had made me several Arbors to sleep in with my Women in the heat of the day, in these I and my women passed the time away, they being never willing to be out of my company. (p. 68)

In due course, they vowed not to leave one another or the island itself. In this respect they differ from Robinson Crusoe whose bid to escape ends in failure. He refrains from continuing the attempt, not from a positive desire to stay but due to his fear of falling into cannibal hands. Furthermore Crusoe, who has no sexual history in the island sequence of the narrative, disciplines himself through labour; far from making things, as Pine does, merely to give himself something to do, Crusoe must work in order to survive, the text informs us, in spite of his residence on an initially deserted Caribbean island.

After sixteen years, 'perceiving my eldest Boy to mind the ordinary work of Nature, by seeing what we did' (p. 68), Pine must consider what to do with his offspring. Free on either side it seems from guilt or shame, he provides his son with a mate, whether a sister or half sister he neglects to say, 'and so I did to all the rest, as fast as they grew up, and were capable' (p. 68). In this contented state Pine spent his final years. At sixty, having outlived his wives, including his favourite (his master's daughter), he marries the males of one family to the females of another, no longer permitting incest 'as we did formerly out of necessity' (p. 69). He expires, in the end, at the ripe age of eighty, but not before he has assembled his descendants to count them, in a fashion consistent both with his book-keeping background and his status as something of a biblical patriarch. To his satisfaction, they now amount to 1,789 individuals.

We can speculate on Neville's purposes for composing this story which may have arisen from an interest in underpopulation, in polygamy, or simply from a wish to delude naive readers of travel literature with an elaborate hoax.[22] But the main interest of the work, and the reason it provoked an exceptional response, centres on its exploration of sexual fantasy.[23] It shares with some of its predecessors a fascination with patriarchy, with naturalized male rule that remains uncontested. Female docility in matters of domestic management joins with sexual availability, with the lack of resistance to male desire, and, what is more, to peaceful coexistence with multiple wives. Beyond that, Neville offers a tale of exceptional fertility that foregrounds incest as part of the plot. He achieves this within the limited stylistic terms of authentic travel narratives, by circumscribing the extent of erotic and salacious detail. But this technique merely invites the (male) reader's imagination to expand the episode more fully, contemplating the possibility of an island retreat, free from the demands of labour, where the days and nights have no greater responsibility than coition.

As a work of fantasy, Neville's text explores male desire, offering a form of wish-fulfilment achieved at a narrative level. The appeal of his work depends on the presentation of willing female participants who respond unproblematically to male advances (and even make some of their own), together with an acceptance of male political authority. But Neville makes an important move by presenting the story as authentic, and in such a way as to convince a wide group of contemporary readers of its veracity. Whatever his intentions for doing so, he placed the reader in the position of consuming a fantasy while reacting, ostensibly, to a genuine account of how the English social and sexual order might be reconfigured. On the one hand, this way of telling it served as an alibi; on the other, it meant that even the reticent confronted a possibility shown to exist, if not in their own nature, then at least in the nature of one group of shipwrecked travellers who departed with a certain set of moral conventions and ended up with quite another.

Notes

1. See Danielle Clarke's essay in this collection, pp. 109–21, which discusses the available discourses for representing sexual fantasy in the early modern period.
2. There are of course exceptions, notably in the seventeenth century. See Susan Wiseman, 'Read within: gender, cultural difference and Quaker women's travel narratives', in Kate Chedgzoy, Melanie Hansen and Suzanne Trill, eds, *Voicing Women: Gender and Sexuality in Early Modern Writing* (Keele, 1996), pp. 153–71. James F. Gaines and Josephine A. Roberts, 'The geography of love in seventeenth-century women's fiction', in James Grantham Turner, ed., *Sexuality and Gender in Early Modern Europe: Institutions, Texts, Images*

(Cambridge, 1993), pp. 289–309, gives an account of the geographical component of romances by women.

3. Richard Baxter, *A Christian Directory* (London, 1673), tome IV, p. 133.

4. Francis Osborne, *Advice to a Son* [1656], ed. Edward Abbott Parry (London, 1896), pp. 75–6.

5. John Burbury, *A Relation of a Journey of the Right Honourable My Lord Henry Howard, From London to Vienna, and thence to Constantinople* (London, 1671), pp. 95, 170.

6. *The Travels and Controversies of Friar Domingo Navarrete 1610–1686*, ed. J.S. Cummins, 2 vols, Hakluyt Society, 2nd ser. 118–19 (London, 1960), vol. 2, p. 220. Anxieties associated with sexual transgression and homosexuality, registered in the writings of English and Spanish representatives in the New World, have been discussed by Jonathan Goldberg in *Sodometries: Renaissance Texts, Modern Sexualities* (Stanford, 1992), part 3.

7. Sandys's account, which appeared in 1615, was reprinted in Samuel Purchas, *Hakluytus Posthumus or Purchas his Pilgrimes* [1625], 20 vols (Glasgow, 1905), vol. 8, pp. 150–1.

8. Abraham Duquesne, *A New Voyage to the East-Indies in the Years 1690 and 1691* (London, 1696), pp. 95–6.

9. Nicolas Villault, *A Relation of the Coasts of Africk Called Guinee*, 2nd edn (London, 1670), p. 141.

10. W. Glanius, *A New Voyage to the East-Indies*, 2nd edn (London, 1682), p. 26.

11. George Warren, *An Impartial Description of Surinam* (London, 1667), pp. 23–4.

12. For further examples and discussion see Annette Kolodny, *The Lay of the Land: Metaphor as Experience and History in American Life and Letters* (Chapel Hill, 1975), ch. 2.

13. Sir Walter Raleigh, *The Discoverie of the large, rich and beautifull Empire of Guiana* [1596], ed. V.T. Harlow (London, 1928), p. 73. Raleigh goes on to extend the metaphor, saying that the country was 'neuer sackt, turned, nor wrought, the face of the earth hath not beene torne ... It hath neuer been entred by any armie of strength, and neuer conquered or possessed by any Christian Prince.' In spite of these inducements, Raleigh insisted elsewhere that the sailors and soldiers who accompanied him proved examplars of sexual restraint, even though 'we saw many hundreds [of women], and had many in our power, and of those very yoong, and excellently fauored which came among vs without deceit, starke naked', p. 44.

14. For discussion see Louis Montrose, 'The work of gender in the discourse of discovery', in Stephen Greenblatt, ed., *New World Encounters* (Berkeley, 1993), pp. 177–217.

15. Daniel Denton, *A Brief Description of New-York* (London, 1670), pp. 3–4.

16. For the relationship of travel and drama specifically see Julie Sanders's chapter in this volume, pp. 137–50, and the essays collected in Jean Pierre Maquerlot and Michèle Willems, eds, *Travel and Drama in Shakespeare's Time* (Cambridge, 1996).

17. The poem first appeared in *The Harmony of the Muses: or, The Gentlemans and Ladies Choisest Recreation* (London, 1654). Although the emphasis is more commercial, a similar connection emerges in Falstaff's amorous expectations in *The Merry Wives of Windsor*. Plotting his joint adultery with Mrs Ford and Mrs Page, he announces: 'I will be cheaters to them both, and they shall be exchequers to me: they shall be my East and West Indies, and I will trade to them both' (I.iii.65–8). See also Danielle Clarke's essay in this volume, pp. 109–21.

18. Two subsequent editions explained the provenance of the text by inventing a Dutch sailor who conveyed it as part of a relation of his experiences in the South Sea, including the discovery of the island. For an illuminating reading of the politics of the text in its expanded form see Susan Wiseman, '"Adam, the father of all flesh": porno-political rhetoric and political theory in and after the English Civil War', *Prose Studies* 14:3 (1991), pp. 134–57; Amy Boesky, *Founding Fictions: Utopias in Early Modern England* (Athens, Ga., 1996), ch. 5.

19. Consider also Francis Godwin, *A Man in the Moone* (1633; London, 1638): 'Againe their Females are all of an absolute beauty: and I know not how it commeth to passe by a secret disposition of nature there that a man having once knowne a Woman, never desireth any other', p. 103. In the eighteenth century, Robert Paltock explored sexual themes in his fictional travel fantasy *Peter Wilkins* (London, 1751).

20. The text is reprinted in Worthington Chauncey Ford, *The Isle of Pines 1668: An Essay in Bibliography* (Boston, 1920). The quotation is from pp. 65–6. Subsequent references are given in the text. A more widely available but less reliably edited version of the first edition appears in Philip Henderson, ed., *Shorter Novels Volume Two: Jacobean and Restoration* (London, 1930).

21. The hesitation in the text over interracial intercourse is well described in Harold Weber, 'Charles II, George Pines, and Mr Dorimant: the politics of sexual power in Restoration England', *Criticism* 32:2 (1990), pp. 193–219.

22. See A. Owen Aldridge, 'Polygamy in early fiction: Henry Neville and Denis Veiras', *Publications of the Modern Language Association*

65 (1950), pp. 464–72; Geoffrey Bullough, 'Polygamy among the reformers', in G.R. Hibbard, ed., *Renaissance and Modern Essays* (London, 1966), pp. 5–24.

23. For an account of the readership Neville attracted and remarkable publishing history of the work see Daniel Carey, 'Henry Neville's *The Isle of Pines*: travel, forgery and the problem of genre', *Angelaki* 1:2 (1993–94), pp. 23–39.

Research for this essay was supported by the John Carter Brown Library, Providence, Rhode Island.

11 *Jenny Voss: the fantasy of female criminality*

Barbara White

Early modern female rogues exert a fascination today as they did once over their contemporaries. While Mary Frith (1584–1659), better known as Moll Cutpurse, was the inspiration for Middleton and Dekker's *The Roaring Girl* of 1611, another highwaywoman, Catherine Ferrars (*c.*1634–1660), has been the subject of two film versions of *The Wicked Lady*, with Margaret Lockwood and Faye Dunaway playing the title role. Daniel Defoe's *Moll Flanders*, whose heroine is a fictitious composite of real-life female rogues, still enjoys great popularity. It is not surprising therefore that early modern criminal biography has provided fertile ground for examining why criminals were fictionalized by popular writers to serve the needs of an avid readership. Lincoln Faller voices this interest: 'our concern is not so much with the real as with the highly selective ways in which the real was represented'. He argues that criminal biography was absorbed into two principal myths of crime, one imitating the picaresque novel, the other a form of spiritual biography found especially in cases of domestic murder. In the latter myth the personality of the accused was given detailed attention and every effort was taken to create a real world, 'even to the extent of inventing what would otherwise seem to be actual facts'. Conversely, Faller argues, criminal picaresque narratives such as *The English Gusman*, a biography of the highwayman James Hind, 'move toward the fantastic, edging away from a "solid" and "realistic" appraisal' of the lives of the criminals described. By suppressing the personality of individual criminals and turning them into roguish stereotypes, Faller argues that reality was distorted to serve as an escape for readers from the concerns of the everyday world, 'not the least of which was the increasingly troublesome business of hanging men merely for crimes against property'.[1] It is to this category of criminal biography that accounts of the petty thieves and tricksters, Jenny Voss and Mary Carleton, belong.

The focal point of this chapter are the two biographies of Voss, the most detailed being an anonymous publication entitled *The German Princess Revived: or The London Jilt* of 1684.[2] Its title explains why the life of Carleton is also included in this study. The biography describes Voss as 'the London Jilt', suggesting her dexterity at picking locks and opportunist thieving, but she is also 'the German Princess Revived'. Carleton, the original German Princess, had been dead twelve years when Voss's biography was published. Her attempt in 1663 to ensnare a rich husband by disguising herself as a German princess had led to a charge of bigamy in a celebrated court case. Although guilty, her brazen outfacing of her detractors in court led to her acquittal and to over twenty-seven publications about her life which made her the most famous female felon of her day. These included attacks and counter-attacks on her by her aggrieved husband John, official and unofficial reports of her trials in 1663 and 1672, poems, ballads, a play, several biographies written by anonymous hacks and one by Francis Kirkman, the bookseller and author, as well as two purported autobiographies.[3] In 1663 her duped husband dismissed the publications about Carleton as 'Stories, Fancies, dayly encreasing Fables', but they were a publishing sensation.[4] Kirkman believed Carleton herself could have made £500 'of those that would have given 6d. and 12d. a peece' just for the chance of seeing her.[5] To join Voss and Carleton together in the title of *The London Jilt*, and thus in the public imagination, was therefore a shrewd and calculated stratagem by *The London Jilt*'s anonymous biographer to cash in on this previous publishing success. It signalled to a readership, clamorous for sensationalist criminal biography, that *The London Jilt* would provide a tale of criminal adventure and sexual exploit to rival that of the Carleton narratives.

The London Jilt gives a colourful version of Voss's life which may have had little bearing on the facts. It portrays her as an ungovernable child who, as an eleven-year old, was stealing money from her parents but who was wily enough to frame the family pet monkey for one theft in order to escape suspicion over her others. According to *The London Jilt*, by the age of fifteen she had developed a licentious nature, a violent temper and what was euphemistically described as 'angry rhetorick'. She had abandoned her family to range around the west of England with a gypsy gang of thieves and within a year had become their ringleader, for none was a greater 'Crafts-Mistress in the Art of Deceit than her self'.[6] A year later, so *The London Jilt* continues, Voss had left the gang in the company of a gypsy lover (one of many reputed husbands in her life) to rob on her own; when one such attempt went wrong she escaped in male disguise. Maintaining this disguise, Voss took to a life of highway robbery before being caught near Wiltshire and jailed. *The London Jilt* claims that she escaped from prison by seducing the jailer's wife, and made her way to London disguised as a maid. In London, Voss became an 'applauded artisan' in the arts of stealing, cheating and pickpocketing, most notably being involved in the theft of the Lord Chancellor's Mace for which she was transported. The close similarities between the lives of Carleton and Voss as seen in their biographies extends beyond their notoriety as masqueraders, daring tricksters and bigamists. Both had travelled to and tricked their ways around Holland, both had been transported, and both were hanged at Tyburn for the theft of a silver tankard, Carleton in 1672 and Voss in 1684.

The second Voss biography is taken from the *Account* of her confession and last dying words, recorded by Ordinary Samuel Smith, prison chaplain of Newgate jail.[7] The Ordinary of Newgate's ministry was to prepare felons for death by bringing them to a full confession of and repentance for their crimes, with their confessions and details of their lives forming the centre-piece of the *Accounts*. The Ordinaries advertised the purpose of the *Accounts*, which by the beginning of the eighteenth century were a semi-official periodical being published five or six times year, as serving the public good and warning others of the dangers of sinfulness. However, these publications also provided Ordinaries, and certainly the more enterprising ones, with a substantial and regular income.

Although Voss's biography in the *Account* is much less detailed, it is an important counter-balance to the exuberant fantasies of freedom and irresponsibility portrayed as the life of Voss in *The London Jilt*. The *Accounts* served a crucial function within the genre of rogue literature by providing an overarching moral framework which ensured that criminals paid the penalty at Tyburn, where they were left 'in the Armes of Death to pass into a vast

Eternity' for a life lived beyond the boundaries of conventional society.[8] At Tyburn, the society which they had so long subverted and eschewed was seen to exact its dues.

The *Accounts* are also significant because they reached such a large readership. 'Usually sold for 3d. or 6d. and run off in printings of thousands, they enjoyed one of the widest markets that printed prose narratives could obtain in the eighteenth century.'[9] This readership is important. By understanding 'how that fraction of the population with access to the popular press wrote and read about [crime]', we will also understand the assumptions which the eighteenth-century reading public found attractive in such fictions, and why biographers found it necessary 'to move toward the fantastic' and away from factual accounts in their portrayal of criminals.[10]

In general terms, this readership has been regarded as naive and lower-class. Spufford, in her seminal work on popular fiction and the seventeenth-century readership, argues that 'in the popular mind, there were really likely to be giants in the fens, and dragons in Northumberland' and that chapbooks merely reflected the fantasy world in which most people must have lived.[11] Voss, the Carleton biographers, and certainly the author[s] of the Carleton autobiographies appealed to a wide cross-section of the reading public by constructing a range of larger-than-life personae appropriate to their targeted readership derived from the bare bones of their mundane criminal lives. Both Carleton and Voss were variously reinvented as virtuous romance heroines, as stereotypical rogues carrying out audacious thefts, and, particularly in Voss's case, as cross-dressing highway-robbing sexual predators. The repeated reinvention of these women found resonance in the imaginations of their readers. Criminal biography enabled readers to live vicariously beyond social regulation. The freedoms that these felons were portrayed as enjoying were, by extension, offered to their readers, who could also escape momentarily their responsibilities to conventional society and their allotted place within it. Readers could ally themselves with those who had triumphed over society and against those who were their victims. The biographies also created for the reader a potent fantasy image of subversion and sexual power. For the male reader, the subversion of sexual roles derived from the portrayal of women as dominant and predatory provided safe sexual fantasies, whilst for the woman reader,

the portrayal of self-determined independent women who chose
their own destinies created 'a favourite fantasy for many an
adventurous young woman who understood that as a female she
could expect little latitude or freedom in her life'.[12] John Richetti
believes that popular literature 'must have appeared to the educated literate elite of the eighteenth century precisely what comic
book and television seem to the contemporary guardians of cultural standards'.[13] Yet we know that the biographies of Voss and
Carleton attracted the attention of this very elite, although in the
case of the *Accounts* they were not necessarily the targeted audience. Fielding, Gay, Goldsmith, Pope, Swift, and especially Defoe
read the *Accounts* in order to satirize them. The Carleton narratives attracted a wider interest. We would expect Carleton's
biographer Kirkman to have been 'supplyed by Books, which
have bin formerly written of her', but Pepys's argument with
Lady Batten while visiting her and her husband after church on
7 June 1663 suggests that they too were conversant with the
details of Carleton's life:

> my Lady Batten inveighed mightily against the German Princesse
> and I as high in the defence of her wit and spirit, and glad that she
> is cleared at the Sessions.

Pepys's interest in Carleton had still not abated almost a year later
when, on 15 April 1664, he went to see '*The German Princesse*
acted by the woman [Carleton] herself; but never was anything so
well done in earnest, worse performed in jest upon the stage'.[14]
Aphra Behn knew of Carleton, referring to her in the Epilogue to
her play *The Dutch Lover* (1673), and Defoe also made reference
to her in *Roxana* (1724).[15]

Disguise was the hallmark of the lives of both Carleton and
Voss.[16] The main set-piece in *The London Jilt*, the seduction of the
jailer's wife, depended upon the wife being duped by Voss's disguise, and Carleton 'had such an art in disguising her self, that it
was very difficult to know her, she could upon occasion alter, not
only the aire of her Countenance, but also some of her Features
would seem to be different'.[17] Thus in order to rob tailors, mercers
and weavers of their cloth, landladies of their valuables, and lovers
of their money, Carleton would transform herself into a variety
of personas. Her favourite disguise was 'a splendid gallant Garb'
reflecting her obsession with escaping 'the grim social fate defined

as [her] portion'.[18] At her 1663 trial she portrayed herself as a distressed and educated woman of quality who was wrongly accused, but she was 'ready to represent any quality she pleased' and was thus equally at home in widow's weeds, in the dress of a demure young virgin or a country gentlewoman.[19] Weber has argued that 'continual dissimulation' gave the rogue

> the perfect freedom of being 'everyday what he pleased himself'. In the literature of roguery this perpetual disguise leads to a fantastic world dominated by mobility and randomness.[20]

For Weber, this fantastic world is defined as freedom from a set identity, permitting the rogue individuality. Yet rogue literature demands a moral balance whereby the rules of society are reaffirmed by the downfall of the rogue, who repents for his or her life beyond the boundaries of the socially acceptable and acknowledges that the penalty is death. For a while Voss's disguise gave her the freedom of the road, normally the preserve of highwayman, as well as sexual freedom, economic independence, and 'release from the rigorous demands of social identity'.[21] Similarly, Carleton's impersonation of rank while enabling her to dupe willing victims also created for herself, and the women to whom her *Case* was addressed, 'romance fantasies of female grandeur', complete with aristocratic friends, expensive jewels, servants and coaches drawn by fine horses from Flanders.[22] In this, Carleton shared much with her own biographer Francis Kirkman, who also 'tried to rectify the accident of [his] birth by writing fantastic accounts of [himself]'.[23]

Rogue literature, in its creation of a fantastic world of sexual freedom and independence, is concerned with the violation of rules of social conduct and the traditional values of everyday life.[24] For women of good reputation these values confined them to the home and to male supervision. In a sermon preached at the funeral of Anne, Lady-Dowager Brooke in 1691, the Right Reverend Gilbert, Bishop of Sarum, gave the orthodox view of virtuous womanhood:

> The Affections of that Sex are more tender, they are less hardy and bold; they are under a greater Regularity of Form; *Decency* and *Modesty* are great Defences: They are not so much exposed to the Temptations that are in the World; they live at home, and do not range abroad ... so that they are out of that loose Ramble, which is the great Corruption of Mankind.[25]

It is not surprising that the *Accounts* of the Ordinaries, whose ministry was with felons held in the condemned cells of Newgate jail, confirmed implicitly that any breakdown in filial, paternal and marital control led women into crime, and inevitably to the dark reality of Tyburn and execution. Most of the women whom the Ordinary comforted were without families to guide and protect them. For example, the confession of Lorina Cary, who was executed for felony on 25 May 1687, reads thus:

> Aged eighteen Years, Born in *Hereford-shire*. Parents are Dead ... Afterwards she lived with a Gentlewoman in this City. She hath not been three Years in *London*: she acknowledged that she had not spent her time so well as she ought to have done; but that a Covetous mind prevailed upon her, to supply her Excess in unlawful ways.[26]

A focal point of the *Accounts* was therefore the Ordinary's description of his painstaking efforts to bring the criminals in his charge into repentance for filial disobedience and into a recognition that a lack of early moral guidance had been the first step toward their untimely deaths. Jane Langworth, executed for infanticide on 21 December 1684, acknowledged that 'she had been well Educated by honest Parents, and might have continued happy had she not associated her self with Leude Persons'.[27]

By contrast rogue literature regarded a lack of parental or marital governance, and alienation from defined social roles, as a first step toward freedom, self-determination and independence, although the gallows were still the final destination. We have seen that *The London Jilt* established Voss as unruly from childhood, unfettered by notions of filial duty or social convention. Thus, Voss was presented from the outset as a self-possessed woman on a 'loose Ramble' and poised to enter a 'golden world many people persist[ed] in imagining [as existing] before the imposition of social forms of behaviour'.[28] By thus permitting controlled flights from the reality of accepted social or sexual behaviour, fantasy extended and tested the boundaries of the norm. As Rosemary Jackson explains, 'presenting that which cannot be, but *is*, fantasy exposes a culture's definitions of that which can be: it traces the limits of its epistemological and ontological frame'.[29] In the case of Carleton the very fact that she 'inscribed herself textually' or at least had a hand in the writing of her autobiography was in itself, as Parker has shown for the following century, 'a revolutionary act'.[30] The autobiographies themselves demonstrate a testing of social boundaries, for, 'in propagating conflicting myths of herself as virtuous romance heroine and fraudulent rogue', Chalmers argues that Carleton amplified 'divisions inherent in the attempt to speak as a female subject in her culture'.[31] However, it is in the treatment of female sexuality in rogue literature that the testing of cultural boundaries finds particular expression.

Both women were portrayed in the biographies as sexually voracious and as contemptuous of marriage.[32] We know that Carleton was at least bigamous, and Voss purportedly had anywhere between seven and eighteen husbands, some concurrently. Yet Kirkman claims that John Carleton told him that his wife was not

> a Common Prostitute; not to be enjoyed by every one that Courted her, that she had not great Inclination that way, and if she did, it was not with any that brought their half Crown, Crown, or half a Piece; it must be greater Kindnesses then these, and some considerable acquaintance, and knowledge of the Party.[33]

As portrayed in the biographies, sexual freedom meant economic independence if only because it gave access to the bedrooms and treasure chests of their lovers. More than in contempt for marriage, however, alienation from social convention was most strongly encoded in the image of transvestism in *The London Jilt*, and to a lesser extent in the Carleton literatures. Only one publication foregrounds Carleton's enjoyment of a male identity. It describes her entrance into the White Hart Tavern in Smithfield where she passed undetected until she chose to reveal herself to her obvious satisfaction,

> she so compleatly behaveing her self, and with such a gallant deportment in that habit as though she had been some Mounsier of great rank and quality; her habit was rich, with a half shirt, a Perewig, down to her shoulders, and a Rapier by her side.[34]

As we have seen, according to *The London Jilt*, Voss first took on manly appearance when she and her gypsy lover had held up two travellers on the highway and forced them, at pistol point, to exchange clothes in an attempt to avoid discovery after committing an armed robbery at their lodgings. Voss committed many more robberies in the male disguise which her first adventure as a foot-pad had given her, before being apprehended and imprisoned. We may bridle at Reginald Hargreaves's suggestion that 'women do not, apparently, possess that resourcefulness – or is it self-sufficiency? – which would enable them to dispense with the company of others' and endure 'the isolation, the loneliness, to which the Knight of the Road was condemned'.[35] However, it is true that whilst women in breeches were commonplace in rogue literature, highwaywomen (apart from a few well-known women like Mary Frith, and Joan Bracey, who appeared in Captain Smith's *A History of the Lives and Robberies of the Most Notorious Highwaymen*) were rare. Thus, by doubly contravening the law of sexual differentiation in marrying male disguise with highway robbery, the biographer of *The London Jilt* ensured that the adventures he created for Voss would be fantasies of the highest quality. The fantasies were safe, however, for rather than being disturbing symbols of the female usurpation of male roles, Voss's potential for armed aggression is diluted in *The London Jilt* into comic entertainment. This dilution and makeover from petty crook to 'favourite fantasy' was achieved by means of a climactic comic set-piece with complicated lesbian undertones concerning the seduction of the jailor's wife (this is reproduced in the documents section below, pp. 273–4). When the jailer's wife lusts after Voss, the readers, in company with Voss and her lover, know she is lusting after a woman. Intercourse does takes place but it is in the dark and with Voss's lover; nonetheless it is Voss's face that the jailer's wife imagines and thus by transference it is Voss that we see having intercourse with the jailer's wife.

Voss's final days are most fully recounted in the Ordinary of Newgate's *Account*. Concerned that 'since the last Sessions there have been Published divers false accounts of the Execution of the Prisoners, pretended to be their last Confessions when indeed Printed before they went to be Executed', the *Account* which included Voss's confession was published on 20 December, 'the Morning after the said Executions, which is as soon as any true account can be Printed'.[36] *The London Jilt* was clearly one such 'false account', although it insisted on being a 'true account' and 'taken from her own confession'. As *The London Jilt* does not include her farewell speech, so amply recorded in the *Account*, it suggests that the biographer never actually interviewed Voss while she was under condemnation, and that the biography was rushed off the presses before her death, in order to beat the official publication. It must have been particularly irritating to Voss's Ordinary Samuel Smith, with his reputation for greed and for '[getting] out of the Criminals what you can', to discover himself in competition with the racy and sensationalist *London Jilt*.[37]

As recounted by Smith, Voss the individual was shaped, and her death manipulated, to answer the stereotypical religious purpose of the *Accounts* and to endorse 'the legitimacy of the power which had brought [the condemned] to their sad end'.[38] Thus, Voss's biography in the *Account* was used to warn against the inevitable consequences of an ill-spent life and her final journey to execution at Tyburn was recounted in such a way as to recast her in the image of a redeemed religious penitent. As a result, descriptions of Voss's wicked career and final condemnation were overlaid with conventional religious expressions of the justice of her sentence and of her repentance. References to her life on the road, and to her adventures as a transvestite including the scene with the jailor's wife, disappear completely, to be replaced by details of her career as a London thief. Unusually, Smith's *Account* does once lapse into prurience more suited to sensationalist rogue literature when it reports that she had been common-law wife to at least seven men, some of whom had also been 'turned off' at Tyburn. This claim has some basis in fact, for although the Ordinary did not make the connection himself, he had attended Francis Robinson, named in *The London Jilt* and executed on 23 May 1684 for robbery and burglary. In that *Account*, with heavy-handed piety, Smith recorded that Robinson had told him that Voss,

(now in *Newgate* under Sentence of Death, but Reprieved upon pleading to be with Child, etc.) was his Wife, desired him to remember him to her, and to desire of her she would Reform her Life; and begged that he would give her good Council, and endeavour what lay in him, to reclaim her.[39]

The *Account* for 19 December 1684 confirmed that Voss had been in and out of Newgate jail at least a dozen times, sometimes under sentence of death, but that she had always managed to escape the noose. We glean that the intervening months, between being apprehended in April 1684 and hanged on 19 December, had seen frantic efforts by Voss to procure a pardon or a reprieve.

She had immediately pleaded her belly,[40] and when that failed she applied herself to friends and persons of quality,

> but her Offences being so many and former Grace and Mercy, not being of force to Reclaim her, no place was found for such a favour, which she perceiving, greatly lamented her unhappy state.

Amongst the cold detail of the Ordinary's *Account* is some sense of what Voss might have been like, stripped of the roguish stereotypes created about her by the author of *The London Jilt*. An echo of her own voice rather than the Ordinary's formulaic overtones can be heard in his reported conversations with her. For example, her repentance under condemnation sounds shallow and, as she promised 'amendment if her days might be prolonged', her desire for life at any cost makes her both very human and pathetic, not at all the devil-may-care rogue heroine of *The London Jilt*.

In an unusual incident on the scaffold, the *Account* claims that Voss joined Samuel Smith and the father-in-law of Richard Jones, a fellow sufferer who had refused to confess to his crime of murder, in begging Jones to make a gallows confession. 'Laying before him the danger of Concealing a known Crime, and minding him he shortly must appear before his Maker', their entreaties were to no avail. Smith had been accused elsewhere of fabricating stories to increase sales of his *Accounts*, and with such a high-profile criminal in his charge this may well have been an attempt to turn Voss into a best-seller by upgrading and sensationalizing her death. Again, perhaps in deference to her 'celebrity status', Voss's farewell speech was the only one published in the *Account*. It was stereotypical in its repentance for an ill-spent life and its belief that 'it was a Mercy she had so much time to repent'. In this account of Voss's final journey to Tyburn, and in her solicitious concern for the spiritual welfare of others, we have a woman who is a far cry from the 'German Princess Revived'.

No *Account* exists for Carleton. However, a description of her scaffold behaviour shows that she too was presented as conforming to what was expected of her in the last stages of her fantastic journey.[41] Although she did not give her farewell speech herself (her voice, we are told, being too low to be heard), it conformed to the form of a good address in that she also repented of an ill-spent life, warned the crowd to beware of ill company and begged God's forgiveness. There are, however, clues to suggest that even in death, Carleton was not completely vanquished by the conventions of society. 'This Vitious Woman, guilty of such gross Immoralities, did dye well satisfied and unconcern'd, with a Resolution and Courage beyond the weakness of her frail Sex.' Moreover, she rejected the ministrations of the Ordinary of Newgate and died a Roman Catholic. In so doing she, in company with all Catholics, undermined the role of the Ordinary and the Church of England as the legitimizing authority at Tyburn.[42]

Carleton, rather than being a German princess, was, in fact, a fiddle-player's daughter from Canterbury. This does not, however, help to separate the real-life Carleton from the fantasies created around her. As with Voss, the self was subsumed under a need to reinvent her as a stereotypical rogue inhabiting a world that existed outside the experience of ordinary people. The two worlds only collided at Tyburn, where spectators could watch a society exact its penalty for the rogues' subversion of societal values. At Tyburn, the wheel turned full circle as fantasies of rogue freedom from societal conventions were replaced by fantasies of abasement, repentance and retribution. Thus, male readers who had taken pleasure in the adventures of transgressive, sexually powerful women might also enjoy their downfall and the re-establishment of male dominance, while women readers, seduced by the notion of self-determination, could see, in the cold light of morning, its terrible consequences.

We can be a little more successful in separating the real-life Voss from the created fantasy figure for there is an unexpected but telling reference to her in a pamphlet by Elizabeth Cellier, midwife to Queen Maria of Modena, wife to James II. 'The Popish midwife' was acquitted of treason in 1680 and in the same year published *Malice Defeated* in which she defended herself against charges of being involved in the Meal-tub plot and conspiring with the Catholic party to introduce a false heir.[43] *Malice Defeated* also described her activities in Newgate jail at the time of the Popish Plot, when she tried

> to bring relief to those Catholics suffering in prison because of the machinations of Titus Oates and other Whigs, such as Shaftesbury and Waller. At a hazard to her safety and reputation, she went

daily to Newgate to document the torturing of prisoners, which she witnessed.[44]

Contained within *Malice Defeated* is 'A Brief Account of the Tyrannical Barbirism inflicted on the Kings Prisoners in his Majesties Goal of Newgate'. It appears that Voss was one of many who suffered abuse at the hands of her jailers. The marginalia describes 'Jane Voss. The Jaylors Own Entries in his Book of Commitments for the 7th month in the year 1667' and the text of complaint reads:

> the Jaylor has suffer'd persons after a commitment, to go forth with a Keeper and Steal, to the intent of satisfying his Avarice incest; of which the said Prisoner [Voss] was taken, and the second time committed without any discharge from the first commitment.[45]

Thus, Cellier's 'Brief Account', in order to highlight the abuses of Newgate prison, portrays Voss as a pathetic victim of corruption and intimidation who was forced to risk commital by stealing to order for her jailers. What this singular example demonstrates is that criminals were manipulated to become whatever their authors intended for them. In the major categories of biography, criminals represented either fantasies of triumphant freedom or fantasies of redemption and penitence. The sensationalist *London Jilt* stereotyped Voss as a wild and reckless highwaywoman in order *to* create a bestseller to rival the Carleton narratives by engineering a harmless inversion of the status quo, enabling women momentarily to escape their defined roles and men to enjoy safely their own armchair fantasies. It is only in the Ordinary of Newgate's *Account* that Voss had any input into how she was presented. She did not refuse to be interviewed by the Ordinary as a small number of other criminals did, so she would have supplied him with most of the details of her life. Yet she had no control over the way this was used to transform her into the stereotypical rogue of the *Accounts*, a figure of penitent redemption.

Notes

1. Lincoln B. Faller, *Turned to Account: The Forms and Functions of Criminal Biography in Late Seventeenth- and Early Eighteenth-Century*

England (Cambridge, 1987), pp. 3–4. My findings on the escapist elements of criminal biography differ from those of Julie Sanders and Lesley Mickel in this volume, whose examinations of Jonson and Brome reveal a resistance to the notion of escapism.

2. *The German Princess Revived: or the London Jilt: Being a True Account of the Life and Death of Jenney Voss, who After she had been Transported for being concerned with Sadler about Eight Years past in Stealing my Lord Chancellors Mace, and several times since Convicted of repeated Fellonies was Executed on Friday the 19th of December, 1684. at Tyburn. Published from her own Confession* (London, 1684).

3. The purported autobiographies were Mary Carleton, *An Historical Narrative of the German Princess, Containing all Material Passages ... Written By Her Self* (London, 1663) and *The Case of Madam Mary Carleton, Lately Stiled The German Princess ...* (London, 1663). For a discussion of Mary Carleton and a full list of the Carleton pamphlets see Janet Todd and Elizabeth Spearing, eds, *Counterfeit Ladies: The Life and Death of Mary Frith, The Case of Mary Carleton* (London, 1994) pp. xxvi–liii. See also Hero Chalmers, ' "The person I am, or what they made me to be": the construction of the feminine subject in the autobiographies of Mary Carleton', in Clare Brant and Diane Purkiss, eds, *Women, Texts and Histories 1575–1760* (London, 1992), pp. 164–94.

4. John Carleton, *The Replication, Or Certain Vindicatory Depositions ...* (London, 1663), p. 1.

5. Francis Kirkman, *The Counterfeit Lady Unveiled. Being a Full Account of the Birth, Life, Most Remarkable Actions, and Untimely Death of Mary Carleton, Known by the Name of The German Princess* (London, 1673), p. 92.

6. *The London Jilt*, p. 3.

7. *A True Account of the Behaviour, Confessions, and Last Dying Words, of Capt. James Watts, Capt. Peter Barnwell, Daniel D'Coiner alias Walker, Richard Jones, and Jane Voss alias Roberts, who were Executed at Tyburn, on the 19th of December 1684. for Robbing on the High way, High Treason, Murther, and Fellony, etc.* Printed by Order (London, 1684).

8. Ordinary of Newgate *Account* (19 December 1684), p. 4.

9. Peter Linebaugh, 'The Ordinary of Newgate and his Account', in J.S. Cockburn, ed., *Crime in England 1550–1800* (Princeton, 1977), p. 250.

10. Faller, *Turned to Account*, p. 3. See also John J. Richetti, *Popular Fiction Before Richardson: Narrative Patterns, 1700–1739* (Oxford, 1969), pp. 1–13.

11. Margaret Spufford, *Small Books and Pleasant Histories: Popular Fiction and its Readership in Seventeenth-Century England* (Athens, Ga., 1982), pp. 249–50, 258.

12. Lillian Faderman, *Surpassing the Love of Men: Romantic Friendship and Love between Women from the Renaissance to the Present* (London, 1981), p. 61.

13. Richetti, *Popular Fiction*, p. 9.

14. Kirkman, *Counterfeit*, p. 3. J. Smith, ed., *Diary and Correspondence of Samuel Pepys, F.R.S., Secretary to the Admiralty in the Reigns of Charles II and James II*, 3rd edn, 5 vols (London, 1851), vol. 2, pp. 170, 315.

15. Daniel Defoe, *Roxana* (Harmondsworth, 1982), p. 317.

16. Todd and Spearing, *Counterfeit Ladies*, pp. xxxvi–xxxviii.

17. Kirkman, *Counterfeit*, pp. 156–7.

18. Harold Weber, 'Rakes, rogues, and the empire of misrule', *Huntington Library Quarterly* 47:1 (Winter 1984), pp. 18–9.

19. Kirkman, *Counterfeit*, p. 160.

20. Weber, 'Rakes', p. 26.

21. Ibid., p. 28.

22. Elspeth Graham *et al.*, eds, *Her Own Life: Autobiographical Writings by Seventeenth-Century English Women* (London, 1989), p. 133.

23. Todd and Spearing, *Counterfeit Ladies*, p. xliv.

24. See, for example, H. Cox, *The Feast of Fools: A Theological Essay on Festivity and Fantasy* (New York, 1969), p. 59.

25. Gilbert, Lord Bishop of Sarum, *A Sermon Preached at the Funeral of the Right Honourable Anne Lady-Dowager Brook, Who was Buried at Breamor, the 19th day of February, 1691* (London, 1691), p. 11.

26. *The True Account of the Behaviour and Confession, Of the Condemned Criminals, at Justice-Hall in the Old-Bayly; on the 12th and 13th of May, 1687* (London, 1687), p. 3.

27. *A True Account of the Behaviour, Confessions, and Last Dying Words, of Abraham Bigs, Richard Cabourn, Jane Langworth and Elizabet Stoaks. At Tyburn, on Wednesday 21th December, 1684 for High-Treason Murther, Felony and Burglary* (London, 1685), p. 3.

28. Weber, 'Rakes', p. 28.

29. Rosemary Jackson, *Fantasy: The Literature of Subversion*, (1981; London, 1988), p. 23.

30. Alice Parker, 'Madame de Tencin and the "mascarade" of female im/personation', *Eighteenth Century Life*, n.s. 9:2 (1985), p. 69.

31. Chalmers, 'Autobiographies', p. 174.

32. This is not true of the Carleton autiobiographies where Carleton was keen to present herself as a fine lady of noble birth wrongly accused of bigamy.

33. Kirkman, *Counterfeit*, p. 107.
34. *The female-Hector, or, The Germane lady turn'd mounsieur. With the manner of her coming to the White-Hart tavern in Smithfield like a young lord in a mans apparel . . . How she deceiv'd an inn-keeper at Sandwitch in Kent . . . How she made her escape from the Kingsbench* (London, 1663), p. 8. I am grateful to Jeff and Irene Burds for their help in obtaining a copy of this pamphlet.
35. R. Hargreaves, *Women at Arms: Their Exploits throughout the Ages* (London, 1930), p. xxiv.
36. Ordinary of Newgate *Account* (19 December 1684), p. 4.
37. Robert R. Singleton, 'Defoe, Moll Flanders and the Ordinary of Newgate', *Harvard Library Bulletin* 24 (1976), pp. 407–13. Singleton argues that Smith was the model for the corrupt and drunken Ordinary in Defoe's *Moll Flanders*.
38. James A. Sharpe ' "Last dying speeches": religion, ideology and public execution in seventeenth-century England', *Past and Present* 107 (1985), p. 156.
39. *A True Account of the Prisoners Executed at Tyburn on Friday the 23d of May 1684. With their Behaviour in Newgate, since their receiving Sentence at the Old-Bayly and Dying Confessions at the place of Execution* (London, 1684), p. 4.
40. Pregnant women could not be executed.
41. *The Deportment and Carriage of the German Princess, Immediately before her Execution* (London, 1672).
42. For a discussion of this argument see my article, ' "The Inferior Sort of the Kingdom of Ireland": Irishmen and Tyburn Tree', *Irish Studies Review* 6:1 (April 1998), pp. 17–26.
43. 'A Brief Account of the Tyrannical Barbarism inflicted on the Kings Prisoners in his Majesties Goal of Newgate' in *Malice Defeated Or, a Brief Relation of the Accusation and Deliverance of Elizabeth Cellier, Wherein her Proceedings both before and during her Confinement, are particularly Related, and the Mystery of the Meal-Tub fully discovered. Together with an Abstract of her Arraignment and Tryal, written by her self, for the Satisfaction of all Lovers of Undisguized Truth* (London, 1680).
44. Janet Todd, ed., *A Dictionary of British and American Writers 1660–1800* (London, 1987), p. 76.
45. Cellier, *Malice Defeated*, p. 7.

Part Three
Twentieth Century

12 *The grotesque utopias of Jeanette Winterson and Monique Wittig*

Lucie Armitt

Fictional utopias can be deceptively unsatisfactory. Elsewhere I have even claimed they may be threatened by redundancy, being 'among the most rigid (and rigidly reductive) of generically bound forms'.[1] Literary fantasy in general has always had to negotiate the establishment's determination to trivialize it as mere narrative formula. While increasingly successful challenges to these attitudes are mounted by such magic realist writers as Allende, Carter, Márquez and Rushdie, utopia still tends to carry a reductive stigma. This is largely, if ironically, due to what is also its greatest strength: utopia's natural aptitude for the depiction of alternative ideologies.

During the 1970s and 1980s, a noticeable increase in the number of feminist utopias published accompanied the more general expansion in the availability of women's writing. The reason for this disproportionate interest in the utopic seems predominantly political rather than literary, as feminism's strength has always relied on a sustained belief that the 'not-yet' can and must become the here and now. Angelika Bammer's in-depth study of 1970s feminism sets utopianism at its core: 'to the extent that feminism was – and is – based on the principle of women's liberation ... it was – and is – not only revolutionary but radically utopian' ...[2] But the strength of Bammer's work is that she refuses to restrict this utopian impulse to that set of texts which satisfy themselves with closed narrative visions. Instead she defines utopia as 'partial vision', a concept in process. This is an important shift in understanding, for however radical the political vision of the 'closed' feminist utopia, women's writing is often at its most transformative (read influential) when looking to transform its own narrative structures similarly. In the process such texts take on a 'riskier' dynamic, in that they positively invite disruption rather than closing off dissenting voices. In refusing to shut up, they invite readers in, desiring us to enter into the discursive spaces they leave. Such texts will never be guilty of putting words in our mouths; on the contrary, they leave us to do that to them.

Such lacunae embody the crux of my title: the oxymoron which couples utopianism with the grotesque. Like the gaping mouth defined as one of its central images, the grotesque body has collective as much as individual significance, being an anti-establishment carnival force which, in its excesses, forms the epitome of all that most threatens order. According to Mary Russo, the grotesque is therefore a crucial asset to contemporary feminism. As 'nice' women, she warns, we have no voice at all; instead we must look to construct a female body politic which is 'heterogeneous, strange, polychromatic, ragged, conflictual, incomplete, in motion and at risk'.[3] The same might be said for the structures and preoccupations of a new, more radical, literary utopia which likewise eschews squeaky-clean lines and accommodates more thoroughly that which 'revolts'. Few writers achieve this more effectively than Jeanette Winterson and Monique Wittig, both of whom, in their joint commitment to feminism and the fantastic, situate open-ended narrative structures at the core of their work.[4]

To date, the attention paid by critics to Winterson's key role as a contemporary writer of fantastic fiction has been to some extent over-shadowed by her perceived importance as a writer on alternative representations of sexuality. Rebecca O'Rourke's reading of *Oranges Are Not The Only Fruit* (1985) is characteristic in this regard, in that although she pays close and detailed attention to how and why differing groups of readers experience the novel differently, her own focus for these responses rests almost exclusively upon the realist aspects of the text, its non-mimetic elements being relegated almost to the level of a single after-thought: 'As well as telling this story, the novel has fairy tales interspersed throughout and some chapters are just [why "just"?] short reflections on topics such as history'.[5] Of course the realist elements of the novel are important, but they are absolutely not the full story. In fact, the text's anti-conventional narrative structure reminds us continually that *Oranges* is, above all, a novel which actively celebrates the fantastic potential of story-telling. As the central protagonist Jeanette well knows it is in the realm of fabulation that the most transformative possibilities reside:

> One day I learned that Tetrahedron is a mathematical shape that can be formed by stretching an elastic band over a series of nails.
> But Tetrahedron is an emperor ... The emperor Tetrahedron lived in a palace made absolutely from elastic bands. To the right, cunning fountains shot elastic jets, subtle as silk; to the left, ten minstrels played day and night on elastic lutes. (p. 49)

Winterson is certainly not a writer of utopias in their static, *perfect*ed sense. In intermingling the convincingly realist and the manifestly unreal, Winterson develops a new and renewing version of the utopia as an enticing but endlessly receding horizon. Such horizons need not always project us into the future. Amalgamating the loss of the melancholy with the fascination of ongoing yet insatiable desire, in one of the most important scenes of the novel, Winterson takes us back beyond time and space to a place where utopia and loss are inseparable:

> On the banks of the Euphrates find a secret garden cunningly walled. There is an entrance, but the entrance is guarded. There is no way in for you. Inside you will find every plant that grows growing circular-wise like a target. Close to the heart is a sundial and at the heart an orange tree ... All true quests end in this garden, where the split fruit pours forth blood and the halved fruit is a full bowl for travellers and pilgrims. To eat of the fruit means to leave the garden because the fruit speaks of other things, other longings ... It may be, some other day, that you will open a gate by chance, and find yourself again on the other side of the wall. (p. 123)

This deceptively important passage is rooted right at the heart of *Oranges*, just as an orange is rooted, in turn, at its heart. The recurring tension set up between enclosures and openings (an inviting secret garden but one which is walled, a beckoning entrance which is guarded, an enticing quest that must end here, delicious fruit split open, but only in order to lead to expulsion) affirms the type of disruptive impulse that redefines the utopic in more interrogative terms. Also deeply embedded within this fantasy image are two of the realist preoccupations of the narrative; and it is crucial for our purposes that we recognize they *do* erupt from beneath and within the realm of fantasy, rather than taking precedence over it. The first manifests itself as the realization that Jeanette's developing lesbian sexuality also follows this same dynamic of enticements and denials. The second parallels the image of the labyrinth, set up here to prevent Jeanette from ever clearly plotting a route back to the space and place of her own origins, being the daughter of not one but two mothers: a fallen but present adoptive mother, and the lost (hence utopian) biological mother – that site of the 'split fruit' which 'pours forth blood'.

This fruit motif and its association with maternal loss and desire is further developed in Winterson's more complex fourth novel, *Sexing The Cherry* (1989).[6] Set primarily during the seventeenth century, the linear aspects of the novel concern themselves with a perceived loss of innocence caused by civil unrest at home and an attendant fascination with the exploration of the unknown in the form of sea-voyages to newly discovered lands. Although pineapples, peaches, oranges and bananas are all included in the resulting exotic plunder, in the context of the postlapsarian domestic situation of England, such travails prove fruitless in their attempt to recapture Eden. Again, utopia is not offered to us on a plate and nor is the structure of the text closed off to dissenting voices. Although journey narratives are often presumed to be linear, *Sexing The Cherry* is, despite its seventeenth-century thematic concerns, an exemplary late-twentieth-century postmodern narrative comprising clashing spatio-temporal planes, multiple narrative perspectives and competing, even contradictory, versions of history.[7] Jordan the male protagonist is, like Jeanette, an adoptive foundling and hence cannot ever fully 'come home'. Instead he is driven endlessly onwards by a compulsive desire to search out glimpses of utopia that will always evade him:

> Curiously, the further I have pursued my voyages the more distant they have become . . . I begin, and straight away a hundred alternative routes present themselves . . . Every time I try to narrow down my intent I expand it . . . The Buddhists say there are 149 ways to God. I'm not looking for God, only for myself . . . Perhaps I'm missing the point – perhaps whilst looking for someone else you might come across yourself unexpectedly, in a garden somewhere . . . (pp. 115–16)

In the context of *Oranges* we have already encountered such a search for this elusive/utopian other who turns out to be the self's other half. But whereas, in that case, the alter-ego takes on shape in the form of the desired other/self of same sex eroticism, in *Sexing the Cherry* it takes on a heterosexual orientation, but emerges less as physicality than as narrative echo. The novel opens: 'My name is Jordan. This is the first thing I saw', before opening out onto an apparition of the self as a ghosted double image: 'I began to walk with my hands stretched out in front of me, as do those troubled in sleep, and in this way, for the first time, I traced the lineaments of my own face opposite me' (pp. 1–2). Only much later on does Fortunata, the other in question, suddenly reveal herself in the guise of Jordan's echo: 'My name is Fortunata . . . This is the first thing I saw' (p. 104).

In the work of Monique Wittig, we find a similar preoccupation with the nature of origins and their relationship to self-definition. Here, though, as the title of her second novel *Les Guérillères* (1969) makes clear, such originary identities are always seen as collective in nature and can be specifically related to Russo's grotesque female body-politic. The journeys undertaken in this text function as metaphors for the development of the women's movement, in the literal, mobile sense of the term. In a passage describing a sustained insight into collective self-realization, the body politic starts to reflect upon itself:

> What was the beginning? they say. They say that in the beginning . . . [t]hey open their mouths to bleat or to say something but no sound emerges . . . They move over the smooth shining surface. Their movements are translation, gliding. They are dazed by the reflections over which they pass . . . Vertically and horizontally, it is the same mirror . . . the same brilliance that nowhere holds them fast. They advance, there is no front, there is no rear. They move on, there is no future, there is no past . . . They are prisoners of the mirror.[8]

As with Winterson's work, *Les Guérillères* does not fall into the trap of an unproblematic progression into a limited utopic horizon. Its structure is deeply complex, prophetically delineating the ongoing but determined struggle in which feminism will remain engaged during the ensuing decades. Later in the text the women, standing in huge numbers alongside the lake shores, peer into watery depths which are rippled, rather than smooth, finding their multiple reproductions 'all identical, [but] all distorted' (p. 69). What is anticipated here is Russo's metaphor of 'fun-house mirrors' which, in challenging the clean lines of passive female beauty, offers up a fantastic and destabilized vision of positive resistance to patriarchy's neutralizing and normalizing codes. The result for Russo is access to a series of unfixed subject positions which, as a collective 'mutant anatomy', offers 'an extra exit, a different way out', potentially enabling women to break free from the shackles inherent in Wittig's term 'prisoners of the mirror'.[9]

Throughout Wittig's work, both fictional and non-fictional, the greatest concern is with how to employ utopia as a means of freeing women from the biological shackles of maternity.[10] To that extent her use of narrative journeys often forces women to cross and re-cross a variety of waters, confronting them with the abject excesses of birthing, but only so that they might be empowered to move on beyond them. Hence, in her fourth novel *Across the Acheron* (1987), her protagonist, also called Wittig, underlines her horror for 'anything to do with grottoes, cellars, subterranean passages, trenches'.[11] Wittig's sustained exploration of how to re-conceive the female genitalia in ways that disconnect them from their status as reproductive apparatus, anticipates the work of another feminist thinker, Luce Irigaray, whose work we will see to have much in common with Wittig's, not least in her superimposition of a 'crosscurrents' metaphor upon the female anatomy. Its lips, she claims,

> adopt a cross-like shape that is the prototype of the crossroads, thus representing both *inter* and *enter*, for the lips of the mouth and the lips of the female sex do not point in the same direction ... those 'down below' are vertical.[12]

Wittig's situation of feminism upon a number of similar crossing-points is inferred by the title *Across the Acheron*. These crossroads provide positive opportunities for change as much as they do problematic dilemmas, as is made clear from the nature of the character Wittig's quest. Beginning in confusion, 'what crossing? There's no river here. There's no sea' (p. 8), this protagonist has to learn that the crossing in question refers, in utopian terms, to a movement set up between two figurative planes which, like the double-face of a sheet of paper, one side filled, one side blank, reveals a palimpsest of possibility underlying the here and now. As her guide, Manastabal, informs her, 'There's nothing where we are going, Wittig, at least nothing you don't know already . . . I'm taking you to see what can be seen anywhere in broad daylight' (p. 8).

We may be forgiven for dismissing Manastabal's words, for many of the magical creatures Wittig meets on her way are anything but 'what can be seen anywhere' – at least from the blinkered perspective of realism. One such is the gigantic, hence grotesque, warrior butterfly:

> Its suctorial proboscis . . . though rolled up on itself, seems able to transform itself into a redoubtable weapon if needs be. As it unfolds its wings . . . they beat in silken fashion . . . At a given moment it descends . . . Its proboscis is unwound like a lasso and, without pouncing down . . . without arresting its flight, it encircles the waist of a swordswoman and lifts her fully armed into the air. (pp. 60–1)

Such ariel forms also appear in *Les Guérillères*, the labial analogy provided by the silken wings obviously rendering this image appropriate as an analogy for the various crossing-points these writers associate with female identity and its connections with fantastic possibility. In this novel she further develops the auspices of the grotesque, creating a new species of woman who amalgamates aerielism with spinsterhood, as if to show just how threatening anti-conventional feminine forms can be:

> Spinning-glands are at work on each of their limbs. From their many orifices there emerge thick barely visible filaments that meet and fuse together . . . giv[ing] the women a sort of wing on either side of their body. When they resemble giant bats with transparent wings, one of them comes up and, taking a kind of scissors from her belt, hastily divides the two great flaps of silk. (p. 132)

Aerielism, then, proves central to contemporary explorations of women's utopia, centred as they are upon the need to resist being tied down. According to Russo, aerielism can even reverse reductive *put*-downs of women, operating as a fantastic prosthetic application which, if 'put on . . . with a vengeance suggests the power of taking it off' (and presumably, in aeriel terms, of take-off). Challenging the common identification of the grotesque with the 'low', Russo speaks of aerielism introducing a 'principle of turbulence' into the equation, which will not only shake up patriarchy but also continue to stir up the female body politic.[13]

It is at this point that we come to the crucial ariel form in *Across the Acheron*, a reconceived reading of the angel motif. Here Wittig exorcizes the oppressive associations the angel takes on in nineteenth-century literature, whereby the 'angel of the house' – the idealised wife and mother – turns out to be little more than a passive tool of patriarchy.[14] Wittig's use of the angel once again links up with the theories of Irigaray, who steps into the realm of fantasy herself in utilizing the angel as one of the primary signifiers by which we might rethink sexual difference. As an icon whose flight plays fast and loose with a variety of cross-currents ('horizontal and vertical, terrestrial and celestial') and whose form transcends traditional gender identities (angels traditionally being read as androgynous), the angel is a perfect symbol for the construction of a new, utopic reading of woman. Its full potential, she claims, is harnessed by means of an 'envelope' which, in locking away secrets within a series of folds and, more actively, embracing the other from within the boundaries of the self, gives coherence to the feminine on its own terms. Being, for Irigaray, a 'figurative version of a sexual being not yet incarnate', in Wittig's work the angel opens up a space-between, a zone of fantasy perfect for expressing this search for a utopian reconception of fantastic femininity.[15]

Other aeriel forms also have currency within this debate. For Nicola Bown it is not the angel but its secular partner, the fairy, which operates as a fantastic manifestation of feminine possibility. In re-evaluating this creature which again, during the nineteenth century, became an icon of feminine coyness, chastity and what we now term 'kitsch', Bown reveals the potential for subterfuge remaining beneath superficial conventionality. What makes the traditional fairy so appealing, she notes, are its 'diaphonous draperies and butterfly wings'. But as we have seen, these are the very parts Wittig employs as metaphors for labial folds. In the process Wittig manages to reverse what Bown sees as the usual aeriel pattern of 'representing something difficult or unbearable [feminine sexuality] as something small, sweet, and harmless'. Her work also anticipates the cautionary note Russo adopts in her reading of contemporary Anglo-American feminism. Never, Russo asserts, will we overcome the tyrannies of a patriarchy hell-bent on reading us as monstrous simply by appealing to its better nature. She is right;

fairies may appeal and may even be high-flyers, but to patriarchy, as Bown warns, they are 'the lowest rank of a hierarchy of spiritual forms'.[16] Neither Wittig nor Winterson settles for that.

In *Sexing the Cherry* aerielism is largely associated with Jordan's dream lover Fortunata. Looking to escape marriage from the fairy fortunes offered by a prince, Fortunata 'flew from the altar like a bird from a snare and walked a tightrope between the steeple of the church and the mast of a ship weighing anchor in the bay' (p. 61). Refusing to stop here, like Wittig's freedom fighters, she then teaches others to succeed in taking flight, before 'releas[ing] them] like butterflies over a flowering world' (p. 76). In *Oranges* an even more intriguing form emerges, intriguing because it suddenly erupts out of nowhere from within the earthy realms of mimesis. Neither fairy nor angel, in this novel it is the orange demon that initiates Jeanette into the allures of fully fledged sexuality. Musing upon the conflict between her church's reading of lesbian desire and the natural sense she has of her own identity, Jeanette ponders:

> Can love really belong to the demon?
> What sort of demon? The brown demon that rattles the ear? The red demon that dances the hornpipe? The watery demon that causes sickness? The orange demon that beguiles? . . .
> Leaning on the coffee table was the orange demon. 'I've gone mad,' [Jeanette] thought.
> 'That may well be so,' agreed the demon evenly. 'So make the most of it.' (p. 108)

The demon, we might think, is antithetical to angels and fairies, for where the latter take on the clean lines of perfect miniatures the demon is, the Bible tells us, 'Legion', multiple, its proper inhabitation an overrunning herd of pigs.[17] On the other hand, one may equally argue that where common parlance affirms the 'little devil' as mere playful endearment, 'fairy' has a more abusive function as homophobic pejoration. These texts rupture all such stereotypical readings and, in Winterson's orange demon, we have an aerielist who 'beguiles' (p. 108) while appalling the establishment in the manner applauded by Russo. In fact it is the intervention of this figure that helps to give validity to Jeanette's view of the maternal as an anti-normalizing state, rather than validating the mother's reading of her own child as a freak. Russo, referring to twin mothers as 'a reproductive stunt' (and remember Jeanette is the product of two mothers), suggests that this apparent obstacle can, in certain ideological contexts, be transformed into a positive experience of multiple subject-identifications.[18] It is this awareness that enables Jeanette to enquire of the orange demon himself, rather than taking her mother's word for it, 'Demons are evil, aren't they?', and, on obtaining the reassuring response, 'Not quite, they're just different, and difficult' (p. 108), to then decide to follow her own different and difficult path.

The difficult, even at times the unbearable, also confronts the reader of Wittig's *Across the Acheron*, in which, in order to reach a utopian space/place where

> angels pass, carrying baskets and bowls of fruit . . . cherries, straw-berries, raspberries, apricots, peaches, plums, tomatoes, avocados, green melons, cantaloups, water-melons, lemons, pawpaws, pine-apples and coconuts (p. 119)

we have first to digest passage after passage of violence against women ('The women stand without flinching . . . and they are hardly shaken when a bullet, an arrow or a knife perforates their thorax' (p. 77)). Much is made of the fact that *Across the Acheron* adopts a shocking and at times dystopian vision even though it searches out utopia in the end. But, to reiterate, the route to utopia is neither easy nor clear-cut and, like Russo, Wittig recognizes the need to jolt us out of our complacent willingness to accept what some may see as the 'good enough' point that 1980s and 1990s feminism has reached. If our journey is to move forward rather than backwards into the unknown territory of a new millenium, we must not lose sight of the fact that the struggle against patriarchy may sometimes get ugly. Even *Les Guérillères*, published on the brink of the new decade of the 1970s (a period of relative optimism in these terms), is read by Cecile Lindsay as a novel 'contaminated by the rejected past, which it carries along with it into some improbable future'.[19] Returning to the point at which we began, we remember that critics tend not only to diminish the significance of the narrative lacunae in *Oranges*, but also the role played by Winterson's rewritings of history as meta-narrative. In contrast, Bammer reads history as being central to Wittig's larger project which, she claims, 'proposes women's history as a counter-narrative . . . marked to a large extent by that which is not there: the unnoticed, the unrecorded, the forgotten, the lost'.[20] The same is clearly true of her fictive utopias.

In summary, then, all four of these novels take us towards a new understanding of utopia which *envelopes* the grotesque. In the process they collectively carve out a fictive zone which reaches out into the beyond, including the *unknowable* beyond, while engaging with the unsatisfactory here and now of perceived liberation. Using aerielism as a fantastic manoeuvre to overcome spatio-temporal boundaries is very different from the futile escapism of taking flight. As the orange demon reminds us, you cannot have the different without choosing the difficult and Winterson and Wittig both give us hell, but only as a necessary impulse towards offering us utopia.

Notes

1. Lucie Armitt, *Theorising the Fantastic* (London, 1996), p. 183.
2. Angelika Bammer, *Partial Visions: Feminism and Utopianism in the 1970s* (New York, 1991), p. 2.
3. Mary Russo, *The Female Grotesque: Risk, Excess and Modernity* (New York, 1994), p. vii.
4. According to Kathleen L. Komar, Wittig originally planned to leave blank pages in the middle of her novel *Les Guérillères* as an open invitation for readerly introjection. This would be anathema to a conventional utopia, which always shuts off conflicting voices. Apparently it was also anathema to the publisher, who 'could not be persuaded' of the efficacy of this narrative device. See 'The communal self: remembering female identity in the works of Christa Wolf and Monique Wittig', *Comparative Literature* 44 (1992), p. 53.
5. Rebecca O'Rourke, 'Fingers in the fruit basket: a feminist reading of Jeanette Winterson's *Oranges Are Not The Only Fruit*', in Susan Sellers, ed., *Feminist Criticism: Theory and Practice* (Hemel Hempstead, 1991), p. 62.
6. Jeanette Winterson, *Sexing the Cherry* (London, 1989). Page references are included in the main text.
7. See also essays in this volume by Daniel Carey, pp. 151–65, and Julie Sanders, pp. 137–50.
8. Monique Wittig, *Les Guérillères*, trans. David Le Vay (Boston, 1985), pp. 30–1. Further page references are included in the main text.
9. Russo, *Female Grotesque*, pp. 86, 127.
10. See also Peter Stoneley's essay in this volume, pp. 223–35.

11. Monique Wittig, *Across the Acheron*, trans. David Le Vay (London, 1987), p. 105. Further page references are included in the main text.
12. Luce Irigaray, 'Sexual difference', in Margaret Whitford, ed., *The Irigaray Reader* (Oxford, 1991), pp. 174–5, original emphasis.
13. Russo, *Female Grotesque*, pp. 70, 29.
14. For a fuller discussion of this concept see Sandra Gilbert and Susan Gubar, *The Madwoman in the Attic: The Woman Writer and the Nineteenth-Century Literary Imagination* (New Haven, 1984).
15. See Irigaray, 'Sexual difference', p. 173.
16. Nicola Bown, ' "There are fairies at the bottom of our garden": fairies, fantasy and photography', *Textual Practice* 10:1 (1996), pp. 77, 73, 63. See also Carolyne Larrington's essay in this volume, pp. 32–47.
17. Mark 5:9–13.
18. Russo, *Female Grotesque*, p. 18.
19. Cecile Lindsay, 'Body/language: French feminist utopias', *French Review* 60:1 (1986), p. 55.
20. Bammer, *Partial Visions*, p. 126.

13 Fantasy, childhood and literature: in pursuit of wonderlands

Karín Lesnik-Oberstein

'Fantasy' as a concept is, in the Western world, strongly linked to the idea of childhood and to books classified as having been written for children, such as Hans Christian Andersen's fairy-tales and Lewis Carroll's 'Alice' books. Childhood is described, in its traditional Romantic manifestation, as an era of the imagination, fantasy and dream. Children are habitually referred to as being more imaginative than adults, as engaging more frequently and more extensively with fantasy, and, in relation to this, as retaining the ability to make-believe, play and dream. Charlotte Huck, for instance, writing about children's books, sees them as helping the child to 'experience the delight of beauty, wonder, and humor . . . He will be challenged to dream dreams . . . cynicism and despair are not childlike emotions . . . Children see beauty where there is ugliness.'[1] In this respect people writing, or writing about, children's books, do not share the attitude that Lucie Armitt discerns in adult literature, where fantasy in a literary context creates a problem: 'Suddenly it is something dubious, embarrassing (because extra-canonical). Suddenly we need to justify our interest in it.'[2] Children's literature, in contrast, has since its invention (usually placed in the late eighteenth century, when books are seen as being produced for the first time to 'amuse' children, instead of primarily to educate them) freely produced works of 'fantasy', and included them at the heart of children's literature in the marketing, criticism and discussion of the books.[3]

Yet Armitt's comment is in fact doubly relevant to children and children's literature: adult critics not only marginalize fantasy as a

genre within adult literature, but also marginalize children's literature, whether fantasy or not. Authors who write children's books
and critics who study them repeatedly have to justify their work.
Children's books are seen as being unworthy of, or even incapable
of study – the idea that there is nothing there to explain or understand. They are viewed as simplistic, 'childish' and, indeed, 'child-
ishly' fantastical. They are, in other words, seen as suitable for the
child but not for serious adult consideration.[4]

Such ideas of self-evident simplicity and obviousness ignore
two major problems to do with the concepts of the child and children's literature. Firstly, 'children's books' are written, published,
marketed and usually bought by *adults*.[5] Secondly, the idea of what
children are like, what they think and feel, changes in different
historical and cultural settings. Although people usually assume a
level of common understanding of what children are, and although
they look to disciplines such as biology, child psychology or education to tell them what children are like, these ideas change over
time, from place to place, and between people who hold, for instance, different views on morality, politics or gender. As sociologists
Allison James and Alan Prout argue,

> childhood is . . . to be understood as a social construction. That is,
> the institution of childhood provides an interpretive frame for
> understanding the early years of human life. In these terms it is
> biological immaturity rather than childhood which is a universal
> and natural feature of human groups, for ways of understanding
> this period of human life – the institution of childhood – vary
> cross-culturally.[6]

Children's literature, then, expresses the adult *creation* of childhood; these books are spoken of as the repository of the child's
consciousness, and are even discussed as if written by adults who
somehow are or have become children again. Moreover, because
fantasy, imagination and dream are allocated to the child, so the
books 'for' children are regarded as embodiments of these ideas.
This approach raises further questions in relation to the concept
of fantasy: if childhood and the child are themselves creations, for
instance, are they then to be seen as forms of cultural fantasy?
And if childhood is indeed a fantasy how can we talk of a separate
and distinct notion of fantasy within children's literature? This
chapter will show how these issues might be formulated in relation

to two texts: A.A. Milne's 'Introduction' to *Winnie-the-Pooh* o.
1926 and Larry Clark's 1995 American film *Kids*.[7]

Firstly, then, the question of how, if childhood is a construction, we can distinguish between cultural constructions of childhood and cultural fantasies of childhood. In a similar approach to
that of James and Prout, Peter Berger and Thomas Luckmann
argue that reality itself is a construction too:

> reality is socially constructed and the sociology of knowledge must
> analyse the process in which this occurs . . . Sociological interest in
> questions of 'reality' and 'knowledge' is thus initially justified by
> the fact of their social relativity. What is 'real' to a Tibetan monk
> may not be 'real' to an American businessman.[8]

In other words, that which conforms to public rules which function in that particular society for the creation of reality, counts as
real. Institutionalization, public policy, media, custom, ritual and
language, for instance, may function as rules for the real. For what
we can call the discourse, the rules, of the real child we can look
to the language of medicine, developmental psychology, education
and family life (the stress on these topics here has to do with the
language they employ, not with attributing to them a status as
truth). This childhood also defines, and is defined by adulthood
and its discourse.

A particular idea of childhood can become fantasy when, in
some way, meanings are developed which transgress the rules for
real childhood. Disagreement about what real children are produces meanings which may either fall into a category seen as
realistic or possible but nevertheless incorrect, or, from another
perspective, into the category of the fantastic. Aside from any
construction of a reality and its fantasy, the relationship between
fantasy and childhood remains peculiarly strong because childhood is created around notions of consciousness which engage
specifically with the imagination and fantasy, and because adulthood defines itself around ideas to do with a departure from this
realm of the child into reality and the world of fact. In other
words, childhood relates to fantasy on three levels. The discourse
of childhood is a fantasy produced, even when it is attributed with
the reality of the real child, which in turn produces and underpins
adult senses of reality. Valerie Walkerdine describes this paradox
when she writes about education:

the 'reality' of the child-centered pedagogy seems to be the object of an elaborate fantasy. It appears that here in the practices there circulates a vast and complex network of meanings, in which the play of desire, of teachers for children, of children for each other, envy, jealousy, rivalry, and so forth are continually created and re-created. It is not necessary to counterpoise fantasy to reality, but to demonstrate how fantasies themselves are lived, played out and worked through in their inscriptions in the veridicality of discourses and practices.[9]

Secondly, there are the versions of childhood which some designate as fantastical in opposition to their real child. Finally, there are the fantasies defined by and within childhood.

We can trace the negotiation between these three levels of fantasy in the shifting narrator in A.A. Milne's play of, and on, voices in his 'Introduction' to *Winnie-the-Pooh*. Initially, the reader is directly addressed by the narrator: 'if you happen to have read another book about Christopher Robin, you may remember that he once had a swan (or the swan had Christopher Robin, I don't know which), and that he used to call this swan Pooh'. The narrator directly introduces himself as a story-telling adult in his control both of a history of, and knowledge about, Christopher Robin, Pooh, and Pooh's names and incarnations. Although the narrator is adult in his initiation of a story-to-be-told, the 'I don't know which' also creates a space for the narrator to be without knowledge, to identify with the status of the reader – who is yet to be told the story – in terms of uncertainty. There is also an immediate engagement with word-play: who possesses whom (Pooh or the swan) is made an uncertain issue.

Word-play of this kind, dealing with a self-consciously paraded lack of knowledge or control, particularly of language itself, is a trait characteristically associated with fantasies of childhood. The tradition of nonsense associated with Lewis Carroll and Edward Lear is classified as part of 'children's literature' too. *Winnie-the-Pooh*'s nonsense seriously reveals the inherent instabilities of language while depending on the drive to make sense that *is* language. Names, and the changing of names, are an important issue in Milne's 'Introduction', and these are closely linked with questions of identity and with the linked instabilities of both language and identities. The narrator continues:

that was a long time ago, and when we said good-bye, we took the name with us, as we didn't think the swan would want it any more. Well, when Edward Bear said that he would like an exciting name all to himself, Christopher Robin said at once, without stopping to think, that he was Winnie-the-Pooh. And he was.

Names are like possessions, to be discarded or taken away when no longer needed: the end of identity and the end of the story ('when we said good-bye'). When the name is found and a story brought to life with Christopher Robin's saying of 'Winnie-the-Pooh', to whom does the name (and therefore the story) actually belong? In other words, is Christopher Robin indeed himself 'Winnie-the-Pooh' ('Christopher Robin said at once ... that he was Winnie-the-Pooh. And he was'), or is the discovery of the name a revelation of that which belongs as an inherent quality to 'Edward Bear'? In so ostentatiously playing with the notion of who creates whom (or what), the narrator emphasizes his power in having created both Christopher Robin and Winnie-the-Pooh.

The text ostentatiously reveals the mechanisms whereby it constructs its children within its narrative. Precisely when the narrator's own control and presence are most repressed, the narrator acts out the fantasy of becoming a child himself:

Pooh is the favourite, of course, there's no denying it, but Piglet comes in for a good many things which Pooh misses; because you can't take Pooh to school without everybody knowing it, but Piglet is so small that he slips into a pocket, where it is very comfortable to feel him when you are not quite sure whether twice seven is twelve or twenty-two. Sometimes he slips out and has a good look in the ink-pot, and in this way he has got more education than Pooh, but Pooh doesn't mind. Some have brains, and some haven't, he says, and there it is.

The narrator moves from the voice of the adult story-teller, to inhabiting the child's mind as created by him, and then to presenting the perspectives of Piglet and Pooh. The self-consciousness of this exercise is so intense that it becomes a paraded pretence of fantasy: a simultaneous presentation of a fantasy and of its mechanisms, which effectively subverts its status as artless escape from the discourses constructing adulthood. This is, then, a sceptical text: an adult narrator creating a fantasy about the creation of the fantasy of the child as fantasizing. In the geographical metaphors employed in the text, as well as in the map by E.H. Shepard of the world of *Winnie-the-Pooh*, the narrator colonizes the child's mind and imagination:

> when Christopher Robin goes to the Zoo, he goes to where the Polar Bears are, and he whispers something to the third keeper from the left, and doors are unlocked, and we wander through dark passages and up steep stairs, until at last we come to the special cage, and the cage is opened.

When Christopher Robin goes to the Zoo he is accompanied by a score of ghosts (the narrator and the readers) who constitute the 'we' for whom Christopher Robin becomes the vehicle of access to the 'dark passages' and the 'special cage'. The creation of the child serves a function for the adult narrator and the readers: it allows for the entry into a fantasy of being and consciousness which is 'other' to themselves, but well-controlled. Similarly, the statement 'drawn by me and mr shepard helpd [sic]' underneath the map of the world of *Winnie-the-Pooh* tells us that this is the map of Christopher Robin's imagination, now made visible to give access to that imagination. The hand-writing and the mis-spellings on the map ('rabbits frends and raletions') are parallel, as we will see, to the ostensibly hand-held camera in *Kids*. Here are adult narrators using formal devices to create *themselves as children*, as well as to create a conventional fantasy *about* children (that children are not experienced with cameras and writing and spelling – language – and therefore their camera is unstable, and their spelling incorrect).

Although apparently quite different from *Winnie-the-Pooh*, Larry Clark's *Kids* negotiates similar issues around fantasies of childhood, and the relationship of the adult to it. Presented as contemporary, this story of a group of teenagers in New York was alternately critically viewed as a shocking, realistic, revelatory depiction of the real lives of adolescents, and as a near-pornographic fantasy about their lives (significantly, adolescents were often barred from watching this film purportedly about themselves).[10] The film portrays scenes of a group of teenagers aged roughly between eleven and eighteen as they talk, argue, party, engage in sexual relationships, drinking, drug-taking, stealing, rape and physical violence. The action is centred on the possible infection of a number of the girls with the HIV virus by one of the leading characters,

Telly. There are almost no adults shown to have any role in the teenagers' lives other than that of being absent, failures, or unaware of their offsprings' activities and whereabouts. How can it be decided whether Clark's film functions as a revelation of real adolescence or whether it functions as a fantasy, without simply relying on the traditional claims and counter-claims (usually grounded in either anecdotal experience and morality, or in the professional discourses such as psychology) about the evidence that such adolescents exist?[11]

Yet *Kids* functions as a fantasy because the film foregrounds its own fictionality. Seemingly plot-less scenes are juxtaposed with a plotted narrative, and with scenes contrasted to produce irony and oblique moral comment. There are jump-cuts between a group of girls and a group of boys in discussion, contrasting their concerns and language; a girl, previously shown having her first and only experience of intercourse, is told by a nurse that she has contracted HIV, while a promiscuous girl is told that she does not have HIV; a song plays, while a black man is battered.

As with *Winnie-the-Pooh*, the film alternately suppresses and foregrounds the role of the narrating adult – in filmic terms, the camera. As Jacqueline Rose writes of children's literature,

> realism in children's writing cannot be opposed to what is 'literary' or truly 'aesthetic', once it is seen that realism does not refer just to the content of what is described, but to a way of presenting it to the reader. Realism is a fully literary convention ... Realism – in the sense in which we have seen it defined here for children – is that form of writing which attempts to reduce to an absolute minimum our awareness of the language in which a story is written in order that we will take it for real ... To this extent, it shares with other theories of language which I have looked at ... a conviction that the best form of expression is that which most innocently ('no dishonesty', 'no distortion') reflects the objects of the real world.[12]

Although *Kids* is not part of the 'children's literature' Rose is referring to, the idea that realism involves reducing 'to an absolute minimum our awareness of the language' operates widely in art about children because, as Rose argues, childhood itself is formulated as the fantasy of an ultimate reality unmediated by language. *Kids*, however, makes no effort to sustain its formal realism. Its use of an unstable camera, familiar from television programmes such as *N.Y.P.D. Blue*, to suggest a hand-held video-recording initially points to a documentary style. However, the introduction of the film through a scene in a bedroom, where the older (eighteen or so) male Telly is shown initially persuading and eventually forcing a much younger (twelve- or thirteen-year-old) girl to have intercourse with him, reveals the camera to be participating in the supposedly private scene. In a scene of the HIV test sequence, on the other hand, the camera focalizes through the girl's consciousness, becoming her glance, inhabiting her identity. In these ways the film allows for a self-conscious slipping from formalistic suggestions of documentary directness and realism, to an emphasis on the camera as a voyeuristic, exhibiting eye, with an ability to penetrate 'secret' worlds through being suppressed as necessarily present, to the camera as inhabiting and occupying the most 'secret' world of all: the mind's eye/I.

There are differing views on whether children can be given a voice (or to what extent), or whether childhood is actually produced as silence (that the acquisition or possession of voice equates with an adulthood), but in the case of *Kids* and children's literature, these are adult-controlled productions and creations of childhood. The control by the camera of perspective corresponds to the frequent changes in narratorial positions used in *Winnie-the-Pooh* to create the narrator as 'adult'; such control is part of the adult eye/I. The camera in *Kids*, the narrational shifts, provide an adult framing of the child.[13]

Kids overtly reveals the fantasy of adolescence as the remainder of a childish pure experience, free from language, but expressed through a sexuality and a consciousness (frequently shown as 'liberated' from language by drugs) which moves towards adulthood. The film heavily engages in fantasies of gender, often associated with fantasies of adolescence, and used sometimes to sustain conservative gender roles as 'natural' and sexually 'hormone-bound', but also used, paradoxically, to depict freedom from traditional roles – adolescence as anarchy. *Kids* obviously subscribes to the patriarchally convenient fantasy of the sex-object girl, as 'adolescent' removed from any feminist liberation for the pleasure of both the male characters in the film and the male gaze of the viewer. Girls are presented as being 'adolescent' through a more adult than adult femininity, existing almost solely in their relationships to and fantasies about the boys.

In short, *Kids*, in its form, appears to create a 'realism' which it disrupts by drawing attention to its fictional devices of plot, counter-plot, musical score and camera perspective. The film's emphasis on the camera's ability to construct the supposedly secret worlds of adolescent violence, sexuality, speech and drug-taking, and, ultimately, the adolescent mind, while slipping from remaining invisible itself to drawing attention to itself, reveals the film as a fantasy. This camera claims both the status of being adolescent, not as intruder, but as a participant in this adolescent scene – and as such revels in a wish-fulfilling denial of its adult control and identity – and of being the controlling (adult) eye invisible to the adolescents, and therefore by definition voyeuristic.

Both *Kids* and *Winnie-the-Pooh* illustrate how childhood is a cultural production, underpinning the fantasy of reality within which childhood is seen as fantasy. At issue is not primarily the analysis of differing images of childhood in texts, histories or cultures, but the need of the narrators to create, control, and finally to become the child themselves. It is this colonization which is usually extravagantly praised as 'seeing through the eye of the child' or 'capturing the child so perfectly one would say the author must be a child herself'. We may wonder, however, whether this is a praiseworthy expression of an adult's intimate knowledge of a child, or whether it is an adult need to create and control a cultural fantasy.

Notes

1. Charlotte Huck, *Children's Literature in the Elementary School* (New York, 1976), pp. 4–5.
2. Lucie Armitt, *Theorising the Fantastic* (London, 1996), p. 1.
3. More extensive histories of the development of children's literature include F.J. Harvey Darton, *Children's Books in England: Five Centuries of Social Life*, rev. Brian Alderson (Cambridge, 1982); John Rowe Townsend, *Written for Children: An Outline of English-Language Children's Literature* (London, 1990).
4. See, for instance, Frederick Crews's well-known *The Pooh Perplex: A Student Casebook* (first published 1964). In this book Crews attempts to parody the burgeoning of schools of literary criticism by applying their approaches to the most ridiculous example he can apparently conceive of, A.A. Milne's *Winnie-the-Pooh* (1926).

5. Jacqueline Rose, *The Case of Peter Pan or: The Impossibility of Children's Fiction* (London, 1984 and reprint 1995); Karín Lesnik-Oberstein, *Children's Literature: Criticism and the Fictional Child* (Oxford, 1994).

6. Allison James and Alan Prout, eds, *Constructing and Reconstructing Childhood: Contemporary Issues in the Sociological Study of Childhood* (London, 1990), p. 3. For historical changes in ideas of 'childhood' see especially the classic study by Philippe Ariès, *Centuries of Childhood: A Social History of Family Life*, trans. Robert Baldick (New York, 1962).

7. A.A. Milne, 'Introduction' to *Winnie-the-Pooh* (1926; London, 1992), pp. ix–x; *Kids* (Excalibur Films/Independent Films/Miramax Films, 1995); dir. Larry Clark; writers: Larry Clarke, Leo Fitzpatrick, Harmony Korine and Jim Lewis.

8. Peter Berger and Thomas Luckmann, *The Social Construction of Reality: A Treatise in the Sociology of Knowledge* (1966; Harmondsworth, 1991), pp. 13, 15.

9. Valerie Walkerdine, *Schoolgirl Fictions* (London, 1990), pp. 140–1.

10. Roger Ebert writes in his review in the *Chicago Sun-Times* (28 July 1995) that 'the film is intended as a wake-up call, and for some kids it may be a life-saver ... Most kids are not like those in *Kids*, and never will be, I hope. But some are, and they represent a failure of home, school, church and society. They could have been raised in a zoo, educated only to the base instincts.'

11. I will not be considering Clark's own widely publicized claims concerning the authenticity of his film (often related to the writing of the dialogue by nineteen-year-old Harmony Korine, who, according to Roger Ebert, 'lived in the world of skateboarders and suggested the casting of some of his friends to Clark'), or his own knowledge of adolescent life in New York. The film – as with any art-form – depends not on Clark's claimed intentions, but on how it is interpreted by the viewer, and which aspects seem to become operative in an interpretation. Otherwise any film/text would have to be accepted as 'real' or 'fantasy' simply on the basis of the author's intention. I make this approach explicit because claims to knowledge or experience of children still seem to be widely attributed with a truth value.

12. Jacqueline Rose, *The Case of Peter Pan*, p. 65.

13. Children's books written by children do not disprove this assertion: these books are still selected, edited and published by adults. They are therefore created as written by children by adults: sometimes as examples of how clever (some) children are seen to be ('like an adult writer'), and sometimes as an example of what is enshrined as the purest idea of how the real child would/should write.

14 *The decline and fall of the great English ghost story*

Julian Thompson

The great age of the English ghost story runs roughly from Joseph Sheridan Le Fanu's *Ghost-Stories and Tales of Mystery* (1851) to the outbreak of the First World War. A number of reasons have been put forward as to why the ghosts paled and 'thinned away'[1] in or about 1914. Perhaps the physical terrors of the trenches banished more ideal ones, though Kipling's great wartime ghost story, 'A Madonna of the Trenches',[2] argues a contrary view. Perhaps Freud turned the subconscious, the ghost's domicile, into territory for the pathologist, not the poet? Perhaps the irresistible rise of science fiction might be to blame? Or perhaps with the coming of Modernism, and the Modernist scrupulosity about ordering emotion as the best means of presenting it, the ghosts might have seemed too unruly? Or maybe they simply did not like the new electric light. It is, of course, probable that a little of all of these reasons might have held sway. But it is my particular suggestion in this essay that the form declined, even temporarily fell, when it became too schematic, and as a consequence too self-aware, its authors too determined to enforce the latest political, psychological or sociological speculations.

The best ghost stories, like the best supernatural poems – Christina Rossetti's 'Goblin Market', for example – engage our imagination so deeply that the moral ceases to matter, indeed, becomes subordinate to, or even exorcized by, the mysterious perspectives that are 'momently',[3] in Coleridge's word, opened up. In Kipling's 'They' (1904),[4] a very high quality ghost story, the reader finds the shimmering greenwood where the children walk, or the lavish shadows of the House Beautiful, far more engrossing than the author's attempts to explain the workings of the human imagination which sustains them. The effect at the heart of a good ghost story is perhaps most usefully described by Keats's celebrated definition of the characteristic of literary achievement, *negative capability*, 'that is when man is capable of being in doubts, mysteries, uncertainties, without any irritable reaching after fact & reason'.[5] Robert Aickman, possibly the form's finest analyst, has a useful metaphor to expand the point:

> The successful ghost story does not close a door and leave inside it still another definition, a still further solution. On the contrary, it must open a door, preferably where no one had previously noticed a door to exist; and at the end, leave it open, or possibly ajar. A door ajar is often, of course, more teasing to the imagination ('worse', as children put it) than a door wide open.[6]

Like the poignant frieze on Keats's Grecian Urn, that half-open door 'teases' us 'out of thought / As doth eternity'.[7] Though the ghost story may bring along with it a pleasing shock of terror, its suggestions are akin to the 'immortal longings' of poetry. We murder as we dissect them. The temptation is to impose an interpretive scheme on the story: the best stories impressively resist, as does Henry James's *The Turn of the Screw* (1897), by refusing to yield their consummate ambivalence to rationalist probings. Persist in reducing James's novella to a study of tortuous sexual malaise, and his story has a way of getting its own back. You might wish, for instance, to ascribe all little Miles's sufferings to the abusive imagination of his governess. If you do, you find yourself trapped into sketching out nasty little fondlings and couplings – those for which, presumably, the story's spectral machinery symbolically stands. Thus the reader's imagination is pressured into a prurience more extreme than that of the governess. Better to stick with the otherworldly leer of Peter Quint, and the girl's fear and desperation.

Thus the main constituent of the classic English ghost story, under the memorable charm and fear, is its central impenetrability. Though much may be said about the psychological predicament of the main character, or the social and cultural pressures of the age in which he or she is situated, ultimately the story must resist the secularization that comes with a purely intellectual exposition. Unfortunately the ghost story writers of the early twentieth century – perhaps fazed by encroaching materialism, perhaps lured by the explicatory grails of Marx and Freud – were all too keen to key an interpretive mechanism to the story itself. This chapter examines four major ghost stories of the early twentieth century in which the author's purposes are clearly didactic as well as poetic, in which the ghost becomes, intermittently at least, the primary level in an allegory, or is too rapidly and obviously reduced to a psychological emission. Notwithstanding these overt designs, however, whether accidentally or on purpose all four authors have succeeded in retaining an appropriate atmosphere of mystery. Though Aickman's door is grappled shut, it is not close-fitting, and remains unlocked. A way is left out of the mental box-room in which the solution was meant to be imprisoned. Thus the present stories remain distinct from other supernatural writings of the twentieth century in which the whole purpose of the otherworldly mechanism is to embody a psychological insight: Saki's few genuinely supernatural stories, for instance, where the point seems to be to dramatize the disturbance in conventional life when adolescent sexuality manhandles the Great God Pan through the French windows and into the drawing-room;[8] or *Peter Pan*, where Barrie ironizes his own most creative effects, expounding the meaning of Peter's Napoleonic heartlessness for the benefit of the over-eights in the audience.[9] In the four stories I have chosen the ghosts are not reduced to icons. They remain disturbing, refreshing and releasing. Nevertheless, as I have suggested, in each case the author's overlying purpose is plain, its insistence adjusting oddly with the teasing suggestiveness of the chosen form. Oliver Onions's 'The Beckoning Fair One', the least keen of the four stories to supply a programme, and thus the most subtle achievement, is nevertheless earmarked in several ways as a story about the workings of sexual tension, sometimes with disturbing explicitness. H.G. Wells, a champion creator and explicator of popular scientific theory, attempts to reconcile the Romantic with the rational; May Sinclair was a committed Freudian, keen to test the latest psychoanalytic theory in fictional form; while D.H. Lawrence regularly undertook to reorganize the whole of Western civilisation by means of literary propaganda, not least in his supernatural fiction.

'The Beckoning Fair One', by Oliver Onions (1873–1961), appeared in the collection *Widdershins* (1911).[10] Robert Aickman has judged this one of the six finest ghost stories ever written, and 'an almost perfect story', praising the teasing 'slenderness of the ghostly mechanism', and 'the unusual but indispensable length' to which the story is sustained (pp. 10–11). But notwithstanding the subtle insidiousness of the spectre, and the patient obliquity of Onions's exposition, the human predicament beneath the other-worldly suggestiveness is always sharply defined. A middle-aged novelist takes and does up part of a big old house as a flat, and arranges his belongings with 'spinster-like precision and nicety' (p. 40). Even before his longstanding girlfriend enters the story it is clear that Paul Oleron is undergoing a mid-life crisis, and drifting into a familiar solution. For the first time in his life he takes a mistress – or, rather, a mistress presents herself in the form of the in-house ghost. Then the duel is on between heavy, florid Elsie Bengough and her wispy supernatural rival, who may be no more than the shadow of Oleron's solipsistic decline. The feeling that the 'Beckoning Fair' may be no more than an implosive sexual fantasy is borne out by the tenuousness of her appearances in the story. Oleron is enthralled by glances and hairsbreadths: a glimpse of his own eighteen-penny comb tracing the outline of an antique coiffure, a lovesong played by the notes of a dripping water-tap, the faint impress of a body on the coverlet of a made bed, a wrenching, half-intermitted kiss. The more perfect Oleron's infatuation, the more sinewy the ghost-girl's blandishments, until they are indistinguishable from the shadow of the moon on the blood-red curtains that shield him from the prying eyes of the world. With knowing deftness, Onions sketches the impact of Oleron's eccentricities on his prurient neighbours, and their self-appointed moral spokesman, the long-nosed street-preacher, Barrett. They merely see an arty decadent, up to no good with the affections of blowsy, loyal Elsie Bengough. At the end of the story their vigilance is gratified: an unshaven Oleron is carted off to the police station to face murder-charges, while the remains of Elsie emerge on a hooded stretcher from the fatal house. The quaint appurtenances of its eighteenth-century past, so ravishing to Oleron when they seemed the poor remnant of his spectral Lady's boudoir, are reduced to a novel means of secreting the body: Elsie is shrouded in a harp-case, and hidden in a powder-closet. Thus Onions has shown how closely Romantic aspiration and murderous incontinence are linked in the human psyche. Without obscuring anything from the reader, the author's supernatural mechanism protects Oleron from the sordid details of his own decline; at the same time pursuit of the elusive girl-ghost gives a freshness and poignancy to the hardly original theme of artist's frustrations in his quest for perfect beauty.

For all the story's accomplishment, however, close inspection of 'The Beckoning Fair One' reveals, as with so many early-twentieth-century ghost stories, an elaborate theoretical pattern. Oleron is as much a prisoner of the imagination as the 'madwoman in the attic' of Charlotte Perkins Gilman's 'The Yellow Wallpaper' (1892), his story's human agenda and sexual politics just as clear. The wraith winding insidiously about his soul represents the fatal power of the human imagination to override the practical exigencies of the universe; battling, laughing Elsie Bengough, with her 'dim shape emblematic of mortality' (p. 52), represents the hardwearing answer of reality, whose stuff will nevertheless endure only so long. Onions has dramatized the distance between the ideal and the absolute, the imagined and the everyday, and, in doing so, has explored what Philip Larkin, in a study of Hardy's poems, has called a 'basic insincerity in human affection'.[11] Just as the ghost of Hardy's first wife, immortally young and girlish, is bound to overpower memories of the time-stained woman she became, so Elsie is inevitably at a disadvantage in her fight with the ageless and bodiless 'Beckoning Fair'.

For the most part, Onions has succeeded in concealing his purposes more effectively than the other writers I shall go on to consider. There are, notwithstanding, moments of over-explicit rationale when Aickman's so delicately propped 'open door' at least quivers on its hinges. A number of passages in the story seem to insist on its status as a late-Romantic complaint about the limits of mortality, and the artist's responsibility to test those limits to breaking-point. We hear Elsie urging the perfectionist Oleron to 'remember you're human, and live in a world' (p. 47); the 'crucial importance, in his artistic development' (p. 41), of the novel he is working on when the ghost interrupts, is emphasized many times. At the ghost's insistence he destroys his original manuscript, and tinkers with the idea of recasting the book in her image: the icon that emerges is a little too obviously the Pateresque Mona Lisa, the 'Woman all men desired', and Onions's account of the agony of following such a fatal Cleopatra is a little overwritten, as if he had read a textbook on chasing the 'reflex' of Wordsworth's star.[12] Here is a taste:

> [the novelist] must weep wretched tears, as Oleron did, must swell
> with vain presumptuous hopes, as Oleron did, must pursue, as
> Oleron pursued, the capricious, fair, mocking, slippery, eager spirit
> that ever sees to it that the chase does not slacken. (p. 90)

In *Wuthering Heights* the 'intolerable torture'[13] to which the
dead Cathy subjects Heathcliff is evoked as delicately as the
entrancement of Oleron; but Emily Brontë remained far too
wise (or 'negatively capable') to descant on the meaning of her
enigma.

A writer who is never loath to comment on the fantastic events
in his fiction is H.G. Wells (1866–1946), author of my second
chosen story, 'The Door in the Wall',[14] the first of three in which
the desire to explain the inexplicable seems to have unfortunate
side-effects, even in some of the most evocative ghost stories ever
written. Like many ambitious and productive writers, Wells intermittently found himself drawn to the sportful irrationalities of the
ghost story. Some of his efforts, like the much anthologized 'The
Inexperienced Ghost', are unashamedly flippant; but in characteristic texts like 'The Red Room' (1896), Wells gets into his stride of
fantasizing extravagantly ('The Red Room' is a splendid shocker)
while offering simultaneous commentary on the probable psychological bases of the supernatural. Nowhere is this blend of
approaches more conspicuously or successfully applied than in
'The Door in the Wall' (1906). This is the story of Wallace, a self-
aware careerist who by the age of thirty-nine has climbed to the
rank of Cabinet minister. Wells's purpose is to investigate the
status in his life of a recurring dream of, or visitation from, a
picturesque garden, reached through a green door in a white wall.
The mode Wells employs in the story is very close to allegory:
Wallace's garden of joyful fellowship is as meaningfully fantastic
as any landscape in Spenser. It dramatizes the approach to life
of 'dreamers, these men of vision and the imagination' (p. 72),
privileging the speculative over the known and seen, the timeless
over the temporal. In the garden panther cohabits with monkey,
children play at life as if it were a game, and every prospect and
artefact is 'full of the quality and promise of heart's desire' (p. 61).
The book Wallace is shown when he visits the garden at the age of
five is a perfect, living record of 'all the things that had happened
to me since ever I was born' (p. 61), abolishing the interface

between art and life. In fact the garden is something like a perfected Romantic vision; yet it arises, like so many Romantic visions, out of a commonplace setting, the streets of West Kensington, circumscribed by the graphic remembered details of natural history, the yellow chestnut leaves, and human inconsequence, the ironmongers' shops. As Wallace works his way down the years he never manages to return to the garden. He has penetrated its secrets once, in earliest childhood. Thereafter the exigencies of an increasingly crowded daily life keep him pavement side of the beguiling door. At school the demands of the timetable squeeze him past it; as a lover, his girl generates more romance than a lost garden; while climbing the greasy pole to Cabinet Office, appointments in Eden never seem to fit the spaces in a crowded diary. It is only with the 'feeling of forty' (p. 68) that the bright, elusive possibilities of the garden claim him again, with fatal results: deluded into thinking a workman's doorway over a 'deep excavation near East Kensington station' (p. 71) is his elusive door in the wall, the poor man falls to his death. There is more than a hint that Wallace has become a fading Romantic visionary, desperate to recover the lost allure of youth.

The structure of Wells's allegory is admirably clear – nevertheless, the 'ideas man' in Wells leaves nothing to chance. He inserts the device of a framing narrative, in which Wallace's extraordinary story is told to a keenly analytic friend and contemporary. Thus the story is mediated through a commentary that is always drawing attention to the gap between the two planes of Wallace's divided inclination. Unable fully to credit the possibility of a Cabinet minister with a secret life in which he desires a fairy-tale garden, the narrator suggests that the garden story may only be a means of conveying 'experiences it was otherwise impossible to tell' (p. 57). He insists upon the equivocal status of the evidence presented, resolutely refusing to judge the truth of Wallace's case: 'but whether he himself saw, or only thought he saw, whether he himself was the possessor of an inestimable privilege or the victim of a fantastic dream, I cannot pretend to guess' (p. 57). Even after Wallace's death has been dissected by the newspapers and clubmen, the narrator reiterates his dialectical moral in a curtain-lecture. It is as if Wells were determined to remind us that the ghost story is at bottom just another convenient literary method of mounting a 'raid on the inarticulate':[15]

Was there, after all, ever any green door in the wall at all?

I do not know. I have told his story as he told it to me. There are times when I believe that Wallace was no more than the victim of the coincidence between a rare but not unprecedented type of hallucination and a careless trap, but that at least is not my profoundest belief. You may think me superstitious, if you will, and foolish; but, indeed, I am more than half convinced that he had, in truth, an abnormal gift, and a sense, something – I know not what – that in the guise of a wall and door offered him an outlet, a secret and peculiar passage of escape into another and altogether more beautiful world. At any rate, you will say, it betrayed him in the end. But did it betray him? There you touch the inmost mystery of these dreamers, these men of vision and the imagination. We see our world fair and common, the hoarding and the pit. By our daylight standard he walked out of security into darkness, danger, and death.

But did he see it like that? (p. 72)

The narrator's theorizing is so explicit it goes a long way to reducing Wallace's mysterious garden to the mechanism of a parable. At least the 'knowledge' thus re-emphasized turns out to be the relatively hospitable moral – in ghost story terms – that 'we do not know'.

The parables expressed in the supernatural fiction of Wells's friend, correspondent and near-contemporary May Sinclair (1863–1964) are even more strikingly didactic – at times, indeed, they read more like sermons than parables. A journeywoman intellectual, who had little formal education save for a year at Cheltenham Ladies' College, Sinclair lived precariously as a poet, reviewer and philosophic essayist, taking every opportunity to engross herself in the tumultuous intellectual life of late-Victorian and Edwardian England. Her preponderantly cerebral outlook resembles that of George Eliot, and, like George Eliot, she is the rare instance of an accomplished creative artist who conceives fiction in the mould of philosophic and psychological theory, and who is nevertheless able to produce work of intrinsic literary merit, rather than a drily didactic treatise. She moved through several creative phases, as her various intellectual orientations dictated, beginning in the 1890s with *Robert Elesmere*-style spiritual odysseys,[16] and moving on to Wellsian social realism in the Suffragette years (she was part of the movement's think-tank). Eventually she fixed on translating the new psychoanalytic theories of Freud and Jung into fictional form, at the same time, with characteristic energy and enthusiasm, becoming a founder-member of H.N. Brailsford's Institute of Psycho-Analysis. It is to this phase of her work, beginning roughly with her autobiographical novel *Mary Olivier* in 1919, that the present short-story 'Where Their Fire is not Quenched' belongs, though its closest affinities are with a bleak, spare novel of 1922, *The Life and Death of Harriet Frean.*[17] *Harriet Frean* is the somewhat claustrophobic vision, in stream-of-consciousness form, of the seventy-year life of a woman who prefers to 'behave beautifully' (p. 182), rather than prosecute her subconscious desires, and who dies on the operating table, having given birth to a monstrous tumour, the product of her repressed libido. The novel is written in Sinclair's characteristic clinical-poetic prose, and is quite unrelenting: Harriet Frean's errors of judgement, ambition and policy constitute the drily tragic record of a life where sexual repression was neither sublimated nor mastered. The novel is all the more harrowing because its heroine is completely aware of the psychosexual omissions of her underpowered libido. In reading the book T.S. Eliot claimed he was moved to the purgative emotions of 'terror and pity' (p. viii). Sinclair's psychological ghost stories can be comparably cathartic, and equally cerebral. The supernatural mode gives Sinclair readier access to the deep places of memory and desire on which Freudian analysis depends. In the present story, 'Where Their Fire is not Quenched',[18] Sinclair reduces the life of her protagonist, Harriott Leigh, to a series of sexually charged memories, from first love at seventeen through an unrequited affair in her twenties, and on through tedious thirtysomething adultery to her final years as a devout but hypocritical 'Sister' and helper in an Anglo-Catholic parish, professing an 'intense repugnance' for the sins of the fallen women she chooses to raise (p. 117). Harriott dies at about the story's halfway point, whereupon Sinclair pursues her into the afterlife, illustrating the Freudian conviction that sexual repression infects every aspect of human potential, its consequences telescoped into a terrible eternity in which nothing has significance beyond the consummation of unwanted desire.

Sinclair's writing throughout the story is pin-sharp, often harrowingly economic. It is disconcerting to see the life of an averagely intelligent, averagely well-meaning woman reduced in this fashion to a series of acridly poetic literary postcards, leading to a crisis in which even her 'innocent' memories collapse into the horror and boredom of a never-ending furtive love. With the logic of a revealing dream, Harriott's history is opened to the reader's analysis. Throughout life, she has blocked her sexuality, preferring, in Freudian terms, to 'sublimate' it. The result is a series of liaisons in which Harriott loves 'with her soul' in a rather gushy, 'unearthly way' (p. 108). Back in youth the pale poet Stephen Philpotts was the recipient of this kind of love. He preferred someone else. In middle-age she reacts similarly to her spiritual mentor, the Revd Clement Farmer. He holds her quivering hand until it is 'wrenched from him in the last agony' (p. 107). Only heavy, cynical Oscar Wade can make anything of Harriott's sexuality, and he leads her to a few afternoons of guilty coupling in a Parisian hotel. This is the nasty sty to which all roads lead in Harriott's eternity. There can be no refuge from the memory of it: the origins of Harriott's repression lie far back in innocence, and the roots run so deep that innocence itself is tainted. Between bouts of sickly, straying, remembered lust, Oscar explains to her the Freudian determinism that governs her story: 'You think that the past affects the future. Has it never struck you that the future may affect the past? In your innocence there was the beginning of your sin. You *were* what you *were to be*' (p. 125). Harriott's efforts to retreat into her adolescent love-affairs, to dream the dead goldfish back into her childhood pond, and to recover the enfolding maternal arms in the paternal orchard, have all the poignancy and futility of Pincher Martin's attempts to construct himself an afterlife on a barren rock in the North Atlantic in Golding's novel.[19] Ultimately there can be no running from the 'beastly' (p. 114) abomination Harriott Leigh made of her once-innocent love: she must lie in the arms of bloated Oscar Wade, an image of mutually loathing, festering sexual congress. Christianity, or even a less schematically humanist vision of the supernatural, might offer Harriott a chance of escape. Sinclair unyieldingly shows how, once free of her body, Harriott is progressively consumed by the afterlife of her unsatisfied libido, the Freudian subtext becoming insistent, even clamorous, in the scene where the ubiquitous half-living lover, Oscar, usurps the father's place on the latter's deathbed (p. 121).

Jean Radford has called Miss Sinclair 'a logical lady' (*Harriet Frean*, p. vi), and there is certainly a diagrammatic exactitude about the way in which the psychoanalytic programmes emerge from her sparely written tales. In a later story, 'The Villa Desirée' (1926),

she materializes the foetus-like ghost of a sexual degenerate; in
another, 'The Nature of the Evidence' (1923), unfinished sexual
business between a man and his first wife materializes as a solid,
inconvenient presence in the bed of his second marriage; in 'The
Victim' (1922), the ghost of a murdered man returns to reprove
his murderer, not for packing up his dismembered body in seventeen paper parcels, but for having committed the psychological
solecism of having looked on a fellow-creature 'with hate'.[20] Reducing the other-world to a series of graphic emanations of the
subconscious, she imprisons the ghost story in the iron grip of a
deterministic universe, leaving no refuge for her ghosts, because
she believes we have no refuge from ourselves, or ultimately from
the penalty of our misapplied passions.

The work of May Sinclair features in Lady Cynthia Asquith's
anthology of 1926, *The Ghost Book*, to which another deter-
minedly didactic writer, D.H. Lawrence, contributed one of the best-
known ghost stories of the period, 'The Rocking-Horse Winner'.[21]
Though it used to be fashionable to suggest that 'The Rocking-
Horse Winner' is uncharacteristic of Lawrence's major work, in
truth the story unfolds a familiar Lawrentian social philosophy.[22]
Essentially this story of a boy who rides his rocking-horse until he
is '*absolutely* sure' (p. 155) of the winners of important races is a
study of the triumph of the will, the usurpation of terrible consciousness over that part of the psyche which should function
instinctively. The characterization, for all its spare assurance, features characteristic Lawrentian types. The father is an 'absent presence', so despised and ignored by his creator that he is left to sip
whisky in offstage, darkened rooms. Though she can cut a fairy-
tale figure in a doorway, blonde in a green and crystal dress, the
mother is a silky, brutal study of feminine rapaciousness, a woman
for whom talent and vocation is replaced by an icy desire to do
one thing better than everyone else – it turns out to be drawing
fashion-plates of women in fox-furs. The fault-line of the crucial
human tension, as so often in Lawrence, falls between mother and
son. She needs money; the son whips his body up into his soul,
riding out of the story to fetch her some from the racecourse.
Through her guilty straying propensity to 'touch' him for more,
Lawrence explores the cerebral titillation to be had at the fringe
of the cash nexus: gambling, the catwalk, 'piles of iridescent
cushions' (p. 158).

In fact, Lawrence is exploiting the ghost story, as he exploited many other forms in the 1920s, for a satirical purpose. He never articulates the moral, as he so brusquely does in many of his didactic stories of this period, especially those with a supernatural mechanism. Yet it emerges clearly enough. 'Poor devil, poor devil', mutters the boy's perceptive but sly uncle, Oscar Cresswell, after the mad charge for 'luck' on the rocking-horse's back leads to a fever, and ultimately to the boy's death, 'he's best gone out of a life where he rides a rocking-horse to find a winner' (p. 163). Most people attempt to crack the capitalist system with equally desperate gymnastics and frequently, if less spectacularly, perish in the attempt. As Lawrence, just before writing the story, told his friends the Carswells – he was fond of absorbing names – riches have 'a really magical touch to make a man insensitive and to make him wicked'.[23] Though the moral is plain, and probably formed the germ of 'The Rocking-Horse Winner', this is not to say that the story fails. On the contrary, the supernatural agency is presented with combative directness, like everything in Lawrence's best mature work, and without the hymns to the freedom of the blood, or to the enfranchising power of sexuality, that can mar his work at any period. The 'life' of 'The Rocking-Horse Winner' is eerily fleshless: the elvish whispers of the money-seeking house, the acid hopes and frustrations of the turf, the mad mechanical surge of the rocking-horse, possibly the most effective symbolic horse in Lawrence, without the masculinist pullulations of St Mawr's flanks or the anthropological gestures of the dream-horses that end *The Rainbow*. Yet for all the silkiness and understatement of the writing, Lawrence's story stands or falls, as no great ghost story should, by the rigour of its allegoric purposes. Aickman's door is not left ajar, half-shielding, half-gesturing at otherness. It is slammed firmly shut, entrapping the kingdom of Mammon. Lawrence's 'solution' is not to tilt our senses towards a mystery, but to exhibit human guilt and rapacity in all their ugliness. There is no ambivalence, no alternative explanation. Without the reader's collusion in its patterns of allegory, the story seems kinetic but inconsequential; with it, it is clear that once again a writer of the Modernist period is keen to subdue the suggestiveness of the ghost story to the emphatic whisper of satirical or psychological purpose. The house of 'The Rocking-Horse Winner' is 'haunted' not by a ghost but by a chorus of judgemental materialism, 'like people laughing at you behind your back' (p. 156). Lawrence's rocking-horse is as evocative of the capitalist treadmill as Dickens's melan-choly-mad elephantine beam-engine in *Hard Times*.[24] It should come as no surprise that 'The Rocking-Horse Winner', a rare achievement in a phase of writer's block, should have freed Law-rence up for *Lady Chatterley's Lover*, one of the most influential didactic novels ever written.

It would be unreasonable to claim that there have been few great twentieth-century ghost stories because those in a position to excel in this most demanding of forms (at least as demanding as poetry) were too knowing to write them. Two great masters of the genre, Walter de la Mare and Robert Aickman, have, in the middle years of the century, produced a teasing array of phantoms who sidle through the 'half-open door' of possibility and then retreat backwards through it, without a hint of allegoric or sche-matic explanation of their presence.[25] This chapter attempts one possible explanation of how and why the first flowering of the English ghost story seemed to expend itself around 1914. Since then, there has been fresh budding, and conditions look auspicious for a full-blown comeback. Obliquity, ambivalence and suggestive disorientation, the hallmarks of the form, have been the stock-in-trade of the literary art of the twentieth century. The ghost story, in the form of elegantly edited anthologies from major publishing houses, is available in convenient packaging to a larger number of consumers than ever before.[26] Modern literary phantoms, such as A.S. Byatt's 'The July Ghost' (1987), have been much relished, and there is a fertile market for pastiche of the ghost stories of earlier periods, as Susan Hill's *The Woman in Black* (1983), with its stage and television derivatives, has demonstrated.[27] Whether in its traditional form, or upgraded to its fashionable manifestations, angel and alien, the ghost maintains a vigorous presence on the margins of our culture, perhaps the closest approach the history of humanity supplies to an embodied literary text. In the most effect-ive ghost stories there can be no 'conceivable' answer as to why the normative should suddenly be invaded by the irrational. Occu-pying as it does the mental spaces unclaimed by materialist cer-tainties, the ghost story provides aesthetic testimony that the 'inconceivable' remains the deepest truth we have.

Notes

1. Thomas Hardy, 'A Trampwoman's Tragedy', stanza xiii, in *The Complete Poems of Thomas Hardy*, ed. James Gibson (London, 1976), p. 199.
2. Rudyard Kipling, 'A Madonna of the Trenches', in *Debits and Credits* (London, 1926).
3. Samuel Taylor Coleridge, 'Kubla Khan', l. 19.
4. Rudyard Kipling, 'They', in *Traffics and Discoveries* (London, 1904).
5. John Keats, *Letters of John Keats: A Selection*, ed. Robert Gittings (Oxford, 1970), p. 43.
6. *The Third Fontana Book of Great Ghost Stories*, selected by Robert Aickman (London, 1966), p. 7.
7. John Keats, 'Ode on a Grecian Urn', ll. 44–5.
8. I am thinking especially of the stories 'Gabriel-Ernest', 'The Music on the Hill', and 'Laura'.
9. According to Peter Hollindale, a 'strange blend of self-effacement and intrusiveness, of the self-dismissive and the self-assertive, is characteristic of much in Barrie's dramatic practice, both in *Peter Pan* and generally'. See *Peter Pan and Other Plays*, edited and introduced by Peter Hollindale (Oxford, 1995), p. 310; and Hollindale's introduction, pp. xvi–xviii. Other writers of the early twentieth century who characteristically analyse their fantastic effects include Arthur Machen, who in stories such as 'Change' and 'The Great Return' uses the ghost story to embody anthropological or mystical insights; and Algernon Blackwood, who, in stories such as 'Ancient Sorceries' 'The Camp of the Dog' and even the highly impressive 'The Wendigo', is perhaps overly keen to dramatize his encyclopaedic knowledge of folklore and occultism.
10. George Oliver Onions, *Widdershins* (London, 1911). References to 'The Beckoning Fair One' are to its reprint in the more conveniently available *Great Ghost Stories* 3, pp. 35–106.
11. Philip Larkin, 'Mrs Hardy's memories', reprinted in *Required Writing* (London, 1983), p. 147.
12. Walter Pater's celebrated description of the Mona Lisa as Romantic archetype comes in his essay 'Leonardo da Vinci' (1869), later collected in *The Renaissance* (1873), ch. 10; Wordsworth's description of skating across the reflection of the star in the frozen lake will be found in *The Prelude* (1850), Book I, ll. 450–52.
13. Emily Brontë, *Wuthering Heights*, ch. 29.
14. References to this story are to its reprint in *Great Ghost Stories* 6, pp. 56–72.
15. T.S. Eliot, 'East Coker', in *Four Quartets*, Part V, l. 8.

16. Mrs Humphry Ward, *Robert Elesmere*, 3 vols (London, 1888). This novel, exploring the difficulty and resilience of faith in late Victorian England, was widely read, discussed and imitated.

17. Both *Mary Olivier: A Life* and *The Life and Death of Harriet Frean* were reprinted by Virago in 1980, with neat introductions by Jean Radford, providing useful potted background on the writer. There is a biography of Sinclair by T.E.M. Boll.

18. Reference is to the convenient reprint of this story in *Great Ghost Stories* 6, pp. 107–27.

19. In William Golding's *Pincher Martin* (London, 1956) the rather disagreeable protagonist dies on the novel's second page, but prefers to concoct a Robinson Crusoe-like fantasy of survival, rather than submit to the terrible compassion of God.

20. 'The Villa Desirée' appeared in *The Ghost Book*, edited by Lady Cynthia Asquith (London, 1926; reprinted 1970); 'The Nature of the Evidence' and 'The Victim' both featured in May Sinclair's *Uncanny Tales* (London, 1923). 'The Nature of the Evidence' is conveniently reprinted in *The Oxford Book of Twentieth Century Ghost Stories*, ed. Michael Cox (Oxford, 1996), and 'The Victim' in *The Oxford Book of English Ghost Stories*, ed. Michael Cox and R.A. Gilbert (Oxford, 1986).

21. References to 'The Rocking-Horse Winner' are from *The Ghost Book* (reprinted London, 1970), pp. 147–63.

22. In his once highly influential *D.H. Lawrence: Novelist* (London, 1955; reprinted 1976), F.R. Leavis complains somewhat cryptically that 'it is exasperating to find "The Rocking-Horse Winner" so highly regarded (especially in America, it would seem)' (p. 357).

23. Quoted in Harry T. Moore, *D.H. Lawrence: The Priest of Love* (1954; revised edition Harmondsworth, 1976), p. 53.

24. Charles Dickens, *Hard Times: For These Times* (1854), Part I, ch. 5.

25. In my opinion some of the finest and most satisfyingly elusive of de la Mare's ghost stories are 'All Hallows', 'Crewe', 'The Quincunx', 'A Recluse' and 'What Dreams May Come'; Aickman's most impressively enigmatic and atmospheric contributions to the genre include 'Ringing the Changes', 'The Trains', 'The Inner Room', 'The Visiting Star', 'The Swords', 'The Cicerones' and 'The Hospice'.

26. The variety of worthwhile anthologies is too great to list here. Apart from the items documented in the bibliography below, the reader might like to consider the following: Lady Cynthia Asquith, ed., *The First Ghost Book* (1926), *The Second Ghost Book* (1952) and *The Third Ghost Book* (1995); V.H. Collins, ed., *Ghosts and Marvels* (Oxford, 1924) [includes a notable introduction by M.R. James]; Michael Cox, ed., *The Oxford Book of Twentieth Century Ghost*

Stories (Oxford, 1996); J.A. Cuddon, ed., *The Penguin Book of Ghost Stories* (1984); Anne Ridler, ed., *Best Ghost Stories* (1945); Montague Summers, ed., *The Supernatural Omnibus* (1931).

27. A.S. Byatt's 'The July Ghost' appeared in *Sugar and Other Stories* (London, 1987); Susan Hill, *The Woman in Black* (London, 1983).

15 'Never love a cowboy': romance fiction and fantasy families

Peter Stoneley

To desire is necessarily to exist in a state of fantasy: it is to entertain the possibility of obtaining something one does not have – power, love, adventure. Given that all desire is fantastical by its very nature, it might seem odd that some projections of desire are criticized because they seem inauthentic. Popular romance fiction, for instance, has long been derided as the worst kind of fantasy. There is the sense that publishers such as Silhouette, Harlequin, and Mills and Boon provide emotional and erotic titillation for women who are too weak to achieve fulfilment in 'real life'. Only such fools, with no genuine hold on reality, could lend credence to the impossibly beautiful, monolithic creatures to be found in these novels. There is the suggestion that these works are not so much fantasy as false consciousness. The passion is at once euphemized and overstated; this is pornography for those who cannot bear to own up to sexual appetite. Alternatively, such caricatures of desire may provide an excessive compensation in the sphere of the erotic for a variety of other wants: the imaginary lover can requite not merely sexual loneliness, but also a poorly paid job, or a general feeling of insignificance.[1] Of course such criticism could also be offered of the characters and scenarios of male-oriented popular fiction, who are usually every bit as predictable and fantastic: the spy who is equally adept at unlocking women's desires and un-ravelling the plans of evil empires; the silent, unbreakable Western hero; the detective who outwits and outpunches low-life villains. The hard-boiled quality of masculine fictions suggests a claiming of the real, even though we as real readers in the real world may detect the wishfulness of it all.

This essay looks at the recolonization of one particular hard-boiled genre – the Western – by women writers of romance fiction. It asks what is at stake – what is being managed, expressed or denied – in definitions of the real and the fantastic in such novels, focusing on Ann Major's *The Fairy Tale Girl* (1987), Lindsay McKenna's *Heart of the Eagle* (1986), and Robin Morgan's *The Cowboy and His Lady* (1984).[2]

From the outset the Western was a celebration of manliness. It has been argued that as American cultural life became increasingly feminized in the course of the nineteenth century, the demand grew for narratives which would engage the interests and attitudes of men. Appalled by the coy complacencies of late-nineteenth-century 'little women', turn-of-the-century writers such as Owen Wister and Zane Gray offered the male reader something supposedly closer to his own experiences. An oppositional male audience was created, which did not want to read tales of tearful but virtuous heroines. The cowboy is a heroic figure who consciously attempts to evade and transcend the culture of women. In a deliberate turn away from a world of feeling, male American writers developed Western stories of adventure, in which masculine virtues of courage and physical strength were celebrated.[3] The action takes place against a harsh backdrop of deserts and windswept plains, constructed as an unsuitable locale for the niceties of womanly feeling. The moral civilization of feminine domesticity gave impetus to a masculinist counter-culture, in which love was not a long, careful matching of emotional and spiritual compatibilities, but a hard kiss on a reluctant, then accepting, mouth.[4]

There are several questionable assumptions in all this, one of the most important being that women's writing was at one with the domestic sphere. In fact, many domestic fictions subvert the feminine stereotype that they may seem, also, to affirm. Novels such as *Little Women* (1869) show how claustrophobic the home could be. Within a feminine narrative template, women writers could, more or less covertly, express rage over the circumscription of their lives.[5] Furthermore, the Western is nostalgic and escapist, for all that it privileges toughness and violence. This masculine genre is, as much as any women's narrative, filled with pathos. The cowboy is a lonely figure who can bring stability to the lives of small people, but who will always be too big himself ever to fit in. Much of the time he is a misfit, condemned to a life of heroic isolation. Given the emotions that cluster around this notionally anti-sentimental character, we might say that the Western does not wish to get rid of sentiment, so much as find a way of making it masculine. It is founded on this contradiction between the desire for sentiment and the reaction against it, and in this it displays the key to its own incoherence. It represents male emotion as more valid because it is the product of authentic experience. Men's feelings, the Western would have us believe, are not female hysteria, but a legitimate response to the sadness of life; not excessive, but true.

This is not to adjudicate between competing versions of reality, so much as ask what is being sought or avoided in each case. It has been argued that fantasy fiction, and especially formulaic fictions, give us a telling indication of the limits and contradictions of a given social order. Our fantasies can represent and, at the same time, get rid of desires that are either forbidden or simply not met in everyday life. In Rosemary Jackson's formulation, fantasy both tells and expels desire, granting a momentary and vicarious experience of what, otherwise, we cannot have.[6] In a similar vein, Tania Modleski asks why romance fiction endlessly retells almost identical stories: the formula of formula fiction, the same stories over and over again, reconvinces us of what we otherwise cannot believe. We reiterate those scenarios that are at once archetypal and unlikely, that address unspoken contradictions within normative culture.[7] What behaviours and desires need such endless and careful maintenance in the telling and retelling of Western romances? What contradictions are assuaged and what impositions subverted? Do these narratives seem calculated to produce the fantasy of false consciousness? Or should we rather see them as an ambitious rhetorical effort to transform the world to romantic consciousness, to make dreams come true? This chapter argues that we can indeed read these as fictions of wished-for transformation, but that they also encode fears that they cannot quite address.

Silhouette, the New York-based romance publisher launched in 1980 with a $3 million advertising campaign, has enjoyed so much success with its 'Western Lovers' series that it has divided it up into various sub-series, each of which offers a slightly different slant on Western material. 'Reckless Renegades' claims that 'Wild hearts can't be broken', whereas 'Kids 'n Kin' sells the idea that '*Nothing* is stronger than the bonds of family love!'. The other sub-series offer intermediate positions between 'recklessness' and family ties, but regardless of the promise of 'wild' love, all the 'Western Lovers' novels are engaged by questions of child-bearing and responsibility. We noted that the Western originated in part out of a sense of claustrophobia, with a desire to exchange the restraints of family living for the open spaces of a non-urban, non-feminized landscape. But writing in the 1980s and 1990s, authors of contemporary Westerns can no longer take the conventional family unit for granted. In 'Western Lovers' the heroism of the leading characters now lies in the determination to fashion a stable family life in a world of selfish desire and broken homes. In keeping with this, these novels are as much marked by an agoraphobic fear of excessive freedom as they are by claustrophobia. The nostalgic regression of masculine Westerns was back to the 'wild frontier'; for women romance writers the interchange of regression and progression, dependency and independence, is altogether more difficult.

The awkwardness or tension of 'Western Lovers' novels is produced above all by an apparent incommensurability between sexual desire and family values. Amber Johnson is the heroine of *The Fairy Tale Girl*, for instance, a novel which forms part of the 'Denim & Diamonds' sub-series. Amber has gone back to the 'untamed landscape' of Colorado to try to recover from a disastrous marriage to an unreliable husband, when she meets Jake Kassidy. He stimulates in her 'forbidden sensual urges', forcing her to acknowledge that her sexual interest in him threatens to overwhelm her long-term interests and preoccupations: 'She jerked her eyes away, but they returned to watch in breathless need, shamelessly savoring every magnificent inch of him'.[8] Amber is trying to reassemble the broken pieces of her life, but 'her body had a will of its own' (p. 136). Part of her difficulty lies in the fact that sex not only threatens her interests but also offers an escape from her problems. In submitting to her desires she can experience a state of non-being which is at once a self-discovery and a self-forgetfulness: 'She was surrendering to a force more powerful than she'd ever known before. It was like dying, this totality of giving and needing' (p. 117). In keeping with much other romance fiction, in 'Western Lovers' passion is represented as 'melting' and 'shattering', as being 'crushed' and even 'pulverised'.

In a discourse that seems to explicate the romance, Bataille points to sex, violence and death as experiences which offer to transcend the boundaries of individuality. He suggests that the subject is haunted by a yearning for a lost continuity. Our individuation from others leads to a sense of alienation, but an act of love or one's death holds out the possibility of the dissolution of the boundaries between different bodies or between different stages of existence, closing the gulf or discontinuity upon which desire depends.[9] The paroxysms of sex and death both offer to obliterate the constraints of selfhood. A sense of fulfilment or plenitude is only to be gained through a 'radical disintegration and humiliation of the self', an experience of the body that is strong enough to destroy one's psychic organization.[10] By this logic the apparently selfish desire to be appeased is also a desire to transcend selfhood altogether, to lose one's attachment to oneself; it is to be both satisfied and virtuous. Pleasure and pain can, then, stand as metaphors for each other, in that they both offer an escape from the self. The desire for the obliteration of the constraints of selfhood might also be read in the light of Freud's theory of regression, in that we long to enjoy once more the totality of being that the infant is supposed to feel before she realizes her individuation from her mother. In this sense all desire is nostalgic – a fantasy of regression. Although the impossibility of desire may produce the death drive with its motive of transcending selfhood, this in itself represents a wish to approximate the plenitude of infancy. Or we might focus more narrowly on Nancy Chodorow's revision of Freud, as does Radway, to the effect that a mother supplies her own desire to be nurtured, by nurturing her children.

In a reading that supplements Radway's, I want to argue that in the 'Western Lovers' novels there is a privileging of the infantile but also a subliminal fear and loathing of motherhood. In *The Fairy Tale Girl* we discover very early in the novel that Amber's mother felt betrayed by motherhood, which meant a loss of opportunity: 'Her mother continually told her that having Amber had ruined her body and that she wished she'd never had a child at all. Not only that, but having a child had ruined her chances to catch a new man and make a new life for herself' (p. 9). Her mother's last words before she fell into a coma were: 'Amber, you were the greatest mistake of my life' (p. 12). Amber's own path toward a sexual relationship is marked by a fear of replicating the fate of her mother. When she first meets Jake, she is menaced by a rattlesnake. Later she calls him a snake, and, as we have already noted, she is appalled and fascinated by 'every magnificent inch of him' when he removes his underwear. It might be argued that although this novel and others like it glorify the idea of children and the family, the reptilian underside of passion is motherhood. Being a mother is potentially another kind of 'death', and another 'totality of giving and needing'. Indeed, in their endless and de-tailed references to flat, hard, male stomachs, these novels are worshipping not just the male body but the non-pregnant body.[11] Jake's body is the opposite of 'child-bearing': 'He was beautiful as only a man can be. His broad shoulders tapered to a narrow waist, slim hard hips, and long muscular legs' (p. 35). There is a potent and regretful note in the mention that he is beautiful 'as only a man can be', whereby it takes on the sense of 'as only a man is allowed to be'.

This unspoken contradiction between familialism, desire, and the feared betrayal of pregnancy, is often realized by way of relat-ively ephemeral signifiers. In Lindsay McKenna's *Heart of the Eagle*, part of the 'Reckless Renegades' sub-series, Dal Kincaid runs a ranch and monitors the progress of the eagles in her vicin-ity.[12] Jim Tremain meets her because he is investigating a spate of 'nest robbing'; there is a lucrative trade in eagles' eggs, and his first suspect is Dal. It transpires that it is Dal's angry former husband who has been robbing the nests, much as he refused to agree to Dal's becoming pregnant. But in spite of all this concern with the progenitive, *Heart of the Eagle* is as wedded to the ideal of the flat stomach as *The Fairy Tale Girl*. The novel does not end with pregnancy, but with various projections and displacements of the infantile. Jim buys two puppies, a male for him and a female for Dal; but their love for each other is not so much looking toward having a family as creating a space of childishness for and with each other. When Dal tells of how her husband disapproved of her as 'an immature child who needed to grow up', Jim reas-sures her: 'That's one of the many things I like about you. You are a child' (p. 103). He makes her feel 'like a little girl instead of a grown woman' (p. 158). The alliance of the regression to infancy with the death drive is equally apparent. After sex which feels to Dal like shattering 'into a million golden fragments' (p. 170), he brings her 'hot chocolate laced with tiny marshmallows, so that she thought she might cry . . . she thought she might die from happiness' (p. 173). This resolution of adulthood and childhood has its counterpart in the hero himself, who also reconciles contraries. For all the 'cougarlike leanness' of his body, Jim also takes on the gentleness and nurturance of the maternal. As Amal Treacher observes of the generic popular romance:

> The hero is endowed with maternal qualities; he is not simply the phallus but also the maternal phallus: the ideal mother and father ... The wish for the total love of the mother and father becomes the longing for that total love to be located within one's partner in adult life.[13]

Certainly Jim weeps on several occasions, and whereas Dal's husband saw tears as 'a sign of weakness', Jim sees them as 'a sign of trust' and of 'healing' (p. 63). The other binary that Jim breaks down, that of race in that he is part Navajo, is related to his incorporation of the feminine:

> 'As I said before, the Navajo are a people who were ruled by and gave homage to a woman. The Navajo men realize women are stronger in some ways than they are, so we try to open our senses like they do. When a woman sheds tears, she becomes cleansed. Our men have watched this for countless centuries and know the wisdom of her ways.' (p. 64)

Jim is archetypally masculine, but he is also importantly other. Whatever one thinks of this reductive usurpation of the Native American with its ridiculous Indianspeak, in the world of the novel Jim's difference means he can offer Dal a consecration which is not the trap of her abusive conventional marriage: 'Let us be free together and give the other the gift of ourself ... forever ...' (p. 169). *Heart of the Eagle* ends with the two lovers kissing as the puppies play in their laps. By now, however, the puppies do not necessarily signal Jim and Dal's procreative future, so much as their access to the infantile in themselves and in their relationship with each other. Maternity remains as distant, as ideal, as it was at the start.

In keeping with such philoprogenitive sleights of hand, it is interesting that even those novels specifically dedicated to recovering the family – and which have child-characters – also manage to avoid biological motherhood. The fantasy aspires to the ideological privileges of motherhood, but without some of its disadvantages. In this it seems to acknowledge the fact that motherhood both is and is not in women's interests. Child-bearing is always in the novel's prehistory, as in Annette Broadrick's *Hunter's Prey* (1985), part of the 'Kids 'n Kin' sub-series. In that novel, Kristi Cole returns to her marriage and her children after a lengthy break as a fashion model. Given the perfection of her post-child-bearing body, which she has proved in her career as a model, it is as though she has inherited the children rather than given birth to them. The family composed of inherited children is a favourite scenario in Silhouette Westerns: Robin Morgan's *The Cowboy and His Lady*, part of the 'Fabulous Fathers' series, is concerned with the rural West as a place in which to mend the damaged family.[14] Set in and around Paradise, Nebraska, the characters try to relocate themselves in the paradise of a stable home, the paradise of the 1950s that America has since lost. It features Joel Crawford, the champion rodeo rider, and his daughter Lacy, both of whom have been abandoned by Luann, the rodeo queen. Luann turned her back on her husband and daughter with no regrets, seeking only sexual gratification and success in her career. Joel returns to his home town of Paradise, hoping to bring Lacy up properly, far from the glitter and impermanence of the rodeo circuit. Megan Miller, on the other hand, has never left home. Her mother, Patrice, abandoned her when she was a child. Megan has stayed in Paradise, helping her father to bring up her younger sister. When the novel starts, Megan is finally able to leave Paradise for California, where she hopes to find her mother, and have a career in photography. What actually happens is that she falls in love with Joel, on whom she had had a crush as a fifteen-year-old. She also finds herself taking increasing responsibility for Lacy, whose childhood abandonment matches her own. Megan is torn between mending her own broken home by tracing her mother, and mending the broken home before her eyes. Eventually she discovers that her mother has remarried, to a man with a 'high-class chain of restaurants'. Megan's father has sent Patrice continual reminders of her daughters' existence, but this has never produced a response. Megan can give up on her quest to find her mother, because her mother was never lost, so much as uninterested. This leaves Megan free to love Joel and his daughter, making one home out of the two broken halves.

The reconciliation of the contraries of gender feature here as they did in *The Fairy Tale Girl* and *Heart of the Eagle*. Joel is strong and commanding; but he is also a good mother. He even takes on madonna overtones, when, for instance, the heroine sees him with his daughter, 'framed by an aura of love' (p. 25). In other ways, too, the novel depicts exchanges and mergings of roles. Megan was a 'mother' to her sister, once their actual mother had left. And yet this early responsibility meant that Megan was not so carefree as other girls, and failed to develop a romantic life of her own. A 25-year-old virgin, she became a mother, but also remained enclosed within childhood. As Joel reflects: 'The other night, Megan's kiss had seemed fresh and innocent, making him think she'd been locked away in her daddy's store too long' (p. 70). The infantilism of the heroine is part of her virginal attraction, but it also verges on the stale, of having been 'locked away in her daddy's store too long'. There is a tension between freshness and an 'on the shelf' spinsterhood.

Throughout, Megan is defined as both like and unlike a child. Joel is drawn to her because she 'hasn't changed a bit' from her self as a child. He tells her that she looks like 'one of those dolls a person can look at but never touch'. Again, he thinks of her as a 'perfect doll, the kind that comes in a protective box' (p. 116). Megan's sexual maturity is made to seem more available because, in other respects, she has the vulnerability of a child. This aspect of one role containing the values of another is constant. Lacy tucks her toy up in bed 'like a little mother', and tells Megan that the doll, Lacy, and her mother all look like each other (p. 167). When Joel and his daughter hug, Megan is left 'feeling like the odd child left out of the circle, struck by how much it hurt to only stand and watch' (pp. 161–2). As with the previous novels, there is a continuity between roles, with 'responsible adults' who also crave the protective love of a parent, and a child who yearns for the powers of parenthood. There is a freedom of emotional experience for the reader too. He or she has three points of identification within the narrative: those of the two adults, and that of the child. Within the romantic telos of the story of hero and heroine, the regressive subject position of childhood highlights the regressive elements of the romance itself, of how loving or being loved may bear resemblance to the dependencies of parent and child. The willing assumption of the responsibilities of parenthood by Megan and Joel might be seen as maturity, but it also has this opposite and compensatory element of regression to a condition without alienation, before the Fall from Paradise, before the need to grow up.

Desire must be seen to conform to the needs of parenting. Megan's desire, called into existence by the presence of the hero, is always enjoined by a sentimental response to the child. When Lacy has locked herself in a bathroom, and Megan is helping Joel to get her out, Megan is powerfully stirred by the way his T-shirt clings to his 'lean torso', but is drawn back to reality by the child's cry for help, which stirs 'instincts too strong to deny' (p. 40). Megan's responses are always seen as automatic when they involve mothering: 'Though Megan couldn't recall reaching out, seconds later Lacy was up and wrapped in her arms' (p. 44). She clasps the child without thinking, and then implicitly congratulates herself for the fact that her maternal action is not thought out but instinctive. Megan keeps her feelings under constant surveillance, only able to tolerate her own sexual desires when they are naturally subservient to the needs of family. At one point after kissing Joel she thinks: 'She planned to leave Paradise and it was clear that Joel intended to go things alone with his daughter. Whatever had triggered that kiss had best be ignored' (p. 62). Desire becomes an unnameable 'whatever' when it does not have immediate relevance to a family unit. The heroine's sexual fulfilment is tied up to her willingness to mother but not give birth to a child. *The Cowboy and His Lady* manages to admit motherhood to an extent that the other novels could not: Megan mothers her sister, and her boyfriend's daughter. But, crucially, it is constant with the other fictions in that it shies away from – does not actualize – biological motherhood. This novel, like the others, seems to turn upon something it cannot actually address: an ideological rupture between family values and sexual fulfilment, between child-bearing and the lean torso.

In *The Cowboy and His Lady* and other novels like it, the emphasis lies on commitment, on expressing desire but also on re-making the American family. But this dual necessity itself precipitates a series of problems. There is a superficial merging of genders, responsibilities and behaviours, and yet naturalized divisions are also maintained: women romance writers have both subverted and affirmed the traditional Western. Certain wishes are legitimated, but only under certain constraints. Other fears emerge in a displaced or subliminal form, and the tension between desire and family remains. The title of this chapter, 'Never love a cowboy', is taken from Jesse DuKore's novel of the same name, part of Bantam's 'Sweet Dreams Readers' series, designed for girls aged eleven and upwards. A woman should not love a cowboy because he will move on, because he is inimical to a woman's domestic interests. However, the message from DuKore's novel as much as from the 'Western Lovers' series is that the ideal is always in part inimical, irreducibly other. To this extent romance fiction always pivots on fantasy, on an impossible merging of incommensurable desires. The fantasy requites not merely present, possibly sexual wishes, but also nostalgic desires that remain from infancy. Such fantasy is inevitably accompanied by paranoia, haunted by its own impossibility. In this instance it takes the form of an unspeakable fear of maternity in the midst of a vaunting of family values: each novel contains a subliminal discourse on the liabilities of maternity. Given the financial and social marginalization that maternity often causes, one might also argue that the paranoia is not 'excessive'. If the pleasure that our heroines gain seems fantastical, the possibility that they may be left holding the baby does not. That much, at least, is for real.

Notes

1. Ann Barr Snitow, 'Mass market romance: pornography for women is different', in Kathy Peiss and Christina Simmons, eds, *Passion and Power: Sexuality in History* (Philadelphia, 1989), pp. 259–76, and Lynne Segal, 'Sensual uncertainty, or why the clitoris is not enough', in Sue Cartledge and Joanna Ryan, eds, *Sex and Love: New Thoughts on Old Contradictions* (London, 1983), pp. 38–47. I do not, by any means, accept any of these readings as an invariable truth. Studies of non-academic readers demonstrate a variety of responses and motivations, including guilt and an awareness of others' derision. See Janice A. Radway, *Reading the Romance: Women, Patriarchy, and Popular Literature* (1984; Chapel Hill, 1991).
2. How early one might begin a discussion of women's Westerns depends on how open a definition of the genre one will allow. In his excellent recent study, *Westerns: Making the Man in Fiction and Film* (Chicago, 1996), Lee Clark Mitchell includes writers such as Fenimore Cooper and Bret Harte, before moving on to the classic Westerns by Wister, Grey, L'Amour and others. But if Harte fits, then so would

Louise Clappe's *The Shirley Letters* (San Francisco, 1851–52); indeed, Harte is thought to have taken inspiration from Clappe's sketches. Even if we work within a much narrower definition of the Western, we could go back at least as far as Edna Ferber's *Cimarron* (1930). This chapter examines the later merging of genres, the intersection between women's popular romance and the Western.

3. On the gendering of American culture as it became increasingly industrialized, see Ann Douglas, *The Feminization of American Culture* (New York, 1977). For a broader and even dissenting view, see Carl Degler, 'What ought to be and what was: women's sexuality in the nineteenth century', *American Historical Review* 79:5 (December 1974), pp. 1467–90, and Carroll Smith-Rosenberg, *Disorderly Conduct: Visions of Gender in Victorian America* (New York, 1985). For a discussion of the Western as a reaction to this feminization, see John Cawelti, *The Six-Gun Mystique* (1970; Bowling Green, 1984), and especially Jane P. Tompkins, *West of Everything: The Inner Life of Westerns* (New York, 1992).

4. The moral tensions of formula fiction's engagement with civilization and lawlessness are shrewdly analysed by Cynthia S. Hamilton in *Western and Hard-Boiled Detective Fiction in America: From High Noon to Midnight* (Basingstoke, 1987).

5. The ambivalence of domesticity in novels such as *Little Women* – home as trap or haven – has featured in much critical work. Susan K. Harris, in *Nineteenth-Century American Women's Novels: Interpretive Strategies* (Cambridge, 1990), suggests that writers embedded radical possibilities within otherwise conservative thematic and rhetorical frameworks for a variety of reasons, but that their readers were quite capable of extracting the subversive elements from within a safe cover story. Specifically in relation to fiction for girls, *What Katy Read: Feminist Re-Readings of 'Classic' Stories for Girls* (Basingstoke, 1995) by Shirley Foster and Judy Simons argues that although 'the familiar behavioural codes of feminine self-effacement and domesticity are in the end reinforced, there are more suggestive "gaps" in the discourse of many of these texts which allow at least glimpses of alternative possibilities' (p. 6).

6. Rosemary Jackson, *Fantasy: The Literature of Subversion* (1981; London, 1988), pp. 3–4.

7. Tania Modleski, *Loving with a Vengeance: Mass-Produced Fantasies for Women* (Hamden, 1982), p. 111.

8. Ann Major, *The Fairy Tale Girl* (New York, 1987), p. 51. Further page references are included in the main text.

9. Georges Bataille, *Death and Sensuality: A Study of Eroticism and the Taboo* (New York, 1962), p. 12.

10. Jonathan Dollimore gives a usefully synoptic view of this longer tradition of a 'drive to undifferentiation' in 'Sex and death', *Textual Practice* 9:1 (1995), pp. 27–53. He also cites Bersani's essay, 'Is the rectum a grave?', on the idea that sexual practice may produce such a 'radical disintegration of the self'. Bataille's 'principle of loss', however, is framed rather differently, being based on Marcel Mauss's work on *potlatch* or gift theory. See 'The notion of expenditure', in *Visions of Excess: Selected Writings, 1927–1939*, ed. and trans. Allan Stoekl *et al.* (Minneapolis, 1985).

11. I am grateful to Lucie Armitt for suggesting the phrase 'non-pregnant body'. See also Armitt's discussion of the ambivalence of the mother/child dyad in relation to gothic fiction and fear of the metamorphic body in *Theorising the Fantastic* (London, 1996), where she reads *The Strange Case of Dr Jekyll and Mr Hyde* as representing a shift from 'the self-willed bodily changes of the planned pregnancy into a series of unwanted and unwilling maternal transformations' (pp. 131–2); and her essay in this collection, pp. 185–96.

12. Lindsay McKenna, *Heart of the Eagle* (New York, 1986). Page references are included in the main text.

13. Amal Treacher, 'What is life without my love?: desire and romantic fiction', in Susannah Radstone, ed., *Sweet Dreams: Sexuality, Gender and Popular Fiction* (London, 1988), p. 80.

14. This novel was first published as Robin Morgan's *The Cowboy and His Lady* (New York, 1984); it was reprinted in 1994 as by Robin Nicholas, in Silhouette's 'Celebration 1000'. Page references are included in the main text.

16 *Fantasy and the ideal of the individual in twentieth-century English domestic architecture*

Timothy Mowl

> The picture of a cottage crowned with a thatched roof, and with ivy and climbing roses and a small garden foreground suggesting old-fashioned perfume of flowers and a home in which dwell content and happiness, appeals straight to the heart of each of us, and there are few who can resist its quiet, peaceful influence for good.
>
> Sir William Lever, *Art and Beauty in the City*, 1915[1]

Benevolent sentimentality can be an irresistible force. In 1888 Lady Lever cut the first sod for Port Sunlight, a village for the workers of a Merseyside soap factory which idealized the country cottage aesthetic. In the same year, responding to a similar impulse, Charles Francis Annesley Voysey built his first stylized cottage for the middle classes at Bishop's Itchington in Warwickshire. Since that time the steep-roofed, gabled cottage has become so much the standard form of English housing at all class levels that it is hard to decide whether it still sustains a fantasy role for those who demand it, or whether it has become over the years merely a functional vernacular.

In a speech to the Royal Institute of British Architects, coincidentally exactly a hundred years after Voysey's first cottage and Port Sunlight's inauguration, the Classical Revival architect Robert Adam suggested that fantasy would in the long run always triumph over high-tech innovations, would absorb and conceal them.[2] Adam had just designed the Amdahl Computer Headquarters at Winchester, where an efficient, advanced technological interior is concealed within a traditional classical shell of Doric columns and pedimented bays which could pass for a late design by the eighteenth-century

Figure 1: A 'skeuomorph' villa proposed by Robert Adam, who believes that such a fantasy creation on the style of Nicholas Hawksmoor could enclose, without effort, every advance of twentieth-century technology.

architect, Nicholas Hawksmoor. His main point was the paradox that every advance of modern technology – synthetic materials, electronics and computer-ware – could also be used to build traditional gabled and pedimented estate houses. Fantasy, in fact, had fought a battle between historicism and high-tech futurism, and, by popular choice, historicism had won. Market forces, Adam maintained, were on his side and technology would continue to make its advances unhindered by the traditional fantasist outer shells of the buildings within which it was deployed, shells which market forces would continue to demand. Adam christened this process of camouflage 'skeuomorphism', a term used by archaeologists to describe old forms carried on into new cultures.

Considered from a European viewpoint, architectural fantasy got off to a remarkably bad start in England in 1900. In all the expanding cities of the Continent the fashionable style was the futuristic fantasy of the Art Nouveau, the fashion of the next two decades. In England it was virtually ignored as a serious architectural style. In most British towns and cities there are only a few suburban villas or commercial premises that toy thoughtfully with the Art Nouveau in their ceramics, metalwork or window architraves, the former Edward Everard Printing Works in Bristol of 1900 being a prime example of Art Nouveau faience decoration among these. Yet serious street exploration of cities as varied as Budapest, Riga, Vienna, Barcelona, Genoa, Milan, Prague, Brussels or Paris will give a reasonably accurate awareness of the Continent's commitment to stylistic experiment. Milan has over forty large apartment blocks which conceal their rectangularity by writhing metal balconies, upsurges of floral tiles across entire facades and nightmarish harpy faces of stone, stucco and terracotta smirking over their entrance ways. In the European outpost of Riga, the Gertrudes Street is lined with an uninterrupted march of six-storey apartments, all crested like breaking waves with the German version of Art Nouveau, the Jugendstil's inventions, and bristling with the ferocious dragons that were Baltic Russia's particular icons of the style. Even a Renaissance city like Mantua has an outrageously polychromatic Art Nouveau municipal centre. The celebrated Catalan architect Antonio Gaudi was no isolated Barcelona phenomenon. England was the architectural isolate, not for the first time, having largely ignored the seventeenth-century Baroque of the Continent, for a more staid Wrenaissance of predictable brick classicism, and reviving Palladio in the early eighteenth century when he had been 130 years in the grave. At the end of the nineteenth century the popular and acceptable domestic fantasy form was to be that of the homely cottage.

There were reasons, beyond insularity, for this British stand on style. There was a profound middle-class suspicion of living in apartments, however spacious or convenient for nearby theatres and concert halls; in nineteenth-century England apartments were for raffish bachelors or the poor of the Peabody Estates of inner London. There was a decadence implicit in creeping linear patterns, bulbous excrescences and hollow-eyed naiads; 'Tudric' pewterware from Liberty's, with its cautious hint of Celtic romance, was as far as most middle-class housewives cared to venture in matters of innovative design. There was a Romantic idealization of country

Figure 2: In Perrycroft, Worcestershire, a typical long, low ground-hugging house by C.F.A. Voysey, the architect offered spacious middle class accomodation within the illusion of a vernacular country cottage.

living for the well-to-do: a miniaturized country house with a large garden to potter in offered a fantasy of rural life in suburbia. The British bourgeoisie had innoculated itself against decorative excess by its uninhibited indulgence in historicism for the fifty years prior to 1890. That historicist fantasy of stylistic reference – houses in the Italianate, High Gothic, Jacobethan, neo-Norman, Loire Renaissance, Artisan Mannerist and Queen Anne Revival – filled the superior nineteenth-century suburbs. The style we describe, almost despairingly, as 'Victorian' is really no style at all but a mood of individual historicist fantasy, and by the late-1890s it was beginning to breed an exhaustion with decorative role-playing. For some years the mock Tudor had been gaining ground over its rivals. It was patriotic, wholesome in appeal, and rural in association.

This was the mood which Voysey shrewdly assessed. Over the next thirty years he was to satisfy the demand so completely that his tasteful simplicities of steep roofs and gables would become accepted as the standard English house of the twentieth century. Industrial magnates like the Levers and the Cadburys were generous in their social aspirations; and England had a long tradition of building picturesque estate cottages at a polite distance from country houses like Houghton Hall in Norfolk, Milton Abbey House in Dorset, and Blaise Castle House in the suburbs of Bristol. Lever picked this tradition up directly from his Cheshire neighbour, the Duke of Westminster at Eaton Hall, even using the Duke's favoured estate architect, John Douglas, to project the style for Port Sunlight. The result was so obviously superior that a precedent was set: industrial housing should not take the form of tenements or long rows of back-to-back terraces, it should be like an ideal English village with cottages, and preferably cottages of charm. The middle-class fantasy of rural living within a city was passed across to the workers.

In a 1907 Chairman's address to an International Housing Conference, Sir William Lever stated his simple high-minded faith:

> I am positive, from all the statistics available, that the most healthy conditions of the human race are obtained where the home unit exists in a self-contained house, with the living rooms on the ground floor and the bedrooms on the floor immediately over.[3]

Had he offered this and no more to the workers and retirees of his soap factory it would have been a prototype for the indifferent council estates of the twentieth century. What made Port Sunlight so much more remarkable than Bournville for the Cadbury workers in Birmingham was that it inherited from its leading architects, Douglas and Fordham (Douglas and Minshull after 1897), the ambitious and ornate design tradition of the estate houses around Eaton Hall. Gables and steep cottage roofs were the basic forms; in addition John Douglas introduced the expensive pargetting (external decorative plasterwork) and patterned half-timbering, with a mix of brick, terracotta and red sandstone, that he had practised on thirty or more lodges, farmhouses and cottages of the Westminster estates.

Responding to this diversity, Sir William Lever varied his architects, bringing in a different firm for each new range of houses: Grayson and Ould of Liverpool were specialists in half-timbered revivalism, Jonathan Simpson was an Arts and Crafts designer, T.H. Mawson and Sons had a Beaux-Arts background. Mainstream architects of the calibre of Ernest George, Edwin Lutyens and Ernest Newton all designed a house or two. What had begun

Figure 3: A range of several houses at Port Sunlight, Cheshire achieves William Morris's aim of reviving medieval forms for modern housing.

as a picturesque village cluster near the factory gates expanded over the marshy tidal creeks to the north into axial Beaux-Arts vistas laid out to the neo-Classical Lady Lever Art Gallery, the sandstone Gothic Revival Christ Church, the dining hall, the hospital, and Goscombe John's ambitious war memorial. Where the late twentieth century would build leisure centres that are glorified gymnasiums, the Levers built a cultural centre and stuffed it richly with nineteenth-century art. Not quite a town but far more than a village, Port Sunlight was a fantasy of how the future could be realized in the stylistic terms of the past. Constructed to a consistent policy of high decorative standards between 1888 and 1930, Port Sunlight was the perfect anticipation of the utopian architectural vision of William Morris's *News From Nowhere* (1890), where a largely timber-framed revival of Tudor medieval domestic architecture was proposed for everyone.

Port Sunlight was not intended to make any profit, it was a philanthropist's self-indulgence, the ornate late nineteenth century projected into the twentieth. It was Voysey who took those Tudor fantasy forms, stripped them of sixteenth-century detail and evolved a house form which was recognizably English yet timeless. This was what Voysey's former master, John Pollard Seddon, had urged when he wrote: 'we want neither a new nor a universal style, we should know nothing about styles; the very name is a hindrance to architects, however useful to the antiquary ... work simply, neither copying nor striving for singularity'.[4]

Functionalists such as Seddon, trapped in the notion that a utopian style must be one based upon common sense and expressed in common language, rarely notice that fantasy, the escape to another role, is a function second only to sound plumbing. Voysey was more sensitive to middle-class needs when he noted as the real essentials in domestic design: 'Repose, Cheerfulness, Simplicity, Breadth, Warmth, Quietness in a storm, Economy of upkeep, Evidence of Protection, Harmony with surroundings, Absence of dark passages, even-ness of temperature'.[5] It was a modest list of modest qualities. When public buildings in Edwardian Britain were pitching into pompous, civil service Baroque Revival, and Lutyens was moving from his subtle vernacular Surrey houses towards a fruity classicism, it was Voysey who caught the mood of that informed, sophisticated middle class for which E.M. Forster wrote his first novels; Voysey houses are for the Schlegels of *Howards End* and the Bartletts and Honeychurches of *A Room with a View*. They caught so perfectly the mood of their time and, in modified form, the mood of the new century, were both fantasy houses and suavely functional, which explains why Hermann Muthesius admired them so much in his influential, *Das Englische Haus* (1908–11).

The typical Voysey house is long, low and ground-hugging, under sweeping pitched roofs of grey-green slates. Its walls are rendered with white rough-cast for easy upkeep, buttressed more for an interesting profile than for actual support. The interior function of rooms is consciously displayed on the exterior, and well-equipped servants' quarters are thrown off to one side at an angle to produce an external profile of inventive asymmetry. A broad welcoming door leads to an interior of humane, low-ceilinged, cosy rooms. Convenient cupboards, chimney corners, window seats in angled-out bows, frequent shelved alcoves, are all there to enliven an easy flow of spaces upstairs and down. Period detail is noticeably absent – the important innovation. There are, of course, delicate Art Nouveau touches set almost subliminally in locks and light fittings, but the fantasy that this evokes is the fantasy of the nursery:

little rabbits and birds cosy up, half-hidden in metal work and wallpapers. Even the sinuosity of Voysey's wrought iron door furniture is usually a symmetrical sinuosity.

Later-twentieth-century speculative builders took up the Voysey pattern and shortened it to produce detached suburban road-liners, or cut it in two and bonded the identical halves together to create the gabled semi-detached. It was the gable which saved the box from being box-like and gave a sufficient air of the pretentious to the utilitarian. Perhaps the one frustration in Voysey's serene career is that he could have made sense of the cubist Modernism of the late 1920s and 1930s exactly as he had made sense of the mock Tudor; but he was only allowed to do so once. It happened long before Serge Chermayeff, Berthold Lubetkin and the other futurist utilitarians from Germany came in to amuse the interwar intelligensia with flat roofs and balconies that leaked, cantilevered corners that sagged and a 'machine à habiter' that passed with suspicious rapidity through a number of owners. Voysey had already designed several tower houses; in 1891 he was asked to build one in Chiswick for Mrs Forster among all the charmingly fussy, Queen Anne Revival houses of Bedford Park. As usual Voysey was faultless in his handling of abstract shapes. With its wide eaves, bull's eye windows and leaded lights divided by mullions, the house, for all its futuristic boldness and cubist apartness from its traditionalist neighbours, looks completely at ease. While John Betjeman and Osbert Lancaster were mocking Metro-land's Pooterish eclecticism in the 1930s and asking when England was going to produce 'a genuine modern architecture', Voysey's well-mannered answer was overlooked.

Voysey's influence continued, though it was never properly acknowledged. In 1903 the Garden City movement proposed by Ebenezer Howard and projected by a group of philanthropists and industrial directors, Lever and Cadbury included, became a reality at Letchworth in Hertfordshire. The aim was a planned town where the lessees would share in the profits as land values rose through the creation of a balanced whole: parks, schools, factories, and Voysey-type cottages, even down to the hand-made tiles. The Voysey influence could be seen in their eaves, rooflines, white walls, and winsome good looks, though Richard Barry Parker and his partner, Raymond Unwin, got the credit. Letchworth was such a success with its 120 exhibits at the 1905 'Cheap Cottages

Figure 4: Voysey's house designed for Mrs Forster in Bedford Park, West London in 1891 creates the fantasy of living in a tower with perfect suburban good manners.

Exhibition' that its example was followed all over the country. After the Second World War, New Towns like Harlow were developed on the same lines, but because their architects cut costs by removing the cottage fantasy element, Harlow today looks shop-soiled and depressed, whereas Letchworth has kept its value.

The other architect who could have offered the future, long before the Modernists came looking for it, was Charles Rennie Mackintosh. His fantasy interiors were so awesomely complete in their innovation that they were doomed to become museum pieces, something at which the twenty-first century should perhaps aim. Mackintosh houses owe their bewildering perfection to the fact that, designed by a true husband and wife team, Mackintosh and Margaret Macdonald, they respond to a wide range of aesthetic sensibilities. Every stick of furniture has been re-thought, every colour coordinated, yet, unlike those Modernist houses of the 1930s, nothing is crudely ruthless; delicate decorative detail – primroses and Celtic scroll-work – twines around all the geometrical abstractions. Their Glasgow town house, 78 Southpark Avenue, has been recreated within a dismal concrete shell in the city's Hunterian Museum and gains by the contrast. To enter it is to experience how life could be in an impossible aesthetic perfection – white pure and pastel – where one smouldering cigarette stub would be an offence. Yet everything has been conjured out of the ordinary room-set of a two-bay terraced house. The Hill House, Helensburgh, has the same refinement, its spaces carried by Margaret Macdonald into an ethereal delicacy. There, however, the exterior has enough of the Scottish Baronial in its conical capped turrets to satisfy the historicist aspirations of the Glasgow publisher, Walter Blackie, who commissioned it, two fantasies gratified in one house.

Histories of style are full of ifs and buts. Between them, Voysey and the Mackintosh pair could have taken the wind out of the sails of Modernism. But the Great War of 1914–18 left Europe in a mood for stylistic revolution. The two decades that followed were the only richly self-indulgent times for historicist fantasy building in twentieth-century England.

It was a rewarding time. The 'lower orders' were prosperous enough, and working-class labour was cheap enough, for house styles to be chosen at will. Architects had still not cornered the market with their designs; jobbing builders could seize their chance. Best of all, there were dozens of pattern books, full of house designs and plans in all manner of pastiche styles – Spanish, Tudor, Georgian, Dutch, Queen Anne, Sea-side Moderne and Rustic – priced from £250 for a tiny seaside bungalow to £1,500 or a little more for a flamboyant 'Des. Res.'. Now, by contrast, when building firms and capital are better organized, potential buyers on any new estate are limited for choice to perhaps four stylistic models all roughly similar but ranging in price. It is difficult to imagine how far more excitingly open the fantasy field was in the interwar period – difficult until one walks out along a 1930s bypass or around the leafy drives of mature developments of those

years, the Metro-lands which can be found in all commuter zones
of large cities.

John Betjeman, in his lovably bumbling, avuncular style, would
pour out appreciative, if faintly ironic, nostalgia over such houses
in his 1960s and 1970s television programmes. His script for
Metro-land to accompany a tracking shot along Oakington Road,
Wembley, reads:

> The show-houses of the newly
> built estates.
> A younger, brighter, homelier
> Metro-land:
> '*Rusholme*', '*Rustles*',
> '*Rustlings*', '*Rusty Tiles*',
> '*Rose Hatch*', '*Rose Hill*',
> '*Rose Lea*', '*Rose Mount*', '*Rose Roof*'.
> Each one is slightly different from the next,
> A bastion of individual taste
> On fields that were once bright with buttercups.[6]

However, when these houses were going up he disapproved of
their variety and their aspirations. 'Look up at the quiet houses
that flank the interminable avenue', he moaned in a 1937 lecture
entitled 'Antiquarian Prejudice', 'in poorer districts only a variation in the stained glass of a front door, the juxtaposition of gable
beams, or greater or less repulsiveness in the texture of rough-cast
differentiates one house from another'. Soon, he declared, in a
notably false prophecy, these would become the slums of the
future, 'bay windows will be falling out, foundations crumbling,
plumbing leaking, leaded lights letting in the rain ... that little
corner of a loving heart that is for ever Metroland, will be rather
unpleasant'.[7] The implication of Betjeman's article was that this
populist fantasy was indefensible, that these new householders
had no right to try to escape from towns, as the middle classes had
always tried to do, and in so doing despoil the beauties of the
English countryside. Betjeman's solution to the problem of housing the 'lower orders' was straight out of Le Corbusier's *Vers Une
Architecture* of 1923, translated into English by Betjeman's close
friend Frederick Etchells in 1927. 'We must create the mass-
production spirit', Corbusier had written, 'if we eliminate from
our hearts and minds all dead concepts in regard to the house ...

we shall arrive at the "House-Machine", the mass-production house, healthy (and morally so too) and beautiful in the same way that the working tools and instruments which accompany our existence are beautiful.' 'Architects have been too wrapped up in "style"', Betjeman parroted, 'to devote their attention to the only solution of the housing problem – the production of decent and convenient mass-produced houses.' Since the early 1930s he had been writing for the highly influential *Architectural Review* as it championed the cause of Modernism, so there was to be no consideration for Betjeman about continuity or any feeling for place: 'pre-fabrication would make it possible to remove these houses from one place to another when they were wanted, and the land they had occupied could go back to agriculture'.[8] With media manipulators like these swaying public opinion and cost-cutting at the top of the housing agenda, it was inevitable that disastrous errors would be made in the postwar housing regeneration of the 1950s.

The one laureate of suburban fantasy, drawing with precise linear observation and wit, was Osbert Lancaster, and even he seems to have despised the houses which amused him so much in his *Pillar to Post* of 1938 and *Homes Sweet Homes* of 1939. These brilliant parodies mocked everything, reducing a Voysey house to an ugly compact square and all the other suburban varieties to the laughably pathetic efforts of people without taste, their houses described variously as: 'Wimbledon Transitional', 'Pseudish' or 'By-Pass Variegated'. To make his example of 'Stockbrokers' Tudor' look silly, Lancaster parked an ultra modern Jowett Javelin saloon at the front door, introduced an electric pylon to the rear and drew the typical husband striding off to the golf club while his wife dutifully fluttered a duster from the balcony. Only when he came to his last victim, a cubist Modernist house, did a note of reverence creep in:

> Just as the cubist movement in painting produced little of any permanent artistic worth but nevertheless provided a most valuable discipline for number of painters, so it is to be hoped that from this bare functional style will one day emerge a genuine modern architecture that need fear no comparison with the great styles of the past.[9]

We are still waiting and, if Robert Adam's theory of 'skeuomorphism' is correct, may wait forever; there is now no need to wrap a high-tech interior within a banal high-tech facade.

Figure 5: Osbert Lancaster's affectionate parody of a suburban villa of the 1930s in South African Dutch style – green tiles, wavy gable and white walls. The illustration is taken from his *Pillar to Post* of 1938. By permission of John Murray (Publishers) Ltd.

The rich reality which inspired Lancaster's mocking cartoons can be hunted down in any of London's outer suburbs, but Bishop's Avenue in Hampstead seems to have upset his sense of architectural propriety most often. That ugly, multi-gabled scribble which he brands as 'Pseudish' is based on the Avenue's two serene evocations of South African Dutch, designed by Philip Hepworth, Gable Lodge of 1928 and Strathenden of 1931. As a result of Lancaster's effective humour the houses of Bishop's Avenue still tend to be dismissed as over-the-top indulgences. Fortunately the very rich have recovered their confidence and there have been several flamboyant new fantasies added quite recently to the Avenue, notably 'The Georgians' with wilfully spaced Doric columns supporting a giant pediment designed to evoke ante-bellum Missouri.

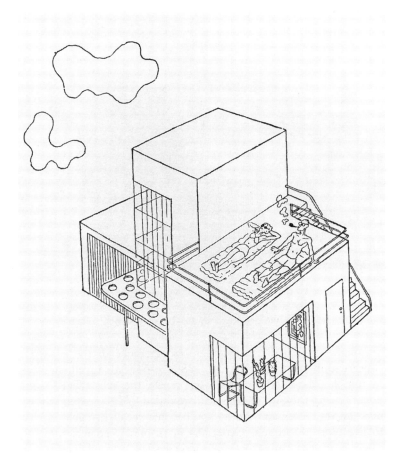

Figure 6: A less affectionate Lancaster parody taken from *Pillar to Post* (1938) of a cubist villa where a cubist couple live out their fantasy of inhabiting a scientific, pipe smoke-filled, minimalist future.
By permission of John Murray (Publishers) Ltd.

Through those dreary decades after the 1939–45 war, a few ageing heroes of classical survival soldiered on, like Raymond Erith and Francis Johnson, designing decent rather than fantasist houses for the gentry-minded, and by the late 1970s nostalgia and the first stirrings of the Heritage Industry gave a few house buyers the courage to demand a show of neo-Georgian columns or a

Figure 7: One of three fantasy villas designed in the late-1980s by Quinlan Terry for a highly desirable site on the edge of Regent's Park, London. The other two are Regency Gothic and Veneto Classical.

notional Tudor gable in shame-faced reference to the past. The conservation movement of the 1980s produced an elitist group of middle-class intellectual conservatives, the self-styled 'Young Fogeys', who took up the classically minded 'old fogies' and moved in wherever Georgian housing had become decayed. Their aim was to live like the original Georgians in ruthlessly correct interiors. Their hero was 'Superfogey' Prince Charles, praised for his controversial 1984 'Carbuncle' speech about a proposed Modernist extension to the National Gallery and for his attempts to build traditionally styled villages on his Duchy of Cornwall estates. As the Fogey fad satisfied both purists and masochists, it had a definite, if limited, appeal but it roused others to the potential charm of regenerated property.

Raymond Erith's main contribution to fantasy architecture was to have trained Quinlan Terry, and Terry has lived on long enough to raise a fantasist's New Jerusalem on the banks of the Thames. His Richmond riverscape is a perfect example of Robert Adam's 'skeuomorphism'. Behind an apparently organic growth of Georgian, Regency and Venetian Gothic facades, all of them modern,

Figure 8: The idea of a Classical skyscraper has always fascinated Robert Adam and he designed this Apollo Tower for BBC's *The Late Show* in 1988 to illustrate how easily a 'skeuomorph' shell could enclose a modern office tower.

Terry accommodated the complex needs of modern office technology. Indeed domestic fantasy has become positively modish, patronized appropriately enough by the politician Michael Heseltine with his summer house at Thenford in Oxfordshire. With even more assurance Terry has since designed and built three 'skeuomorph' villas along the edge of Regent's Park. Outwardly these are three historicist palazzos – one Georgian Gothick, one Ionic Palladian, one 'Veneto' Classical – inwardly they are served with all modern conveniences: three proofs that, for a price, fantasy houses can still be created in the heart of London.

It is in the domestic architecture of England's towns and cities, developments proposed for people on modest incomes, that fantasy fulfilment needs to be asserted, and a new generation of planners educated out of the dreary pieties of postwar austerity. In a crowded country cheap, plain building is one luxury we cannot afford. Two actively fantasist decades out of a possible ten has not been a healthy score for the twentieth century.

Notes

1. Edward Hubbard and Michael Shippobottom, *A Guide to Port Sunlight Village* (Liverpool, 1990), p. 6.
2. Adam's lecture is discussed in detail in Martin Pawley, *Theory and Design in the Second Machine Age* (Oxford, 1990), pp. 63–7.
3. John Brandon-Jones, *C.F.A. Voysey: Architect and Designer 1857–1941* (London, 1978), p. 19.
4. Hubbard and Shippobottom, *Port Sunlight*, p. 6.
5. Brandon-Jones, *Voysey*, p. 17.
6. John Guest, ed., *The Best of Betjeman* (Harmondsworth, 1978), pp. 223–4.
7. John Betjeman, *First and Last Loves* (London, 1960), pp. 54–72.
8. Ibid., p. 66.
9. Osbert Lancaster, *Pillar to Post: English Architecture Without Tears* (London, 1938), p. 80.

EXTRACT ONE

Herodotus 7.12–19, translated by Christopher Pelling based on the Oxford text of Herodotus, ed. K. Hude (1908)

Then night fell, and Artabanus's advice grated with Xerxes. During the night, the king reflected and firmly decided that it was pointless for him to attack Greece. With that resolved, he fell asleep, then in the night he saw the following dream, so the Persians say. He thought he saw a large, handsome man stand over him and say, 'Are you changing your mind, Persian, and deciding not to invade Greece, after telling the Persians to gather an army? You are wrong to change your mind, and there is not one here who will forgive you; just as you chose during the day, keep to that path.'

Then Xerxes thought he saw the figure fly away. Once day dawned he gave no thought to the dream, but reconvened the meeting and spoke as follows:

'Men of Persia, forgive me for changing my plans. My understanding is not yet at its peak, and those who give contrary advice never leave me alone. When I heard Artabanus's advice, at first my youthful temper boiled over, and I hurled words at him which were unseemly and inappropriate to use towards a senior man. Now I have realised the force in what he said, and I will follow his advice. So take it that I have changed my mind and decided not to invade Greece; you can stay at peace.'

When the Persians heard this, they fell at his knees in delight.

Night fell, and the same dream came to the sleeping Xerxes. It stood over him and said: 'Son of Darius, so you make it clear among the Persians that you have abandoned the expedition, and are dismissing my words as if they come from a nobody? Be certain of this, if you do not attack immediately, this is what will result for you: just as you became great and formidable in a short time, so swiftly will you be humbled once more.'

Xerxes was terrified by the dream. He leapt out of his bed and sent a messenger to fetch Artabanus. When he arrived, Xerxes said: 'Artabanus, my immediate response was wrong, when I answered your good advice with foolish words. But I soon changed my mind, and decided I ought to do as you advised. But now I cannot do this, despite my wish. For a dream keeps coming to me now that I have changed and reversed my plans, and it does not approve of my doing this; and now it has gone with a threat. Now, if it is a god who is sending this and it is simply his pleasure that I should attack Greece, this same dream will appear to you and give you the same instruction. My view is that this would happen if you took all my clothing, put it on, sat on my throne and then slept in my bed.'

Those were Xerxes's words. Artabanus did not agree at once to his instruction, for he did not think it right that he should sit on the royal throne; but finally he was left no choice, and obeyed the order with the following words: 'Lord, it is in my view as good a thing to be willing to follow good advice as to have wise thoughts oneself. You have both gifts, but you keep company with bad men who bring you down, just as they say the sea is never allowed by the winds to follow its own nature – the sea, the most useful thing of all to humankind. When you spoke to me harshly, I was not so distressed by your words: it was rather that there were two options before the Persians, the one encouraging arrogant outrage [hybris], the other quelling it and advising that it was a bad thing to school one's heart to be always greedy, and you chose the option which was more dangerous for yourself and for the Persians.

'Now you have changed to the better course and abandoned the Greek campaign, you say that a dream keeps coming to you from some god, not allowing you to give up the campaign. But these things are not divine, my child: I am much older than you, and I will explain to you the truth about these dreams which roam among humans. These dreams tend to represent what one has thought about during the day; and in the last few days we have been particularly occupied with this expedition. If I am wrong in analysing it in this way and if it is something divine, then you have already summed up the matter perfectly: let it appear to me with its commands, just as it did to you.

'But it should not be any more likely to appear if I wear your clothing than if I wear my own or if I sleep in your bed rather than mine, not if it really wishes to appear. Whatever this thing is that appears to you in your sleep, it cannot be so simple-minded as to mistake me for you because it sees me in your clothes. And if it thinks me worthless and does not choose to appear to me, whether I wear my clothes or yours, but comes again to you – well, that is something to discover. If it keeps coming, then I too would agree it was divine.

'If that is your decision, if there is no way of persuading you otherwise and I really must go to your bed and sleep, then let us do that: I shall do as you say, and let the dream appear to me too. Until then, I shall hold to my present view.'

So saying, Artabanus did what he was ordered: he expected to expose Xerxes's words as wrong. He put on Xerxes's clothing, took his seat on the royal throne, then went to bed; and the same dream came to him in his sleep as had come to Xerxes. It stood over Artabanus and said: 'Are you that man who is urging Xerxes not to attack Greece? But you will never – not now, not hereafter – succeed unpunished in deflecting what must happen. What Xerxes must suffer if he is disobedient, he has already been told.' And, Artabanus thought, after delivering these threats the figure was on the point of burning out his eyes with hot irons.

Artabanus let out a great shriek, leapt up, and went to Xerxes. After telling him about the dream, he spoke to him a second time. 'Lord, I am a human being, and I have seen many great fortunes fall at the hands of lesser powers; I would not let you give way to your own youthful temper in everything, knowing what a bad thing was great desire. I remembered the fate of King Cyrus's expedition to the Massagetae and King Cambyses's to the Ethiopians, and I was myself part of King Darius's campaign against the Scythians. With that knowledge, I thought that you would be blessed in the eyes of all mankind if only you remained in peace. But, given that there is some supernatural drive in this matter, and it seems that some divinely wrought destruction is overtaking the Greeks, I too change my mind and reverse my view. Go and tell the Persians what God is revealing; reinstate your previous orders about preparations; with God granting you this opportunity, nothing should be lacking on your part.'

That said, both men were cheered by the dream; and at daybreak Xerxes passed this on to the Persians, with Artabanus, the previous sole opposer, this time openly in support.

A third dream later came to Xerxes, now eager for the campaign; the Magi [dream-experts] interpreted it as relating to the whole world, and indicating that he would enslave the whole human race. He dreamed that he was wearing an olive crown, and the branches from this olive covered the whole earth: then the crown suddenly vanished from his head. After the Magi had delivered that interpretation, all the Persians immediately rode off to their own dominions, full of enthusiasm because of what had been said.

EXTRACT TWO

Tacitus, *Annals* 16.1–3, translated by Christopher Pelling based on the Oxford text of Tacitus, ed. C. Fisher (1906)

Fortune went on to mock Nero: the reason was his own shallowness and the promises of one Caesellius Bassus. Caesellius was a Carthaginian by birth, a man of disturbed mind. As he slept one night he had a vision which he took as an intimation of something quite certain. He travelled to Rome, and bought his way to an audience with the emperor: then he explained that a cave of immense depth had been discovered on his property, containing a vast sum of gold, not minted as money, but in its raw, ancient mass. Lying there were some very heavy ingots, with further piles standing nearby: it had remained concealed for so long, all in the interest of augmenting the prosperity of the present time. It was the Phoenician Dido (he added), so conjecture makes clear, who hid that wealth as she founded Carthage in exile from Tyre; her purpose was to prevent her infant people from moral excess in the presence of too much money, or to stop the kings of the Numidians, always hostile as they were, from being inflamed to war by their greed for the gold.

Nero reacted at once. He did not allow sufficient investigation of the plausibility of his informant or the story itself; he did not send anyone to check on the truth of the report. He even gave additional force to the rumours by sending people to collect the prize as if it were already there waiting for him. Caesellius was given warships and a picked crew to speed everything up. During those days this was the only topic of conversation, the ordinary people accepting it all as true, the sensible folk taking various views [or: 'a different view']. It so happened that the quinquennial games were being celebrated to mark Nero's second five years in power, and poets and orators seized on this as their choicest material to praise the emperor. 'It was not only the usual crops that now grew, nor was gold found mixed with other metals: the earth was producing with unprecedented fertility, and the gods were presenting wealth into our hands.' Such were the servile strains in which they spoke, with heights of eloquence matched only by their sycophancy. They had no worries about their listener's readiness to accept what he heard.

Luxury meanwhile crept upwards among these empty hopes; ancient wealth was consumed, as if a new source had been found which could be squandered for years to come. Public grants were already being lavished from this new wealth, and the expectation of riches became one of the causes of public impoverishment. For Bassus, after digging up his estate and the fields for some distance around, kept saying that this place or that place would be the site of the cave he had promised; and he was followed not merely by soldiers, but by a mass of countryfolk enlisted to carry through the work. Finally he set aside his madness. He said, wonderingly, that his dreams had never proved false before, and this was the first time he had been led astray. He escaped from his shame and his fear by taking his own life. Some authors say that he was put in chains and then later freed, with his property confiscated to replace the royal treasure.

EXTRACT THREE

Plutarch, *Marius* 45, translated by Christopher Pelling based on the Teubner text of Plutarch, ed. K. Ziegler, 2nd edn (1971)

Marius became consul for the seventh time. He came out on January 1st itself, the very first day of the year [86 BC], and executed a man called Sextus Licinius by throwing him from the Tarpeian Rock. That struck both Marius's party and the city as the clearest possible omen of the evils to come upon them.

Marius himself was already worn out by his efforts. He had seen too many terrors and too much toil, and it was as if he had reached the point of saturation and exhaustion in his thought-processes. He reflected that this new war was not going to be against people like Octavius and Merula, leaders of a motley crowd and a faction-ridden mob: now it was Sulla who was approaching, the man who had driven him from his country long before and now had driven back King Mithridates to the Black Sea. Such reflections broke his spirit. Visions floated before his eyes of his own long wanderings, his periods of exile, his perils as he was driven through land and sea. He fell into intense fits of despondency and night-terrors and horrifying dreams, with a voice saying again and again.

Dread is the lion's lair, e'en with the lion away.

His greatest fear was of troubled and sleepless nights, and he hurled himself into carousing and bouts of drunkenness inappropriate for a man of his age: he was trying to achieve sleep as a sort of escape from his own thoughts. Finally news [of Sulla] arrived from the sea. New terrors now beset him, and he developed a pleurisy, influenced both by his fear of the future and by feelings of repugnance and weariness instilled by the present: that is the version of the philosopher Posidonius, who says that he himself visited him during his illness and talked about the subject of his embassy. But a historian called Gaius Piso tells the story differently. Marius, he says, was walking with some friends after dinner, and as they talked he traced his life back through the years. He told them of his many changes of luck, and said that a man of wisdom and insight would no longer trust himself to Fortune. He then embraced his friends, took to his bed, and died a week later.

Some report that his ambition became totally clear during his disease and drove him to a strange delusion. He thought he was fighting the Mithridatic war as commander-in-chief; just as he had in real battles, he threw his body into all sorts of posture and movements, with fierce battle-shouts and shriek after shriek. So intense a lust for that campaign had overcome him, so impossible to deflect, borne of his desire for command and his jealousy. Here he was, seventy years old, the first man ever to hold the consulship seven times, with a household and wealth sufficient to satisfy a host of monarchs: and he was lamenting his own fortune, as dying too soon to achieve the success for which he yearned.

EXTRACT FOUR

Plutarch, *Sulla* 37, translated by Christopher Pelling based on the Teubner text of Plutarch, ed. K. Ziegler, 2nd edn (1973)

Sulla did not merely foresee his own death, but in a way he even described it. He finished the twenty-second book of his Memoirs two days before his death, and he says that the Chaldaean prophets had told him that he would live a good life and meet his end at the height of his good fortune. He also says that his son, who had died a little before his wife Metella, had appeared to him in his sleep, wearing poor clothes and begging his father to cease from anxious thoughts: he should come and join Metella in peace, and live with her a life free of trouble and toil.

EXTRACT FIVE

From 'The Confession of Arnaud Gélis, alias 'Botheler', of Mas-Saint-Antonin de Pamiers, a heretical convert', translated by Mark Philpott from *Le Registre d'Inquisition de Jacques Fournier, Évêque de Pamiers (1318–1325)*, ed. Jean Duvernoy, 3 vols (Toulouse, 1965) vol. 1, pp. 128–9.

The year of Our Lord 1320, 23 February. Since it had been reported to the Reverend Father in Christ, the Lord Jacques, by the Grace of God bishop of Pamiers, that Arnaud Gélis, also known as *Botheler* [butler], of Mas-Saint-Antonin had said that he had seen the souls of dead people and that he had spoken with them, and that he had reported their words to their former friends, and that thus having been deluded by diabolical phantasms he had deluded a number of others; and that moreover the said Arnaud said and believed and, as far as he could, persuaded others to believe many things comprised of heretical perversity about the spirits or souls of dead men and women; the said Lord Bishop, wishing to inquire into the truth about what is written above with the said Arnaud, in the presence of Brother Gaillard de Pomiès, deputy for the lord Inquisitor of Carcassonne (the tenor of whose commission is transcribed below), had summoned before him the said Arnaud Gélis to swear on the Holy Gospels of God to tell the pure, simple and complete truth, as much as a principal concerning himself, as a witness concerning others living and dead. He said and confessed as follows:

First, that when Hugues Durfort, a canon of the church of Pamiers, in whose household and whose servant Arnaud had been, died eight or nine years ago, on the fifth day after the death, when Arnaud was in his bed at night sleeping, in the home which he has in Mas aforesaid; the said canon awoke him and once he was awake he saw one canon in a surplice, with his hood on his head, and he saw this, as he said, by the glow from the fire which had spread out in the hearth, although he had covered the fire when he went to bed.

And, when he saw the said canon he was afraid and asked him who he was and why he had come into the said home. He replied that he was Hugues Durfort. When the said Arnaud said to him that he was dead and that he asked him not to touch him and that he should go away, the said canon told him not to be afraid of him, since he would never do him harm, and that he should come to him the next day in the monastery of Saint-Antonin, as he wanted to speak to him there. When he said to him that he did not know where he could find him as he was already dead, the said Hugues said to him that he would find him in the aforementioned monastery. Having said these things, the said Hugues went away.

And, Arnaud coming the next day to the monastery, found the said dead man, Hugues, standing, leaning against the door of the chapter house at the head of his tomb, wearing a surplice with his hood on his head and was, as it seemed to him, of the same shape and form as he had been when he was alive. And, reaching him, he took off his hood and greeted the said Hugues, and he returned the greeting. And when the said Arnaud said to him that God would give him paradise; the said Hugues replied that God would do this and that he believed he would shortly be in paradise.

And, then the said Hugues said to him that he should tell Brunissende, his sister, the wife of Arnaud de Calmelles of Pamiers, that she should have two or three masses said for his soul and that thus he would go to rest.

And, immediately having said these things, the said Hugues disappeared as he [Arnaud] was leaving. And Arnaud went immediately to the said Brunissende and told her the above, and the said Brunissende had the said three masses celebrated for the said Hugues. And afterwards, before the said masses had been celebrated, he [Arnaud] used to go to the said monastery, and saw the said Hugues two or three times in the aforementioned place, who asked him if he had told his sister the aforementioned things, and he replied that he had. And after the said masses had been celebrated, the said Arnaud did not see the said Hugues, because he had gone to rest.

[*Arnaud then tells how he has met a number of other dead people (Hugues de Rous, Athon d'Unzent, Pierre Durand, canons of St Antonin; Bernard, bishop of Pamiers; Barcelone, the mother of Arnaud de Calmelles; Pons Malet; Barcelone, the widow of Pons Fauré; etc.) who have made of him various requests or merely talked to him.*]

EXTRACT SIX

'Concerning Henry "Nodus" who after his death appeared visibly to many people', translated by Mark Philpott from Caesarius of Heisterbach, *Dialogus Miraculorum*, 12, 15, ed. Joseph Strange, 2 vols (Cologne, 1851), vol. 2, p. 327

In the bishopric of Trier, in which the appearance mentioned above also took place, there was another knight called Henry, surnamed 'Nodus'. Now, he too was an extremely wicked man, accounting as virtues pillage, adultery, incest, perjury and similar vices. After this man had died in the province of Menevelt, he appeared to many people, in a sheep skin which he had been accustomed to wear when he was alive, frequenting above all the home of his daughter. Neither by the sign of the cross, nor by the sword could he be driven away. He was often hit with a sword, but he could not be wounded, only giving out a sound like a soft bed being struck. When his friends consulted the Lord Bishop John of Trier about this, he advised that the house and the daughter and the man himself (if he were there) should be sprinkled with water that had been poured over a nail from the Lord's Cross. When this was done Henry did not appear again. He had fathered this daughter on his maid, although he had a legitimate wife; when the daughter had grown up the wretch corrupted her. It is not long ago that these things happened.

EXTRACT SEVEN

From Ben Jonson, *The Vision of Delight* (1617)

The Vision of Delight Presented At Court in Christmas 1617

THE SCENE

A street in perspective of faire building discovered.

DELIGHT

Is seene to come as afarre off, accompanied with

Grace, Love, Harmonie, Revell, Sport, Laughter

WONDER following.

DELIGHT spake

in song (*stylo recitativo.*)

Let us play, and dance, and sing,
    let us now turne every sort;
O' the pleasures of the Spring,
    to the graces of a Court.

From ayre, from cloud, from dreams, from toyes,
    to sounds, to sence, to love to joyes;
Let your shewes be new, as strange,
    let them oft and sweetley varie;
Let them haste so to their change,
    as the Seers may not tarrie;
Too long t'expect the pleasing't sight
    doth take away from the delight.

Here the first Anti-maske *enter'd.*

A she Monster delivered of sixe Burratines, *that dance with sixe* Pantalones,
which done

DELIGHT, spoke againe.

Yet heare what your delight doth pray
    all sowre and sullen looks away,
    that are the servants of the day,
        Our sports are of the humorous night,
Who feeds the stars that give her light,
    and useth (then her wont) more bright,
    to help the vision of DELIGHT.

Here the Night rises, and tooke her Chariot bespangled with starres.

DELIGHT, *proceeds.*
See, see her Scepter, and her Crowne
are all of flame, and from her gowne
a traine of light comes waving down.
This night in dew she will not steepe
The braine, nor locke the sence in sleepe;
but all awake, with *Phantomes* keepe,
and those to make DELIGHT more deep.

By this time the Night, *and* Moone *being both risen;* Night *hovering over the place,* Sung

Breake *Phant'sie*, from thy cave of cloud,
and spread thy purple wings;
Now all thy figures are allow'd,
and various shapes of things;
Create of ayrie formes, a streame;
it must have bloud, and nought of fleame,
And though it be a waking dreame;
The Quire Yet let it like an odour rise
to all the Sences here,
And fall like sleep upon their eies,
or musick in their eare.

The Scene *here changed to Cloud, and* Phant'sie *breaking forth, spake.*

Bright Night, I obey thee, and am come at thy call
But it is no one dreame that can please these all;
Wherefore I would know what Dreames would delight'em;
For never was Phant'sie more loath to affright'em.
And Phant'sie I tell you, has dreams that have wings,
And dreams that have honey, and dreams that have stings;
Dreames of the maker, and Dreames of the teller,
Dreames of the kitchin, and Dreames of the Cellar:
Some that are tall, and some that are Dwarffes,
Some that were halter'd, and some that weare scarffes;
Some that are proper, and signifie o'thing,
And some another, and some that are nothing:
For say the French Verdingale, and the French hood
Were here to dispute; must it be understood
A feather, for a wispe, were a fit moderator?
Your Ostrich, beleeve it 's no faithfull translator

Of perfect Utopian; And then it were an od-piece
To see the conclusion peepe forth at a cod-piece.
     The politique pudding hath still his two ends,
Tho the bellows, and the bag-pipe were nev'r so good friends:
And who can report what offence it would be
For the Squirrell to see a Dog clime a tree?
If a Dreame should come in now to make you afeard,
With a Windmill on his head, and bells at his beard;
Would you streight weare your spectacles, here, at your toes,
And your boots o' your browes, and your spurs o' your nose?
Your Whale he will swallow, a hogs-head for a pill;
But the maker o' the mouse-trap, is he that hath skill.
And the nature of the Onion, is to draw teares,
As well as the Mustard; peace, pitchers have eares,
And Shitlecocks wings, these things doe not mind 'em.
If the Bell have any sides, the clapper will find'em:
There's twice so much musicke in beating the tabor,
As i' the Stock-fish, and somewhat lesse labour.
Yet all this while, no proportion is boasted
T'wixt an egge, and an Oxe, though both have been rosted,
For grant the most Barbers can play o' the Citterne,
Is it requisite a Lawyer should plead to a Ghitterne?
     You will say now, the Morris-bells were but bribes
To make the heele forget that ev'r it had kibes;
I say let the wine make nev'r so good jelly,
The conscience o' the bottle is much i' the belly:
For why? doe but take common Councell i' your way,
And tell me who'le then set a bottle of hay
Before the old Usurer, and to his horse
A slice of salt butter, perverting the course
Of civill societie? open that gap,
And out skip your fleas, foure and twenty at a clap,
With a chaine and a trundle-bed following at th' heeles,
And will they not cry then, the world runs a wheeles:
As for example, a belly, and no face,
With the bill of a Shoveler, may here come in place;
The haunches of a Drum, with the feet of a pot,
And the tayle of a Kentishman to it; why not?
Yet would I take the stars to be cruell,
If the Crab, and the Ropemaker ever fight duell,
On any dependance, be it right, be it wrong,
But mum; a thread may be drawne out too long.

Here the second Anti-masque *of* Phantos'mes *came forth, which danced.*

PHANT'SIE *proceeded.*

Why? this you will say was phantasticall now,
As the Cocke, and the Bull, the Whale, and the Cow;
　　But vanish away, I have change to present you,
And such as I hope will more truly content you:
　　Behold the gold-haired *Houre* descending here,
That keepes the gate of Heaven, and turnes the yeare,
　　Alreadie with her sight, how she doth cheare,
And makes another face of things appeare.

Here one of the Houres *descending, the whole Scene changed to the*
Bower of Zephyrus, *whilst,* Peace *sung, as followeth*

　　　Why looke you so, and all turne dumbe!
　　　　　to see the opener of the New-yeare come?
　　　My presence rather should invite,
　　　　　and ayd, and urge, and call to your delight,
　　　The many pleasures that I bring
　　　　　are all of youth, of heate, of life, and spring,
　　　And were prepared to warme your blood,
　　　　　not fixe it thus as if you Statues stood.

	we see, we heare, we feele, we taste,
	we smell the change in every flowre,
The Quire	we onely wish that all could last,
	and be as new still as the houre.

The song ended.
WONDER *spake.*

WONDER must speake, or breake; what is this? growes
The wealth of Nature here, or Art? it showes
As if *Favonius*, father of the Spring,
Who, in the verdant Meads doth reigne sole king,
Had rowsed him here, and shooke his feathers, wet
With purple swelling Nectar? and had let
The sweet and fruitfull dew fall on the ground
To force out all the flowers that might be found:
　　Or a *Minerva* with her needle had
Th'enamoured earth with all her riches clad,
And made the downie *Zephire* as he flew
Still to be followd with the Spring's best hue?
　　The gaudie Peacocke boasts not in his traine,
So many lights and shadowes, nor the raine-
Resolving *Iris*, when the Sun doth court her,

Nor purple Phesant while his Aunt doth sport her
To heare him crow; and with a pearched pride
Wave his dis-coloured necke, and purple side?
     I have not seene the place could more surprize,
It looks (me thinkes) like one of natures eyes,
Or her whole bodie set in art? behold!
How the Blew-binde weed doth it selfe infold
With Honey-suckle, and both these intwine
Themselves with Bryonie and Jessamine,
To caste a kinde and odoriferous shade?

PHANT'SIE

How better than they are, are all things made
By WONDER? But a while refresh thine eye,
Ile put thee to thy oftner, what, and why?

*Here (to a loud musicke) the Bower opens, and the Maskers discovered,
as the glories of the Spring.*

WONDER *againe spake.*

Thou wilt indeed; what better change appeares?
Whence is it that the ayre so sudden cleares,
And all things in a moment turne so milde?
Whose breath or beams, have got proud earth with child,
Of all the treasure that great Natur's worth,
And makes her every minute to bring forth?
How comes it Winter is so quite forc't hence,
And lockt up under ground? that every sence
Hath severall objects? Trees have got their heads,
The fields their coats? that now the shining Meads
Doe boast the *Paunce*, the *Lillie* and the *Rose*;
And every flower doth laugh as Zephire blowes?
That Seas are now more even then the Land?
The Rivers runne as smoothed by his hand;
Onely their heads are crisped by his stroake:
How plaies the Yeareling with his brow scarce broke
Now in the open Grasse? and frisking Lambs
Make wanton Salts about their dry-suckt Dams;
Who to repair their bags doe rob the fields?
     How is't each bough a severall musicke yeilds?
The lusty *Throstle*, early *Nightingale*
Accord in tune, though varie in their tale?
     The chirping *Swallow* cald forth by the Sun,
And crested *Larke* doth his division run?

The yellow *Bees*, the ayre with murmure fill?
The *Finches* caroll, and the *Turtles* bill?
Whose power is this? what God?

PHANT'SIE

Behold a King
Whose presence maketh this perpetuall *Spring*,
The glories of which Spring grow in that Bower,
And are the marks and beauties of his power.

                    To *which the Quire answered.*

          Tis he, tis he, and no power els
          That makes all this what *Phant'sie* tels;
          The founts, the flowers, the birds, the Bees,
          The heards, the flocks, the grasse, the trees,
          Do all confesse him; but most *These*
          Who call him lord of the foure Seas,
          King of the lesse and greater Iles,
          And all those happy when he smiles.
                  Advance, his favour calls you to advance,
          And do your (this nights) homage in a' dance.

Here they danced their entry, after which they sung againe

          Againe, againe; you cannot be
          Of such a true delight too free,
                  Which who once saw would ever see;
          And if they could the object prize,
          Would while it lasts not think to rise,
                  But wish their bodies all were eyes.

They Danc'd their maine Dance, after which they sung.

          In curious knots and mazes so
          The Spring at first was taught to go;
          And *Zephire*, when he came to wooe
          His *Flora*, had their motions too,
                  And thence did *Venus* learne to lead
          Th'*Idalian* Braules, and so tread
          As if the wind, not she did walke;
          Nor prest a flower, nor bow'd a stalke.

They Danc'd with Ladies, and the whole Revells followed: after which Aurora *appeared (the* Night *and* Moone) *descended, and this* Epilogue *followed.*

> I was not wearier where I lay
> By frozen *Tythons* side tonight;
> Then I am willing now to stay,
> And be a part of your delight.
>   But I am urged by the Day,
> Against my will, to bid you come away.

The Quire.

> They yeild to Time, and so must all.
> As Night to sport, Day doth to action call,
>   Which they the rather doe obey,
> Because the Morne with Roses strew's the way.

Here they Danc'd their going off,

and Ended.

EXTRACT EIGHT

From Henry Neville, *The Isles of Pines* (1668)

Idleness and Fulness of every thing begot in me a desire of enjoying the women, beginning now to grow more familiar, I had perswaded the two Maids to let me lie with them, which I did at first in private, but after, custome taking away shame (there being none but us) we did it more openly, as our Lusts gave us liberty; afterwards my Masters Daughter was content also to do as we did; the truth is, they were all handsome Women, when they had Cloathes, and well shaped, feeding well. For we wanted no Food, and living idlely, and seeing us at Liberty to do our wills, without hope of ever returning home made us thus bold: One of the first of my Consorts with whom I first accompanined (the tallest and handsomest) proved presently with child, the second was my Masters Daughter, and the other also not long fell into the same condition: none now remaining but my *Negro*, who seeing what we did, longed also for her share; one Night, I being asleep, my *Negro*, (with the consent of the others) got closse to me, thinking it being dark, to beguile me, but I awaking and feeling her, and perceiving who it was, yet willing to try the difference, satisfied my self with her, as well as with one of the rest: that night, although the first time, she proved also with child, so that in the year of our being here, all my women were with child by me, and they all coming at different seasons, were a great help to one another.

The first brought me a brave Boy, my Masters Daughter was the youngest, she brought me a Girl, so did the other Maid, who being something fat sped worse at her labour: the *Negro* had no pain at all, brought me a fine white Girl, so I had one Boy and three Girls, the Women were soon well again, and the two first with child again before the last two were brought to bed, my custome being not to lie with any of them after they were with child, till others were so likewise, and not with the black at all after she was with child, which commonly was at the first time I lay with her, which was in the night and not else, my stomach would not serve me, although she was one of the handsomest Blacks I had seen, and her children as comly as any of the rest; we had no clothes for them, and therefore when they had suckt, we laid them in Mosse to sleep, and took no further care of them, for we knew, when they were gone more would come, the Women never failing once a year at least, and none of the Children (for all the hardship we put them to) were ever sick; so that wanting now nothing but Cloathes, nor them much neither, other then for decency, the warmth of the Countrey and Custome supplying that Defect, we were now well satisfied with our condition, our Family beginning to grow large, there being nothing to hurt us, we many times lay abroad on Mossey Banks, under the shelter of some Trees, or such like (for having nothing else to do) I had made me several Arbors to sleep in with my Women in the heat of the day, in these I and my women passed the time away, they being never willing to be out of my company.

EXTRACT NINE

From *The German Princess Revived: or The London Jilt* (1684)

During all which time *Jenny* our now Knight Errant and her said Comrade Rid onward, Rejoyceing in their Good Success, every Day committing some new Robbery or other, to the great encrease of their Confidence and Store. *Jane Voss* still continuing her Manlike Garb, and Travelling the Country as a Gentleman of Fortune: But as the old Proverb hath it, the Pitcher goes not so often to the Well, but it comes Broken Home at Last: So in the mid'st of this Sun-shine of Prosperity, the Clouds of Adversity fell at length in showers upon her Head: For one Day going into a Fair to sell a Horse which they had worn out, in a Market Town in *Wiltshire*, the Party from whence they Stole the same came by chance thither, and owning the Horse, they were both Apprehended and clap'd into Goal.

This cross Adventure was not a little Baulk to our two Gallants, who were miserably Loaded with *Irons*, and the *Assizes* drawing on, they began to be Apprehensive of that Fate that Threatned them, which set *Jenny's* Brains a Working how to deliver herself, she being all this while in Mans Cloaths and her Sex undiscovered, which made much for her Advantage, for being of a Comely Personage, and having the Beauty of a Woman to add to the appearance of Manhood, the same was taken notice of by the Goalers Wife, who had more than a Months mind to be dealing with her, which *Jenny* soon observed, and improved, insomuch that she grew every day more in Favour than other, and at last by her means got rid not only of her own, but her Comerades *Irons*, and soon after of her Imprisonment: For the Gaolers Wife being very eager to bring her supposed Gallant to her Embraces, (and withal having no good Opinion of her Husband, who was Old and Peevish) appointed her one Evening to come to her Chamber, her Husband being out of the way; and fearing least the same should come to a Discovery, ordered the meeting to be in the Dark, and injoyned each to the other the strictest Silence Imaginable.

The hour appointed came, and *Jenny's* Husband was ordered to carry on the first scene of this Comedy, hopeing thereby to accomplish both their Liberties; nor indeed was he wanting in his Part: tho it answered not his Expectations, but released *Jenny* only, for he gave the Goalers Wife the greatest Satisfaction she could hope for, apprehending it all the while to be *Jenny's* own Person, for whom she had an extraordinary Affection. And the next Morning returning her Thanks accordingly, at which time the Goalers Wife, agreed to give way to her Escape, and run Fortunes with her. To Faciliate which, a Suit of Womens Apparrel was provided to array *Jenny*, and the next Night appointed for her Escape, which tho she would fain have had accompanied by that of her Comerade, yet could she obtain no more than her own, the Goalers Wife being jealous, that if they went out together they would decieve and desert her: Hereupon *Jenny* was forced to leave her first pretended Husband, who the next *Assizes* suffered for the Robbery, whilst in the mean time *Jane Voss* had got far enough from the reach of her Adversary, for by the favour of the Promise aforesaid, at the Hour appointed she found the Door Opened, and the Goalers Wife ready to discharge her, telling her that there was at such a place without the East part of the Town a little House at the Sign of the *Red-Cross*, where if she tarried half an Hour she would come and bring her a Horse and *Pillion*, on which she might Ride to a Place of Safety: But *Jenny* not intending to be so Incumbred took the quite contrary Road, and Travelled with all the speed her Feet could carry her that Night, till the next Morning coming to a Town where the Waggon stood for *London*: She takes place therein as a maid that went to seek a Service in Town, and accordingly Escaped, whil'st the Disappointed Gaolers Wife Lamenting the Infidelity of her supposed Lover, was overtaken by her enraged Husband, who ever after made her lead a worse Life than before this Fault she had done.

Select bibliography

Annotation is by the author of each chapter.

General

Apter, T.E., *Fantasy Literature: An Approach to Reality* (London, 1982).
Argues that rather than repressing unconscious worries which have not
been dealt with, fantasy investigates them. Disputes the claim that
fantasy necessarily produces aesthetically complex or original forms,
as claimed by many literary critics.

Armitt, Lucie, *Theorising the Fantastic* (London, 1996). Examines the
impact that recent literary theory has had upon our understanding of
the fantastic in fiction. Armitt focuses on how the fantastic is engaged in
a dialogue with rules which construct reality, rather than being centred
on particular genres; she looks in particular at the 'other' associated
with somatic distortion, mirroring, excess, lacunae and the grotesque.

Brooke-Rose, Christine, *A Rhetoric of the Unreal: Studies in Narrative
and Structure, Especially of the Fantastic* (Cambridge, 1981). Appeals
to a postmodernist scepticism about knowledge to put fantasy at the
heart of how reality is represented, noting how amenable both are to
modelling by the writer's desires.

Cornwell, Neil, *The Literary Fantastic: From Gothic to Postmodernism*
(Hemel Hempstead, 1990). In its dialogical, interrogative method, and
its strong political and ethical thrust, the fantastic cannot be seen as
marginal; rather, it is the dominant mode of the twentieth century.

Easthope, Antony, *Poetry and Phantasy* (Cambridge, 1989). Uses decon-
struction and psychoanalysis to account for the relationship between
poetry and its readers. Understands art as a publicly available site for
the reader to fantasize. Literary works from the seventeenth century
onwards are examined as phantasies of narcissism and domination,
produced by readers and writers.

Jackson, Rosemary, *Fantasy: The Literature of Subversion* (1993; London, 1981). Reads works of fantastic literature from the nineteenth

century onwards as subversive as much as conservative. Relies on the paradoxical dependence by fantasy on the absent, and thus the desired.

Manlove, C.N., *Modern Fantasy: Five Studies* (Cambridge, 1975). Defends the idea of fantasy as a literary genre, in which texts deliberately answer each other as much as comment on their subject.

Monleón, José B., *A Specter is Haunting Europe: A Socio-historical Approach to the Fantastic* (Princeton, 1990). Details the appropriation of the rhetorics of fantasy and reason to the French Revolution of 1789, the Europe-wide uprising of 1848, and the Bolshevik Revolution of 1917. The fantastic produced a cultural space for the fears expressed by and about the revolutions.

Rose, Jacqueline, *States of Fantasy* (Oxford, 1996). Far from being a solely private mode, a collective ethical fantasy is behind the notion of the social. Israel provides a contentious example: a nation whose origins lie in desire rather than topography, and whose status is threatened by its vulnerability to redescription from within and without.

Todorov, Tzvetan, *The Fantastic: A Structural Approach to a Literary Genre*, trans. R. Howard (Ithaca, 1975). Defines the fantastic as the moment of reception of a text at which a reader is unable to determine whether what has occurred is supernatural (the marvellous) or due to psychological factors (the uncanny).

1   Modern fantasy and ancient dreams

Brenk, Frederick E., 'In mist apparelled', *Mnemosyne* Supp. 48 (1977), pp. 214–36. A sensitive discussion of the function of dreams in Plutarch's *Lives*.

MacAlister, Suzanne, *Dreams and Suicides: The Greek Novel from Antiquity to the Byzantine Empire* (London, 1996). A sophisticated account of the narratological function of dreams in the ancient novel.

Miller, Patricia Cox, *Dreams in Late Antiquity: Studies in the Imagination of a Culture* (Princeton, 1994). Ranges much more widely than the title suggests, setting the early Christian material against its background in the Roman oneiric tradition.

Pelling, Christopher, 'Tragical dreamer: some dreams in the Greek and Roman historians', *Greece and Rome* 44 (1997), pp. 197–213. Argues that dreams gain a different significance as ancient historiography develops, with increasing light shed on the mentality of the dreamer.

Price, S.R.F., 'The future of dreams: from Freud to Artemidoros', in D.M. Halperin, J.J. Winkler and F.I. Zeitlin, eds, *Before Sexuality: The Construction of Erotic Experience in the Ancient Greek World* (Princeton, 1990), pp. 365–88. Discusses the differences between ancient and modern dream interpretation, laying particular stress on the way social status affects the significance of particular dreams.

Winkler, John J., *The Constraints of Desire* (New York, 1990), pp. 17–44. Discusses the light shed by ancient dreams on the protocols of sexuality.

2 The fairy mistress in medieval literary fantasy

Cox, Harvey, *The Feast of Fools: A Theological Essay on Festivity and Fantasy* (New York, 1969). A nuanced, if now somewhat dated, consideration of fantasy and playfulness in religion and ritual from a part-anthropological, part-theological viewpoint.

Jameson, Frederic, 'Magical narratives: romance as genre', *New Literary History* 7 (1975), pp. 133–65. Intelligent discussion of romance as genre, situating it usefully in historical context, but missing some crucial distinctions in the ethics of medieval romance.

Knight, Stephen, 'The social function of the Middle English romances', in David Aers, ed., *Medieval Literature: Criticism, Ideology and History* (Brighton, 1984), pp. 99–122. Useful analysis of medieval English metrical romance from anti-escapist viewpoint, demonstrating how contemporary anxieties are addressed in romance texts.

Tolkien, J.R.R., 'On Fairy Stories', in *Tree and Leaf*, ed. Christopher Tolkien (London, 1992), pp. 9–73. Huge range of material covered; slightly sentimental Christian and humanist approach, but makes many sound points about specific texts.

3 Haunting the Middle Ages

Caciola, Nancy, 'Wraiths, revenants and ritual in medieval culture', *Past and Present* 152 (1996), pp. 3–45. Valuable for its examination of the interaction between popular and learned views of death.

Caesarius of Heisterbach, *Dialogus Miraculorum*, ed. Joseph Strange, 2 vols (Cologne, 1851). The English translation, Caesarius of Heisterbach, *Dialogue on Miracles*, trans. H. von E. Scott and C.C. Swinton Bland (London, 1929), may not be readily available. The *Dialogue* was compiled for educational use by a thirteenth-century German monk; Book 12 includes a collection of ghost stories.

Fournier, Jacques, *Le Registre d'Inquisition de Jacques Fournier, Évêque de Pamiers (1318–1325)*, ed. Jean Duvernoy, 3 vols (Toulouse, 1965; with corrections Toulouse, 1972). There is a French paraphrase, *Le Registre d'Inquisition de Jacques Fournier (Évêque de Pamiers) 1318–1325)*, ed. and trans. Jean Duvernoy, 3 vols (Paris, 1978). A number of those whom Bishop Fournier examined for heresy testified that they had seen ghosts or believed in them.

Gurevich, Aron, *Historical Anthropology of the Middle Ages*, ed. Jana Howlett (Cambridge, 1992). A Russian, Gurevich stands stimulatingly apart from Western studies of the medieval imagination. His conclusions are relevant to accounts of medieval ghosts.

Map, Walter, *De Nugis Curialium: Courtiers' Trifles*, ed. and trans. M.R. James, rev. Christopher Brooke and R.A.B. Mynors (Oxford, 1983). Walter was an educated man and a courtier; his trifles are a fascinating insight into the twelfth-century mind.

Schmitt, Jean Claude, *Les Revenants: les Vivants et les Morts dans la Société Medievale* (Paris, 1994). Undoubtedly the most important study yet made of medieval ghosts, placing them firmly in the history of memory and forgetting. Since this chapter was written, this has been translated by Teresa L. Fagan as *Ghosts in the Middle Ages: The Living and the Dead in Medieval Society* (Chicago, 1998).

4   Chivalry: fantasy and fear

Keen, Maurice, *Chivalry* (New Haven, 1984). The primary work on all aspects of chivalry.

Krueger, Roberta, *Women Readers and the Ideology of Gender in Old French Verse Romance* (Cambridge, 1993). A feminist scholar's analysis of the tensions over gender in Old French literature.

Lacy, Norris, gen. ed., *Lancelot–Grail: The Old French Arthurian Vulgate and Post-Vulgate in Translation*, 5 vols (New York, 1993–96). Lively English translations of the massive corpus of prose romance written in the early thirteenth century.

Strickland, Matthew, *War and Chivalry: The Conduct and Perception of War in England and Normandy, 1066–1217* (Cambridge, 1996). Comprehensive study of conduct in various types of war, honour and piety.

Vinaver, Eugene, rev. P.J.C. Field, *The Works of Sir Thomas Malory*, 3 vols (Oxford, 1990). Latest revision of Malory's classic.

5   Dreaming of Eve: edenic fantasies in John Milton's *Paradise Lost*

Fallon, Stephen, *Milton among the Philosophers: Poetry and Materialism in Seventeenth-Century England* (Ithaca, 1991). A challenging reassessment of Milton's place within the seventeenth-century philosophical debate over the nature of substance. Milton's theory of animist materialism is read as one of a number of contemporary responses to Descartes and Hobbes.

Harvey, Elizabeth D., and Katherine E. Maus, eds, *Soliciting Interpretation: Literary Theory and Seventeenth-Century English Poetry* (Chicago, 1990). Diverse essays on seventeenth-century literature, including works by Donne, Milton, Marvell, Herbert and Wroth. The volume intends to reopen familiar texts to the processes of interpretation by countering received ideas and determined modes of reading.

Harvey, Elizabeth, *Ventriloquized Voices: Feminist Theory and English Renaissance Texts* (London, 1992). An exciting addition to Renaissance studies. Harvey's work assesses early modern texts in which male writers choose to appropriate a 'feminine' voice, and includes analysis of texts by Erasmus, Spenser, Jonson, Donne and Milton.

Lewalski, Barbara K., *Paradise Lost and the Rhetoric of Literary Forms* (New Jersey, 1985). This excellent critical work analyses the structure of *Paradise Lost*, showing in detail how Milton employs the Renaissance genre system to create his 'encyclopaedic' epic.

Rogers, John, *The Matter of Revolution: Science, Poetry and Politics in the Age of Milton* (Ithaca, 1996). Interested in the origins of liberal individualism, Rogers looks at literary texts influenced by the radical thought processes of mid-seventeenth-century England. His discussion of *Paradise Lost*, as a text riven by the conflicting doctrines of vitalist self-determination and Calvinism, is important.

Rumrich, John P., *Matter of Glory: A New Preface to Paradise Lost* (Pittsburgh, 1987). A useful 'reader' to *Paradise Lost*, offering a coherent overview upon the poem and its theology. Concentrating on the themes of free will and monism, Rumrich argues that the epic is a theodicy where the goodness of God is revealed through His material creation.

6 Jonson, the antimasque and the literary fantastic: *The Vision of Delight*

Butler, Martin, and David Lindley, 'Restoring Astrea: Jonson's masque for the fall of Somerset', *English Literary History* 61:4 (1994), pp. 807–27. Demonstrates the vogue for historicist analysis of the Jonsonian masque, and the evolution within masque criticism from a polarized subversion/containment argument to an understanding of the more problematic nature of the form.

Orgel, Stephen, ed., *Ben Jonson: The Complete Masques* (New Haven and London, 1969). An essential work including the texts of Jonson's court masques with explanatory notes and a comprehensive introduction to the form. Orgel also includes Jonson's own notes to the masques.

Orgel, Stephen, *The Jonsonian Masque* (New York, 1981). A seminal work surveying the development of the Jonsonian masque, which the author views as an ultra-conservative promotion of royal propaganda.

Prescott, Anne Lake, 'The Stuart masque and Pantagruel's dreams', *English Literary History* 51 (1984), pp. 407–30. Prescott charts the influence of Rabelais and grotesque fantasy in the antimasque. She shows how medieval images of the topsy-turvy world substantially influenced the development of the Jonsonian antimasque.

Waller, Gary, *The Sidney Family Romance: Mary Wroth, William Herbert, and the Early Modern Construction of Gender* (Detroit, 1993). Includes comments on 'To Sir Robert Wroth', suggesting that Jonson combines praise and irony within the same poem. The author also reflects on the gender politics of the Jonsonian masque.

7   Writing sexual fantasy in the English Renaissance: potency, power and poetry

Freud, Sigmund, 'Creative writers and day-dreaming', in *The Standard Edition of the Complete Psychological Works of Sigmund Freud*, trans. James Strachey (London, 1959), vol. 9, pp. 143–53. Classic account of the connections between literary creativity and unconscious desire.

Hunter, Ian, David Sanders and Dugald Williamson, *On Pornography: Literature, Sexuality and Obscenity Law* (Basingstoke, 1993). Materialist account of the connections between 'obscene' literature and the law.

Merrix, Robert P., 'The vale of lillies and the bower of bliss: soft-core pornography in Elizabethan poetry', *Journal of Popular Culture* 19 (1986), pp. 3–16. Flawed but useful account of eroticism in early modern texts, which uncovers veiled sexual desire in the poems of, in particular, Spenser.

Moulton, Ian Frederick, 'Transmuted into a woman or worse: masculine gender identity and Thomas Nashe's "Choice of Valentines"', *English Literary Renaissance* 27 (1997), pp. 57–88. Situates Nashe's poem in relation to gender discourses and Renaissance literary models, arguing that it can be read as an inscription of male gender anxiety regarding sexual performance.

Stapleton, M.L., 'Nashe and the poetics of obscenity: "The Choise of Valentines"', *Classical and Modern Literature Quarterly* 12 (1991), pp. 29–48. Detailed examination of Nashe's models, especially Ovid and Chaucer, which tries to avoid judging its sexual content, but nevertheless labels the poem as 'obscene'.

8   Silly money, fantastic credit

Agnew, Jean-Christophe, *Worlds Apart: The Market and the Theater in Anglo-American Thought 1550–1750* (Cambridge, 1986). Debates the aesthetics and social ethics of exchange when 'marketing assemblies' arise. Both theatres and trade depend on marketable selves, in the persons of the actor and the merchant.

Halpern, Richard, *The Poetics of Primitive Accumulation: English Renaissance Culture and the Genealogy of Capital* (Ithaca, 1991). Looks at Renaissance culture as a period of transition from feudalism to capitalism, conceived of as both economic and social production. Deals with points where value is manifested, such as in the rhetoric of copia and the literary presentation of the court.

Kerridge, Eric, *Trade and Banking in Early Modern England* (Manchester, 1988). General description of the money market, which describes the form of credit instruments, their legal force, their actual negotiability, and the market needs which created them.

Muldrew, Craig, 'Interpreting the market: the ethics of credit and community relations in early modern England', *Social History* 18:2 (1993), pp. 163–85. Rejects the notion that nascent capitalism was fuelled by Protestant individualism; rather, the language of the market stressed credit relationships which depended on trust, obligation, and a personal knowledge of the debtor.

Shell, Marc, *Language, Money and Thought: Literary and Philosophic Economies from the Medieval to the Modern Era* (Baltimore, 1982). Contends that new forms of money which accompanied new forms of production affected the way meaning was produced, in the interaction between economic and linguistic symbolization.

Stevenson, Laura, *Praise and Paradox: Merchants and Craftsmen in Elizabethan Popular Literature* (Cambridge, 1984). Looks at the role literary representations of the merchant played in changing social theory about trade and its associated vices (including avarice and deception) in order to match the new importance which these possessors of liquid assets had in the early modern economy.

9   The politics of escapism: fantasies of travel and power in Richard Brome's *The Antipodes* and Ben Jonson's *The Alchemist*

Bach, Rebecca A., 'Ben Jonson's "civill savages"', *Studies in English Literature 1500–1800* 37 (1997), pp. 277–93. Links colonialism with the space of the stage.

Butler, Martin, *Theatre and Crisis, 1632–42* (Cambridge, 1984). Butler's thesis sees the majority of public theatre drama at this time less as escapist entertainment than as material directly engaged with contemporary politics in the decade preceding the English Civil War, commonly referred to as the period of Charles I's Personal Rule (1629–40).

282   *SELECT BIBLIOGRAPHY*

Clark, Ira, *Professional Playwrights: Massinger, Ford, Shirley, and Brome* (Lexington, Ky., 1992). Explores the canon of each writer in turn, placing their work in a Caroline social and political context.

Greenblatt, Stephen, *Marvelous Possessions: The Wonders of the New World* (Oxford, 1991). Explores the encounters of Columbus, Diaz, and other actual explorers with the Americas and the tropes of possession which dominated their written accounts of those journeys. It includes a detailed investigation of *The Travels of Sir John Mandeville*.

Maquerlot, Jean-Pierre, and Michele Willems, eds, *Travel and Drama in Shakespeare's Time* (Cambridge, 1996). A collection of essays on the relationship between travel and the theatre, which includes considerations of the use of actual travels and explorations as the subject matter for plays by Shakespeare, Jonson and Brome amongst others, as well as explorations of the relationship between the imaginative journeys undertaken by audiences and the act of travel itself. The dramatic genre is seen to have a particular investment in tropes and concepts of travel and the fantasies of travel.

Parr, Anthony, ed., *Three Renaissance Travel Plays* (Manchester, 1995). Parr's introductory essay, which includes Brome's *The Antipodes*, provides a superb starting point for any one interested in the relationship between travel and drama in this period.

10 Travel and sexual fantasy in the early modern period

Aldridge, Owen A., 'Polygamy in early fiction: Henry Neville and Denis Veiras', *Publications of the Modern Language Association* 65 (1950), pp. 464–72. Relates Neville's pamphlet to contemporary concerns regarding population depletion, seeing the work as 'intended primarily as a fictional representation of a method to increase population'.

Boesky, Amy, *Founding Fictions: Utopias in Early Modern England*, (Athens, Ga., 1996). Concentrates on issues of race and slavery in the extended version of the pamphlet when sexual utopia turns to political dystopia. Drawing on the story of Noah and his descendants, Neville 'complicates and eroticises the relations between master and slave, embedding colonial politics within the structure of the patriarchal family'. To preserve a sense of English identity the progeny from Pine's negro wife must be excluded.

Carey, Daniel, 'Henry Neville's *The Isle of Pines*: travel, forgery and the problem of genre', *Angelaki* 1:2 (1993–94), pp. 23–39. Discusses the complex publishing history of Neville's text in England and on the Continent which alternated between its circulation as a travel fraud and its incorporation into the genre of prose fiction.

Montrose, Louis, 'The work of gender in the discourse of discovery', in Stephen Greenblatt, ed., *New World Encounters* (Berkeley, 1993), pp. 177–217. Valuable theoretical discussion of textual strategies that assisted in the process of exploration and settlement in the New World, particularly the metaphor of virgin land.

Weber, Harold, 'Charles II, George Pines, and Mr Dorimant: the politics of sexual power in Restoration England', *Criticism* 32:2 (1990), pp. 193–219. Situates Neville's pamphlet in the context of satirical and critical comment on Charles II's sexual laxity which allegedly resulted in the monarch's subordination to female authority. Pine, by contrast, establishes his sexual domination over his female companions while at the same time asserting his political control.

Wiseman, Susan, ' "Adam, the father of all flesh", porno-political rhetoric and political theory in and after the English Civil War', *Prose Studies* 14:3 (1991), pp. 134–57. Astute account of the politics of Neville's pamphlet, read in relation to contemporary theories of patriarchal power as well as Neville's earlier satirical writings on the participation of women in the political sphere.

11   Jenny Voss: the fantasy of female criminality

Faller, Lincoln B., *Turned to Account: The Forms and Functions of Criminal Biography in Late Seventeenth- and Early Eighteenth-century England* (Cambridge, 1987). Stimulating in-depth study of rogue literature with comprehensive bibliography and notes. Faller focuses on the way criminal biography reflected the preoccupations and concerns of society, and satisfied its interest in deviant behaviour.

Linebaugh, Peter, *The London Hanged: Crime and Civil Society in the Eighteenth Century* (Harmondsworth, 1991). Seminal study of the labouring and criminal poor who lived in the shadow of Tyburn. Argues that in an era of economic expansion the propertied classes' exploitation of this underclass profoundly influenced the nature of their criminal activity in their fight to survive.

Rayner, J.L., and G.T. Crook, eds, *The Complete Newgate Calendar*, 5 vols (London, 1841). Chronicles the lives of hundreds of criminals (including Mary Carleton) from the seventeenth and eighteenth centuries using contemporary accounts. Other editions such as George Theodore Wilkinson, ed., intro. Christopher Hibbert, *The Newgate Calendar* (London, 1991), are more readily available.

Todd, Janet, and Elizabeth Spearing, eds, *Counterfeit Ladies: The Life and Death of Mary Frith. The Case of Mary Carleton*, (London, 1994). Comprehensive survey of Carleton's life and of the many publications which her life inspired; includes *The Case of Mary Carleton* (1663), a supposed autobiography, in its entirety.

Weber, Harold, 'Rakes, rogues, and the empire of misrule', *Huntington Library Quarterly* 47:1 (Winter 1984), pp. 13–32. The only study to examine the significance of Jenny Voss. A clear and cogent analysis of the various forms of rogue literature and how they relate to the society they reflect.

12   The grotesque utopias of Jeanette Winterson and Monique Wittig

Bammer, Angelika, *Partial Visions: Feminism and Utopianism in the 1970s* (New York, 1991). Taking utopia as the anchor-point for the political trajectory of feminism, Bammer re-evaluates the historical development of the term before applying it as 'partial vision' to the work of a range of American and European women's writing of the 1970s.

Bown, Nicola, ' "There are fairies at the bottom of our garden": fairies, fantasy and photography', *Textual Practice* 10:1 (1996), pp. 57–82. Focuses upon the early-twentieth-century phenomenon of the Cottingley photographs, which captured on film a series of apparently 'authentic' images of children and fairies interacting. Rather than examining them as genuine or fake, Bown utilizes these images to examine cultural assumptions about adolescent fantasy and femininity during this period.

Irigaray, Luce, 'Sexual diffference', in Margaret Whitford, ed., *The Irigaray Reader* (Oxford, 1991), pp. 165–77. For Irigaray late-twentieth-century discussions of sexual difference must engage with a reconception of the discourses of maternity, using philosophical re-readings of the interface between space and time. The angel, transcendent of the limitations of space and time, and fantastic in orientation, functions as the metaphorical pivot of her argument.

O'Rourke, Rebecca, 'Fingers in the fruit basket: a feminist reading of Jeanette Winterson's *Oranges Are Not The Only Fruit*', in Susan Sellers, ed., *Feminist Criticism: Theory and Practice* (Hemel Hempstead, 1991), pp. 57–69. O'Rourke begins with a brief survey and analysis of shifts in feminist criticism from the 1970s to the present, before situating *Oranges* in terms of its reception as a lesbian novel, its function as autobiography, and her own use of it as a teaching text.

Russo, Mary, *The Female Grotesque: Risk, Excess and Modernity* (London, 1994). This ambitious book brings together visual art, literature, cinema and popular history in analysing the manner in which carnival and the grotesque exist as metaphors for the shaping of political feminism in the twentieth century.

13 Fantasy, childhood and literature: in pursuit of wonderlands

Burman, Erica, *Deconstructing Developmental Psychology* (London, 1994). An important analysis of development psychology as a culturally and historically determined narrative, not the 'truth' about children.

Hunt, Peter, *Criticism, Theory, and Children's Literature* (Oxford, 1991). By one of the most eminent critics and theorists of children's literature, this book offers a lucid discussion of the theoretical issues involved in children's literature criticism.

Jenks, Chris, *Childhood* (London, 1996). Involved from early on in sociological thinking about childhood and offering a concise and clear introduction to the field.

Lesnik-Oberstein, Karín, *Children's Literature: Criticism and the Fictional Child* (Oxford, 1994). Argues that the child which children's literature critics constantly refer to as a psycho-biological truth is in fact a cultural construction, and that this argument can be applied to all of childhood. Based on this, an alternative approach is suggested for thinking about adult–child communications.

Rose, Jacqueline, *The Case of Peter Pan or: The Impossibility of Children's Fiction* (London, 1984; repr. 1995). One of the most important books on thinking about theory and children and childhood. Complex and challenging.

Walkerdine, Valerie, *Schoolgirl Fictions* (London, 1990). A meticulous demonstration of how theories of the constructed child may be deployed in understanding and transforming educational practices, children's books and child-raising.

14 The decline and fall of the great English ghost story

Aickman, Robert, ed., *The Fontana Book of Great Ghost Stories*, vols 1–8 (New York, 1964–72). Possibly the most imaginatively satisfying collections of ghost stories available; the shrewd, succinct introductions are essential reading.

Briggs, Julia, *Night Visitors: The Rise and Fall of the English Ghost Story* (London, 1977). Workmanlike and wide-ranging map of ghost-story territory. A very useful textbook.

Cox, Michael, and R.A. Gilbert, eds, *The Oxford Book of English Ghost Stories* (Oxford, 1986). Classic one-volume survey of English ghost fiction from Sir Walter Scott up to the late 1960s. The stories tend, however, to be briefer and more sensational than those in Aickman's collections.

Lamb, Charles, 'Witches and other night fears' (1821), collected in *The Essays of Elia* (1823). Classic literary discussion of the human appetite for tales of the supernatural.

Penzoldt, Peter, *The Supernatural in Fiction* (London, 1952). Excellently organized, creative and urbane study.

15 'Never love a cowboy': romance fiction and fantasy families

Mitchell, Lee Clark, *Westerns: Making the Man in Fiction and Film* (Chicago, 1996). Many of his arguments in relation to gender were pre-empted by Tompkins (1992), but this is nonetheless the best critical study now available. Mitchell moves from works by Fenimore Cooper and Harte to more readily identifiable Westerns by Wister, Grey, L'Amour, *et al.*

Modleski, Tanya, *Loving with a Vengeance: Mass Produced Fantasies for Women* (1982; New York, 1996). This classic study speculates on the complex and often conflicting motivations behind popular fiction.

Radway, Janice A., *Reading the Romance: Women, Patriarchy, and Popular Literature* (1984; Chapel Hill, 1991). This excellent study incorporates theoretical discussion with analysis of a particular group of women-readers of popular romance.

Treacher, Amal, 'What is life without my love?: desire and romantic fiction', in Susannah Radstone, ed., *Sweet Dreams: Sexuality, Gender, and Popular Fiction* (London, 1988), pp. 73–90. A brief but lucid and wide-ranging discussion of the topic.

Tompkins, Jane P., *West of Everything: The Inner Life of Westerns* (New York, 1992). Tompkins offers a lively, thoughtful and accessible approach to many classic Western novelists, including Wister, Grey and L'Amour. She is particularly sensitive to the construction of gendered identity in and through such texts, and to such topics as landscape and horses.

Williams, Linda Ruth, *Critical Desire: Psychoanalysis and the Literary Subject* (London, 1995). Provides a useful overview of the role of the psyche in the literary text.

16 Fantasy and the ideal of the individual in twentieth-century English domestic architecture

Artley, Alexandra, and John M. Robinson, *The New Georgian Handbook: A First Look at the Conservation Way of Life* (London, 1985). A self-conscious style book in photo-journalistic format, derived from glossy magazine articles.

Betjeman, John, *First and Last Loves* (London, 1960). A selection of the poet's magazine, journal and guide-book articles about churches, landscape, towns and architecture.

Lancaster, Osbert, *Pillar to Post: English Architecture Without Tears* (London, 1938). A satirical overview of architectural styles from 'Egypt' to 'Twentieth-Century Functional', accompanied by cartoon-like line drawings.

Lowry, Suzanne, ed., *The Young Fogey Handbook* (Poole, 1985). A tongue-in-cheek analysis of the tweedy, Georgian-obsessed 1980s style-setters, written in photo-journalistic format.

Papadakis, Andreas, and Harriet Watson, eds, *New Classicism* (London, 1990). A lavishly produced series of essays, with many colour photographs, of the latest Classical Revival architecture.

Pawley, Martin, *Theory and Design in the Second Machine Age* (Oxford, 1990). A partial, if instructive, survey of the main influences in architecture and design in the latter part of the twentieth century.

Notes on contributors

Lucie Armitt is Lecturer in English at the University of Wales, Bangor. She is the editor of *Where No Man Has Gone Before: Women and Science Fiction* (Routledge, 1991) and the author of *Theorising the Fantastic* (Arnold, 1996). Her current research centres upon contemporary women's fiction.

Daniel Carey teaches at the National University of Ireland, Galway. His work on travel narrative, natural history, and the history of philosophy has appeared in *Annals of Science, The Seventeenth Century, Common Knowledge* and other journals.

Danielle Clarke is Lecturer in English at University College, Dublin. She is the author of several articles on feminist theory and Renaissance women's writing. Forthcoming publications include *The Double Voice: Gendered Writing in Early Modern England* (Macmillan, 1998), co-edited with Elizabeth Clarke, and an edition of Renaissance women's poetry.

Richard W. Kaeuper is Professor of History at the University of Rochester, New York. His publications include *War, Justice and Public Order: England and France in the Later Middle Ages* (Clarendon Press, 1988) and *The Book of Chivalry of Geoffroi de Charney: Text, Context and Translation* (University of Pennsylvania, 1996), written with Elspeth Kennedy. His present research on public order, religion and violence in chivalric literature will be published shortly by Oxford University Press.

Margaret Kean is the Margot Heinemann Post-Doctoral Fellow at Goldsmiths College, London. She works mainly within Milton studies but her current research interests include the manipulation of dramatic models within texts of the English Civil War period.

Carolyne Larrington has written *The Woman's Companion to Mythology* (Pandora, 1997), *Women and Writing in Medieval English: A Sourcebook*

(Routledge, 1995) and has translated the Old Norse *Poetic Edda* (Oxford University Press, 1996). She teaches medieval literature and is currently researching a book about enchantresses.

Karín Lesnik-Oberstein is a lecturer in English, American and Children's Literature at the University of Reading. She is also an Associate Director of the University's Centre for International Research in Childhood: Literature, Culture, Media (CIRCL). Her publications include *Children's Literature: Criticism and the Fictional Child* (Oxford University Press, 1994) and *Children in Culture: Approaches to Childhood* (Macmillan, 1998) which she has edited and introduced.

Lesley Mickel is Lecturer in English Literature at the University of Northumbria, Carlisle Campus, and is the author of *The Short Bravery of the Night: The Growth and Decline of the Jonsonian Antimasque* (Scolar, 1999) and the co-editor with Alison Thorne of 'Ben Jonson', *Annotated Bibliography of English Studies* (Swets & Zeitlinger, 1997).

Timothy Mowl is Research Fellow in Architectural History at Bristol University. His last two books were *Horace Walpole: The Great Outsider* (John Murray, 1996) and *William Beckford: Composing for Mozart* (John Murray, 1998). *A Study of Rococo Design* is due in 1999.

Christopher Pelling is Fellow and Tutor in Classics at University College, Oxford. His publications include Plutarch, *Life of Antony* (Cambridge University Press, 1988) and *Literary Text and the Greek Historian* (Routledge, forthcoming); he has also edited collections on *Characterization and Individuality in Greek Literature* (Oxford University Press, 1990) and *Greek Tragedy and the History* (Oxford University Press, 1997).

Mark Philpott has taught medieval history at the University of Oxford, Birkbeck College, London and the Queen's University of Belfast; his research interests centre around the medieval Church and the ways in which its doctrines and, in particular, its laws affected people's lives. His comparative study of Archbishop Lanfranc of Canterbury (†1089) and St Anselm (†1109) is to be published in Addison Wesley Longman's *Medieval World* series.

Julie Sanders is a Lecturer in the Department of English at Keele University. She is the author of *Ben Jonson's Theatrical Republics* (Macmillan, 1998) and co-editor with Kate Chedgzoy and Susan Wiseman of *Refashioning Ben Jonson* (Macmillan, 1998).

Peter Stoneley is Lecturer in English at Queen's University, Belfast. His research is, for the most part, on nineteenth-century English and Amercan fiction; he is the author of *Mark Twain and the Feminine Aesthetic* (Cambridge University Press, 1992).

Ceri Sullivan is Lecturer in English at the University of Wales, Bangor, and was a chartered accountant. She is the author of *Dismembered Rhetoric: English Recusant Writing 1580–1603* (AUP, 1995) and *The Rhetoric of Credit* (forthcoming).

Julian Thompson teaches English at Regent's Park College, Oxford. He has edited a number of novels by Anthony Trollope for Oxford World Classics and Penguin, and the *Collected Shorter Fiction* of both Anthony Trollope and Wilkie Collins.

Barbara White is Director of Studies of an American undergraduate programme. She is the author of several articles on early modern sermon literature and her present research interest is seventeenth- and eighteenth-century female criminality.

Index